T0339464

Internationalisation and Strategic Control

This book is a study of the emergence of international business. It immerses itself in the topic of how companies can control income-generating assets in foreign countries, the key element often used to define a multinational enterprise and propounds the notion that control of crucial dispositions by foreign companies can be achieved by other means than direct foreign investment – cash flow and portfolio ownership.

Internationalisation and Strategic Control analyses the extent to which a firm can control the investments of foreign companies in the field of supply and maintenance of production machinery. It achieves this through a case study of how F.L. Smidth & Co., global leaders in providing technology for the cement industry since the 1890s, managed to achieve a vital influence over, and control of, cement-producing companies in Asia in the period of 1890–1938. The study examines how this strategy was promoted by some internal and external factors and circumstances, and hindered by others.

In highlighting strategic tools and initiatives other than cash flow and portfolio ownership, the book applies concepts taken from a broad range of research fields covering social science, cultural analysis, micro history, Actor-Network-Theory and industrial archaeology. It will be of interest to researchers, academics and students in the fields of international business, business history and globalisation.

Morten Pedersen is Head of Exhibitions and the Department of History, Nordjyllands Historiske Museum, Denmark.

Routledge International Studies in Business History

Series editors: Jeffrey Fear and Heidi Tworek

For more information about this series, please visit: www.routledge.com/ Routledge-International-Studies-in-Business-History/book-series/SE0471

Internationalisation and Strategic Control

An Industrial History

Morten Pedersen

Routledge
Taylor & Francis Group

NEW YORK AND LONDON

First published 2022
by Routledge
605 Third Avenue, New York, NY 10158

and by Routledge
2 Park Square, Milton Park, Abingdon, Oxon, OX14 4RN

*Routledge is an imprint of the Taylor & Francis Group, an
informa business*

Library of Congress Cataloguing-in-Publication Data
Names: Pedersen, Morten (Business historian), author.
Title: Internationalisation and strategic control: an industrial
history / Morten Pedersen.
Description: New York, NY: Routledge, 2022. | Series: Routledge
international studies in business history | Includes bibliographical
references and index.
Identifiers: LCCN 2021033486 (print) | LCCN 2021033487
(ebook) | ISBN 9781138333116 (hardback) | ISBN
9781032169798 (paperback) | ISBN 9780429446184 (ebook)
Subjects: LCSH: International business enterprises--History. |
Corporations, Foreign--History. | International trade--History.
Classification: LCC HD2755.5.P43 2022 (print) | LCC HD2755.5
(ebook) | DDC 338.8/8--dc23
LC record available at https://lccn.loc.gov/2021033486
LC ebook record available at https://lccn.loc.gov/2021033487

ISBN: 978-1-138-33311-6 (hbk)
ISBN: 978-1-032-16979-8 (pbk)
ISBN: 978-0-429-44618-4 (ebk)

DOI: 10.4324/9780429446184

Typeset in Sabon
by MPS Limited, Dehradun

Contents

Tables

Acknowledgements

Large projects create many debts. Many people have read and provided helpful comments on some version of this manuscript: Kurt Jacobsen, Kristine Bruland, Caspar Jørgensen, Kristoffer Jensen, Kenn Tarbensen and Jakob Ørnbjerg. I am especially indebted to Per Boje and Jeppe Nevers, both professors at the Center for Maritime and Business History at the University of Southern Denmark, who have provided invaluable help during the years and many phases it took to prepare the manuscript. The responsibility for what has been written rests, of course, on me alone.

During the project period, I have been employed as a curator at the Museum of Northern Jutland, and I am heavily indebted to museum director Lars Chr. Nørbach for providing the opportunity for me to complete what I aimed at from the start.

During part of the project period, I worked as a researcher at the Center for Maritime and Business History at the University of Southern Denmark. My employment at the centre was made possible by a grant from what is today known as the Independent Research Fund Denmark, which is financed by the Danish Ministry of Higher Education and Science. During the last part of the writing phase, I was affiliated as a guest researcher to Aalborg University, Department of Politics and Society, and I am indebted to Professor Marianne Rostgaard for providing this opportunity.

The project could not have been finalised had it not been for the generous financial support received from private foundations: Det Nissenske Familiefond, Farumgaard-Fonden, Aage og Johanne Louis-Hansens Fond and Den Hielmstierne-Rosencroneske Stiftelse. However, nothing would have been written in the first place had it not been for FLSmidth A/S, who have provided unhindered access to the company collections on the early activities of the company in Asia and have refrained from any claims to interfere with my research and the publication of the results.

Finally, I wish to thank translator and language consultant Kirsten Gammelgaard Poulsen for turning my manuscript into good English.

Acronyms and Abbreviations

ACC   Associated Cement Companies (The Merger)
ANT   Actor-Network Theory
CCMA Chinese Cement Manufacturers Association
DAC   Dansk Andels Cementfabrik A/S
EAC   The East Asiatic Company (Østasiatisk Kompagni)
ELL   Ejnar Lassen Landorph Personal Archive
FDI   Foreign Direct Investment
FLS   F.L. Smidth & Co.
FLSA   FLSmidth Company Archives, Copenhagen
MNE   Multinational Enterprise
Rigsarkivet Danish National Archives (Copenhagen)
SSEE   Small Successful European Economy

Introduction

In recent decades, extensive research has been devoted to the subject of international economics and company strategy towards foreign markets. This has specifically included the study of multinational enterprises (MNEs), which have often been perceived as a final phase in the internationalisation of a firm. The ability of a firm to control income-generating assets in more than one country has typically been used as a definition of an MNE. As an indicator of this control, research has focussed particularly on foreign direct investment (FDI) – the magnitude of cash flow and portfolio ownership of companies. The incompleteness of FDI as an indicator has, however, been both recognised and discussed.

The main objective of this book is to contribute to this ongoing discussion. It propounds the notion that firms can control key dispositions of foreign companies by means other than cash flow and ownership, and that a more differentiated understanding of the term *control* may be appropriate. The book consequently undertakes an analysis of the extent to which a firm can control the investments of foreign companies, in this case in the field of supply and maintenance of production machinery.

The analysis is based on a case study of how F.L. Smidth & Co. (FLS), global leaders in providing technology for the cement industry since the 1890s has aspired to – and achieved – control of foreign cement-producing companies by means other than FDI. The study examines how, in Asia in the period 1890–1938, this process was promoted by certain specific elements and influences and hindered or prevented by others. Through a study of activities in several different markets – located in the same part of the world but characterised by very different circumstances – the book examines how internal factors, such as the possession of technological advantages and limited capital reserves, can be of long term as well as fluctuating significance. Similarly, it examines how a non-FDI strategy can be promoted or impeded by external factors.

It is a basic notion that research on non-FDI-driven internationalization cannot be carried out solely by quantitatively focused analyses based on register data. The book discusses the necessity of methodologies with sensitivity to political, cultural and human factors and the need to apply basic approaches and concepts developed by relevant fields of research such as social science, cultural analysis, micro history, Actor-Network Theory (ANT) and industrial archaeology.

The traditional business models that explain the success of multinational companies are thus questioned and challenged through unusual sources and methods that brings the reader to a business world that entrepreneurs of the past in everyday life far away from home had to understand and manage if they were to succeed in markets with other cultural and political rules.

1   The Emergence of International Business: Concepts and Approach

Multinational Enterprise

It is a well-known fact that the activities of companies across national borders and continents have always been a decisive factor in all phases of globalisation.[1] Therefore, it is not surprising that for decades, research in the history of companies, and particularly their internationalisation processes, has been one of the most fruitful tools for understanding globalisation and its driving forces.[2] Major interest has been directed towards the multinational enterprises that began to attract attention in the economic scholarly literature in particular in the 1950s and 1960s. In much early research, multinational enterprise was primarily seen as an American pursuit, but since the 1990s, the topic has been studied as a phenomenon taking its starting point in and directed towards nations across the globe.[3]

At the same time, a consensus was established to speak about enterprises as multinational when they *control operations or income-generating assets in more than one country.*[4] This led to a strong focus on analyses of capital flows and formal ownership. The reason was that the use of *direct portfolio investments* by companies across national borders was seen as a particularly significant indicator of such *control*, i.e. investments linked to formal managerial control. *Green field* investments thus became classic examples of the establishment of multinational enterprise; in these, companies establish subsidiaries from the bottom in a country, or they invest in the purchase and takeover of companies that already exist.

The strong focus on FDI has been accompanied by the recognition that investments may well be important, but considered separately, they are a deficient indicator of situations in which the companies are *controlling income-generating* operations and/or assets across national borders. Rather than focusing narrowly on FDI as an indicator, it may be fruitful to take a broader look at the ways in which enterprise internationalisation may be dependant on – and even based on – other factors than the access to capital. Also across national borders, companies may

DOI: 10.4324/9780429446184-1

be interconnected and influence each other's dispositions in completely other ways than just through capital flows and formal ownership.

These types of connections may be formed in a number of ways, often overlapping and difficult to describe using the concepts normally drawn on in descriptions of companies and their interrelations, whether across national borders or not. In order to connect categories to real-life situations, research has therefore introduced a number of different terms. We may, for instance, point to the use of concepts such as *nonequity arrangements* to characterise licence agreements that transfer the right of use of a technology subject to certain conditions, franchise models, cartels or strategic agreements, etc. In combination, such phenomena have been highlighted as examples of how companies can establish obligations towards each other in ways that involve mutual control of the income-generating assets, leaving out any direct investments.[5] A similar situation is seen in the introduction of categories such as *business groups,* where for instance large commercial companies diversify through contract-bound collaboration with other companies without making moves to buy up or merge, *interfirm networks* for even more decentralised, loose and perhaps occasional collaboration types, *transnational firms* and *metanational firms*.[6]

In other words, an interest in *control* opens the door to a complex world in which companies are interconnected and exercise control of each other's activities in numerous overlapping ways, and where narrow economic and legal concepts and definitions are often inadequate.

The Gradual Internationalisation Process

The introduction of a broad understanding of *control* may challenge our usual understanding of the opportunities of companies to build relations, and consequently of companies as easily definable and autonomous phenomena.

It has long been known how companies can build their presence in foreign markets, gradually and over a long span of time. Since the 1970s, a model consisting of four phases has often been put forward as an example of how this might typically take place; this was known as the *Uppsala model* because it was formulated by the economists Jan Johanson and Jan-Erik Vahlne at the Uppsala School of Economics.[7] On the basis of observations of the establishment of Swedish companies in other countries, primarily companies based on mass manufacturing of products for private consumers, the Uppsala model described a typical *establishment chain,* in which the company builds a solid position in the home market; based on this, it subsequently introduces international involvement in the shape of export/import activities, i.e. the sale and purchase of goods and services across national borders. In the second phase, transactions follow through contract-bound independent collaboration partners using agencies or licence agreements, until the company, in the third phase of internationalisation, establishes its own sales offices and organisations in the recipient country. Finally, the model described how the move into the last phase of internationalisation may be made by investing in the establishment of production facilities in the new market.

In other words, the *Uppsala model* described a process in which *multinational enterprise* based on *direct investment* constituted the final objective and the completion of the strategy of a company towards fully expanded international activities.

The trend towards such gradual development may indeed be explained through the set-up of basic simple explanatory models which may almost seem like natural science laws, and which are focused on how companies in foreign markets are facing a *liability of foreignness*, i.e. the condition that, as a point of departure, companies coming from outside have a weaker position than the national companies, which are acting with ease in well-known contexts.

The market knowledge gained through sales contacts may thus create knowledge about market potential and may form the basis for overcoming the first important step in the *liability of foreignness*. This may create fertile soil for new investments, which can create enough volume to make use of the opportunities – resulting in further knowledge of the new market. In other words, investments may promote a cyclical development where increasing investments lead to increasing market knowledge and an organisation with the strength to make use of the potential, which may result in even more knowledge. Another type of event chain may be sparked by increasing transaction costs.[8] An increase in international activities may involve such great risks in foreign markets – another type of *liability of foreignness* – that it is better and cheaper to integrate the activities through the company's own multinational organisation by establishing offices and factories. This may then result in increased activity, new risks, new investments, etc.

Since the *Uppsala model* was launched, research has demonstrated how the four phases have been nicely followed by large companies such as Singer and Lever Brothers.[9] It has also been demonstrated, however, that companies in the real world often globalise according to more complex patterns that cannot be described and understood through the four phases of the simple standard model.[10] Not least Johanson and Vahlne themselves have formulated this recognition; as part of the explanation, they have pointed out how the internationalisation of companies is not only driven by the simple almost lawful mechanisms originally described in the model.[11]

Actually, it follows from the changed and more network-oriented understanding since the 1970s of the characteristics of a market that there is more to it than overcoming the *liability of foreignness* when companies wish to set up business in foreign markets. Therefore, it is also relevant for the companies to work through other channels and use other tools than those involved in gradual phase-building supported by multinational investments. Whereas a previous more classic market understanding presented an arena with independent suppliers and customers, this image has, since the 1990s, to a large extent been abandoned in favour of a view of markets – as formulated by Johanson and Vahlne – as more or less boundless "networks of relationships in which firms are linked to each other in various, complex and, to a considerable extent, invisible patterns".[12]

In this image of the market, *the liability of foreignness* is not a company's primary challenge. Rather, this is constituted by the absence of network embeddedness, which may impede the opportunities to establish and control the desired activities, i.e. the *liability of outsidership*. The road to success is therefore more likely to run through the creation of relations which may contribute with the necessary and controllable competitive advantages. Such relations may be built through classic investments, but it must be expected that network embeddedness is often created at completely informal levels in which political, cultural and social structures combined with intentions, expectations and interpretations among individuals and groups are key parameters. In other words, conditions that are not easily captured for analysis through approaches focusing on capital, investments and formal ownership structures.

Therefore, it is easy to imagine how an analysis focusing exclusively on FDI can result in a faulty image of which relations have been established, and of the character of these – i.e. the internationalisation of the company. The more formal representation of the investments of a company – agencies, sales offices, production units, etc. – cannot necessarily be viewed as a direct reflection of the extent to which the strategic development of the company has been completed. The decisive factors required to build a market position may to an equal extent consist in more or less formal, not very transparent and rather unstable states of network embeddedness, in the character of the network and its position in the market, and in the opportunities to influence and control the activities in the network.

Born Globals

Another challenge to the image of the prolonged gradual internationalisation process with a fully developed MNE as its ultimate goal derives from the fast-increasing knowledge about companies that internationalise their activities early and at great speed, and which, during the past few decades, have become the subject of an independent research field termed *born globals*. A key question that directly springs to mind is, of course, how such companies can build their globalisation strategies without the prolonged establishment of a solid home market position in the first place, followed by gradual investments and infrastructures in the foreign markets.

Born globals' roads to success – or failure – have attracted great attention, not least because both businesses and state and government bodies have attached great importance to this particular type of enterprise as regards the possibilities to create economic growth. This has resulted in a similarly increased focus on the attempts made by companies to build competitive advantages through network embeddedness and on their possibilities to make profitable use of these competitive advantages to establish and control income-generating assets globally. One reason is that there seems to be no general indication that the born globals are primarily seeking to realise themselves as large monopolistic multinational companies. Rather, they tend to operate within so-called *business ecosystems* consisting of both large well-established multinational companies and younger less well-resourced, but creatively knowledge-operated companies that expand globally at great speed – i.e. born globals.[13]

Thus, born globals seem to be primarily characterised by being driven forward by entrepreneurs/individuals operating at high, specialised technological knowledge levels which they are seeking to translate into global utilisation of new business fields. This means that their activities are often characterised by great uncertainty and – inevitably, since they are new – based on untested and financially weak organisations. In other words, the companies are typically heading towards an uncertain future based primarily on how they imagine this to be. The need for *clever strategising* in order to reach their goal of establishing and controlling global market positions is therefore extremely urgent. This may lead to partnerships in *business ecosystems* with large well established and well-consolidated companies that already have platforms in several countries at their disposal – i.e. existing multinational companies in a more traditional sense. However, born globals may also gain ground through more equally balanced cooperation with other companies in which costs, risks and potentials are spread more equally across more shoulders. When such strategies are used, the risk of restricting creativity by dependence on the rigid structures of existing large organisations may more easily be avoided.

The possibilities of establishing well-functioning *business ecosystems* – globally and in the home market – constitute a key element in the picture of the strategies born globals can seek to follow. It is decisive for their success who they are able to establish collaboration with, as is the way in which they can influence and control the activities in the networks with which they are entwined.

The distribution of burdens, tasks and resources across more shoulders may take place through coordination with other companies with whom collaboration is obvious. These may be companies located close to each other geographically, and which, as a point of departure, constitute parts of what extensive research since the 1980s has termed *clusters*.[14] However, as appears in analyses in cluster research, the co-ordination may include a much broader range of actors than just companies, and it is obvious that this may also apply to born globals. As born globals are often technological and knowledge-driven companies, the conditions for creating knowledge and the possibilities to promote knowledge flows around the companies will often be decisive for their activities. The factors forming the basis of the strategies of born globals may therefore be found across the boundaries between private companies and other types of companies such as state-run institutions and public institutions of education and research. Therefore, the issue regarding the role of the home economy – i.e. the context from which the companies emerge – is essential for the picture of the possibilities of born globals. But this should not only be understood as the possibilities to draw on abundant or insufficient capital reserves when wanting to make direct investments.[15] Attention should also, and perhaps much rather, be directed towards the way in which the home economy may serve as a foundation for the creation of network-based innovation and knowledge advantages to draw on when establishing and controlling global market positions.[16]

Knowledge and Competitive Advantage

Altogether, the issue regarding the possibilities of companies to build competitive advantages through network-based knowledge creation and innovation has attracted much interest from many quarters, and not only when the focus has been on born globals or in other studies of internationalisation processes.

Not surprisingly, the theme has often attracted much political interest addressed directly at creating political regulation and change. This has, for instance, manifested itself in recommendations from the OECD/ World Economic Forum for politicians and business managers regarding the creation of *A Public Model for Collaborative Innovation*.[17] In this context, focus has been distinctly on collaboration between young innovative companies and resource-intensive, more well-established companies as well as on close coordination with the procurement of favourable framework conditions by the government. In other words, drawing a parallel to the *business ecosystems* which have been the focus of research into born globals appears to be logical.

In more recent studies of business history, focus has in several instances been directed towards the basis for creating knowledge/innovation and consequently competitive advantages through targeted collaboration between private technology-based companies and close coordination with the establishment of favourable frameworks and knowledge environments by the government. This has resulted in survey publications as well as a large number of more specific studies.[18]

One example is Johann Peter Murmann's studies of the mechanisms that enabled the completely newly established German chemical dye industry to completely outcompete its well-established British competitors within a short span of time in the mid-19th century. A decisive factor in this appeared to be the development of "… a dynamic model of competitive advantage that has at its center coevolutionary processes linking firms and national institutions".[19] Among the most important components were the patent laws and the educational institutions. The successful firms developed strong links to key activities within research and the development of new knowledge of organic chemistry. This resulted in complex development spirals in which the firms benefited from the most highly developed knowledge and technology from institutions of higher education and, as a consequence, achieved resources and influence for efficient lobbying activities, which secured both continuous knowledge building in the national research environments and efficient patent protection of technologies and products.

Another example is a study of the development of the German aircraft industry during World War II, in which Jonas Scherner, Jochen Streb and Stephanie Tilly explore how decisive competitive advantages were built through innovation based on efficient work distribution among a large group of companies.[20] By staking on a model that split up the production process of aircraft into parts and distributed these across a number of subcontractors – rather than gathering all stages of the production chain in one company – the industry established a structure in which the manufacturers were able to benefit from traditional *economies of scale*, i.e. specialising and upgrading their skills in the production of individual sub-components in large numbers. This resulted in the establishment of a collaboration model in which the market was seen almost as a network where each company refine their skills in their specific field within the larger entirety, and in which the combination of the sub-components into the final product was turned into a specialist field of its own. With the establishment of this collaboration model, which could be spread to other industries, the German industry gained a structural innovation advantage that became decisive for its competitiveness, even after the war had ended.

At a more theoretical level, Bruce Kogut has provided an illustration of how the market may act as a network in his analysis of how networks constitute a market structure based on certain prejudices and rules of game referred to as *generative rules,* i.e. methods and norms that guide the ways in which companies collaborate, and with whom.[21] This structuring makes it possible to establish connections between certain companies – sometimes through primarily cultural and social and personal relations – and consequently to efficiently split up the elements in creation innovation processes across a number of companies, rather than integrating all sub-processes in a singular company. The existence of *generative rules* in the market provides individual companies with the time and ability to focus on specialising and improving their skills within their limited field, which enables them to promote the total innovation effort. This means that the value of the entirety will exceed the sum of the contributions that might otherwise have been provided by the individual companies. Moreover, within technology-intensive fields, a trend will be seen towards creating networks in which several firms centralise around their own separate *research centres,* i.e. firms that have special knowledge-based resources or key technologies at their disposal. The market will therefore often be split into parallel networks that might appear as *competing constellations.*[22] By assuming positions as *research centres*, companies can benefit not only from technological advantages but also from forming the uniting link in the network as a whole. Using a term coined by the network theorist R. Burt, the companies can fill *structural holes/Burt-holes* in which they are particularly powerful because they control and coordinate the information flows between the companies that are closely interconnected with them in the network, but whose mutual ties are otherwise looser.[23] The key point is that the value of an individual company cannot be easily estimated simply by looking at the value of its assets and liabilities; to a large extent, its value is also constituted by the character of the network it is involved in and the *generative rules* of the role assumed by the company in the network. In this context, not least the opportunity to step into a so-called *structural hole* can be added as a particularly lucrative point of departure for control of the values and assets of the network.

Small-Scale State Advantages

A perspective on the significance of the home economy for the companies' use of non-FDI-based strategies can be found in existing research into the reasons why some small-scale countries, and particularly the small Scandinavian economies, became some of the richest in the world in the 20th century. In overall terms, it leaps to the eye that the most muscular European economies such as the British and German have been able to draw on the advantages of large home markets, which has enabled *economies of scale,* diversity and politically powerful contexts, whereas this seems to have been of less importance in the 20th century, when, in relative terms, the large-scale economies were outcompeted by what has been termed *SSEEs* (*Successful Small European Economies*).[24] An explanation may be seen in two areas in particular, both of which address how it has been possible to nurture and control well-functioning *business ecosystems.*

First of all, the SSEEs were tightly seeking to be open economies in order to make sure the companies had optimal conditions for integrating into global markets and were therefore able to divert their focus from the disadvantages of small home markets. Secondly, the SSEEs turned out to be distinctly successful at gaining global leadership in niches primarily in technologically advanced fields such as foods and the pharmaceutical industry (Switzerland), electric products and electronics (the Netherlands) and software (Israel). And, as a prerequisite for this success, they displayed explicit willingness to coordinate and collaborate, as well as the ability to do so. This is important since it is no advantage to be a small economy when you want to approach the technological leadership positions. In this case, there is a need for risk-bearing capital for technological development and implementation, a highly specialised knowledge workforce and the ability to identify the niches available. This means that when a small economy does not have the same critical mass as the large economies, the requirements for coordination and collaboration are great – not least between the private and public sectors, and particularly with the institutions that provide basic knowledge capacity, i.e. train people and conduct basic research, and the companies in which this knowledge is translated into technology development and production. Generally, it seems that the SSEEs were able to accommodate these requirements during the course of the 20th century, not least because they were small and easily manageable and therefore found it easier to identify growth potentials and aim to release these through efficient coordination and targeting of the use of their resources. In other words, being small could be turned into a *small-scale state advantage* based on the fact that the possibilities to coordinate and control one's efforts towards a shared goal are seemingly greater in a small economy than in larger and much more complex economies. Overall, the group of SSEEs appears to be characterised by (1) free, open economies and (2) well-functioning, stable and well-organised labour markets, political systems and institutions, and, in particular, economic equality, little social conflict and high levels of investments in knowledge capital.[25]

The economic development in the Scandinavian countries in particular seems to be able to provide the experience of such patterns. Recent research has reached the overall conclusion that the success history of the Nordic economies has been determined particularly by specific institutional developments which are also found in other small European economies such as the Netherlands and Austria.[26] The decisive factor for the wealth of these countries has been summarised to be their readiness to accept social reforms, their use of income-based pension systems, political regulations, strong unions, state-owned companies and liberal approaches to the establishment of open markets. To this can be added extensive labour market participation combined with large investment rates in knowledge development – *human capital* – and the fact that both of these activities have been accompanied by equality-oriented political trends towards equal access to education, small differences in income and welfare benefits aimed at an efficient and flexible workforce.

In other words, in the overall picture, elements such as income-based transfers/benefits, state pensions and childcare can be linked to historical traditions for collaboration and trust between industrial employers and employees and may therefore be seen as decisive for the establishment of well-functioning *business ecosystems*. And consequently such elements can be perceived as a basis for the existence of economies which can direct their resources in a stable and efficient manner towards the provision of competitive advantages that enable the establishment and control of global market positions within selected niches.

Research on Non-FDI Strategic Control

When summarising research conducted in the past few decades, it may be concluded that this has resulted in solid knowledge of how companies can establish and control their presence in foreign markets through direct investments. At the same time, an increasingly clearer picture emerges that the character and extent of transnational global activities involve more and other elements than FDI. A more differentiated understanding of the concept *control* is required, and consequently analyses of how companies can possibly establish control of global market positions – and *to what extent* they can do so – by means other than FDI. If it can be demonstrated that non-FDI-based strategies have been exercised with great effect in the past, they should be seen as equally important in the general picture of the globalisation of companies – and consequently attract attention in future research.

This is the background of the case study of this book of how a born-global company within one of the key industries in the world has been able to establish competitive advantages, and of *the extent to which* it has been able to utilise these with very little use of FDI to control income-generating assets in countries a long distance away from its own home market.

An analysis focusing primarily on factors other than FDI implies, of course, that the prevailing use of method aimed at exploring FDI must recede into the background. Instead, more qualitative approaches must be applied to better capture political and cultural factors and their importance in social relations. In other words, analyses are called for which, in terms of empirical data, can operate at micro levels, and which can make use of concepts that are relevant for understanding the actors and their relations and actions towards one another in the particular microcosmos in which they are located at the time in question.

It is therefore necessary to identify a basic framework of understanding in order to analyse the particular area within which F.L. Smidth & Co – like so many born-globals – sought (and is seeking) to establish its activities, i.e. the development and transfer of technology.

The Transfer of Technology

Among historians of technology, the concept *technology* is generally used about both the *technique*, i.e. the products and the machinery used to manufacture these, and the competences, production structure and organisations linked to the technique.[27] The idea of technological determinism has long been criticised and abandoned in favour of an understanding of technology as something that, like any other cultural product, is created by humans with a social and cultural ballast and which holds the potential to form part of – and impact – social, economic and political contexts that also comprise organisation types, values and knowledge. This means that the study of technological development has been included among the general approaches in cultural studies to cultural symbols which, as stated by anthropologist Clifford Geertz, can be seen as models both *of* reality and *for* reality.[28]

The dynamics can be understood through analyses of elements and relations in *technological systems*.[29] A technological system – an electric supply system, for instance – can thus be defined as consisting of *physical objects* such as turbo-generators, transformers and power grids, *organisations* in terms of manufacturing businesses, utility companies and banks, and *values* and (scientific) *knowledge* created and stored in books, articles, teaching activities and research. The technological system constitutes a network in the sense that its elements operate with and by virtue of each other. If one component is changed, i.e. legislation concerning power supply, the character of the entire system is affected.

If the technological system is moved from one context to another, changes are inevitable, and its success will depend on the adaptions of a physical, geographical, economic, social, political or cultural character. It might for instance be necessary to expand the infrastructure around newly introduced production machinery, but skilled work-power must also be available, and if this is not the case, competences must be introduced from outside or developed on location by the establishment of new training structures in a private or public setting. Basically, a need for products and services must exist, and if these are not available, they can be created through marketing, adjusted social structures and cultural patterns or perhaps as a consequence of political decisions regarding the building of railways and the resulting demand for iron for tracks and cement for bridges.

The degree of technological embeddedness in a new context can be described as a hierarchy.[30] At the bottom of this hierarchy are *technological projects*, which act as foreign elements, *enclaves*, with well-defined physical, social and economic boundaries towards the local context and with close ties to and great dependence on the sending environment. Ultimately, such enclaves may be much more closely linked to their sending countries than to the new local context in which they find themselves.[31] Further up in the hierarchy, the technology transfer may create *development projects* in which the rub-off effect across the boundaries to the surrounding community is greater. And, finally, the top of the hierarchy is constituted by the fully embedded *technological system* which, at all levels, has both adapted to and shaped its new context.

The character of a technology transfer depends on the opportunity space available to the actors who have access to the technological system and can ensure its integration into the new context. Such actors can be termed *social carriers of technology* to clarify that there is more to the technology transfer than moving machinery from A to B.[32] Social carriers of technology must possess the visions, competences and clout required to make the technological system functional – both physically and as regards its organisational, economic and social aspects. Whether these are individuals, large groups or companies, they must have the *power* to *control* the development of the technological system – and if we turn towards the social sciences, a picture will soon emerge of how power may basically originate from many other sources than capital flows and formal ownership.

Research during the past five decades has often stated with sociologist Michel Foucault that *power* can be viewed as an omnipresent force embedded in social relations and can be understood as closely connected to the *knowledge* that shapes and regulates the world.[33] In this understanding, the right to dispose of the crucial knowledge in relations or networks may result in *knowledge regimes* which are implemented as the right to define what makes sense, i.e. the *discourse* in Foucault's terminology which, incidentally, may quite naturally be juxtaposed with the concepts *generative rules and research centres* used by Bruce Kogut to describe the structuring of the market by networks. If the degree of *homogenisation* (Foucault) is low, understood as the access to and acquisition of this knowledge, the power structure will be correspondingly asymmetrical – and a parallel may be drawn again to Kogut/Burt's notion of *structural holes*.

Another set of concepts may be derived from the field theory of French sociologist Pierre Bourdieu.[34] According to Bourdieu, a field is constituted by a constellation of objective relations between different positions and imposes bindings on the actors that occupy the positions. In this understanding, power is described as the possession of the resources required to enforce decisions and changes among the actors and institutions occupying the positions of the field. The placement of the actors in the different positions and the concrete relations and bindings between them are decided by their relative amounts of capital, which in Bourdieu's framework of understanding does not, as mentioned, only consist of *economic capital* but also of *social capital* in the shape of for instance political network formations, and *cultural capital*, which often derives from access to knowledge and information. The different types of capital within a given field may be concentrated around one actor. However, this may not necessarily be the case, and the extent to which the actors are able to *exchange* one capital type for another and thus change their placement in the relative distribution of power may therefore be decisive for the distribution of positions in the field.

In other words, analyses of one field imply the identification of the actors included in the field and the mapping out of the distribution of capital among them, which may be a basic factor for understanding how the actors can impact and control the behaviour of one another. This applies to all types of social relations – including those in a field where technology transfer is the activity that brings the actors together.

Non-human Actors

When focusing on technology transfer, it is evident how *things* can play a decisive role for the relations of the actors and their possibilities to influence each other. A technological system consists of *things* included in and impacting the entire system in line with the *organisations* and the *knowledge* attached to it. It is therefore important to use methods and sources that make it possible to include the role of things and their impact on relations.

This implies that inspiration can be drawn from the so-called actor-network theory (ANT), according to which things play a key role, and which has, in the most recent decades, exerted such a pronounced influence on theories and methods that in certain parts of culture research, it has become common to speak about not only a *language turn* but also a *material turn*, and to say that *things have returned*.[35] At the same time, this also indicates how the material turn can be considered a renaissance of older theoretical and methodological approaches to the study of social relations and power relations.

The theory behind the so-called actor-network studies has primarily been developed since the 1990s through studies of the sociology of knowledge focusing primarily on exploring the practices in the natural sciences and the processes in the history of technology. French science sociologist Bruno Latour has been a recurrent leading force; his work has been based on the fundamental view that relations in themselves are fragile and unstable if not interwoven with things that can create stability and continuity. As stated by Latour: "It is always things – and I now mean this last word literally – which, in practice, lend their 'steely' quality to the hapless 'society'".[36] A fundamental view expressed by Latour is that *things* must be seen as *active actors* in social relations, and even if this view may seem somewhat affected, it is not, in essence, far removed from the basic view in cultural research since the 1970s that things cannot be seen only as *created* by society, but also as *creators* of society. Directions of research which have taken this as their point of departure and have included the material world, i.e. things, in their analyses of social patterns are the so-called *New Archaeology and Industrial Archaeology.*[37]

In Bruno Latour's research, things are seen as not only a result or an effect of a discursive staging of reality but also as actors *participating* in the social networks and, by means of their very materiality, creating connections and changes spanning across both time and space. Latour defines the role of the actor as a question not about intentionality – which a thing does not possess, of course – but about *effect*. In other words, a question as to whether things make a difference, or as phrased by Latour:

> ... any thing that does modify a state of affairs by making a difference is an actor – or, if it has no figuration yet, an actant. Thus, the question to ask about any agent is simply the following: Does it make a difference in the course of some other agent's action or not?[38]

Thus, the decisive factor is whether things can be seen as *participants* in a network and whether they are making a difference in this network in line with the difference made by the human actors.

In Bruno Latour's viewpoint, things such as factories and production technique can be seen as participants in social relations. If this line of thought is further pursued, they can therefore also be placed in selected contexts, where they can create desired relation types and action patterns. In other words, seen in this perspective, things can potentially be included as an active resource in the establishment and control of network positions by the companies. A key distinction might be that things not only *do* something, they are also *done*, i.e. used actively to make something happen.

A Cultural History Approach

Drawing on ANT – and letting the focus move towards network analyses in general – does, of course, have methodological implications for analyses of relations and control between companies across national borders. Identifying who the actors really are requires the exposure of who (and what) makes a difference, and for that purpose we may again be inspired by Bruno Latour, who suggests that we let the actors point out each other empirically (cf. the slogan "follow the actors"). This means that pointing out the actors and characterising their mutual relationship requires what Latour terms a *close description* of the dynamics at work when networks are formed and when an actor status is assigned to some elements. Action thus becomes an effect of the relations in the network, and in this respect, action is a relational effect. What is important is to explore how humans and non-humans are entangled.[39] Uncovering action patterns as a road to understanding the elements, humans and things of networks, and their mutual relations – and thus their options for reaction in these – is thus the essential concern.

Rather than conducting structural analyses of capital flows, their numbers, sizes and directions, there is a need to approach the inter-human relations in the real world through "close descriptions" – or, what is supposedly referred to by this term, "thick description" in Clifford Geertzk's phrasing.[40] Clifford Geertz is one obvious reference long since drawn on in other studies of relations between innovation, networks and competitiveness.[41] However, more recent cultural history offers several related options. Microhistory is another obvious source of inspiration; through the works of Carlo Ginzburg and Hans Medick since the 1990s in particular, this has specialised in what has been phrased as *not investigating small things, but investigating on a small scale*.[42] Microhistorians have been criticised for sometimes failing to place their central characters in a larger universe, but generally, their aim has been the ambition to uncover and analyse more overall cultural patterns by elucidating their expression in the particular example.[43]

It is by uncovering human action, individual events and (material) conditions immediately close to individuals of the time in question that the actors in the social networks and the character of their relations and power positions may be identified and analysed. According to Bruno Latour, it makes good sense to speak about *renewed empiricism*.[44] Although by this he does not refer to an interest in calling attention to facts or actions as such, but rather to the processes and reaction patterns behind the actions, it is debatable how new this approach actually is. To the extent that such *close descriptions* of networks comprise things, i.e. a material culture, a close relationship does indeed exist to a traditional classic humanist-based cultural history as this has long been implemented, not least in a Germanic and Scandinavian museum tradition. Thus, this tradition has been cultivated in particular in the research into people's lives and manners, i.e. ethnology, in which the *narrative* in itself is seen as a road to recognition in a hermeneutic working method rooted in Wilhelm Dilthey and Hans-Georg Gadamer; this has placed the study of the *artefact*, often at a museum, and its function and position in time, place and social environment in a key position.[45]

This perspective is very far removed from that of traditional economic history, business history and, not least, from the spirit in analytical approaches which, slightly caricatured, focus on how *money talks*, i.e. investments and organisation charts. The distance is not only created by the fact that American-influenced research into multinational enterprise and FDI may seem to be very far removed geographically as well as in terms of spirit from that of a museum researcher studying farming tools, people's clothing and local building traditions in the countryside. The distance is also characterised by the fact that classic humanist-based cultural history does not primarily emanate from a natural science ideal of setting up a hypothesis which can be confirmed or invalidated through controlled tests. In contrast, this working method is characterised by a search for what is likely or forms an entirety; this is a search that takes an interpretive approach towards gaining an understanding of elements, processes, connections which humans are both subject to and the creators of. Culture cannot be easily defined but calls for interpretations of its appearance in manners and physical conditions. The historian's attempt to discover and describe the big picture in the small details, through small traces, is decisive as a method to elucidate the culture which, at the same time, both permeated and embraced the people living in it.

Inductive Hermeneutics

The analysis of F.L Smidth & Co.'s establishment in the Asian markets will draw on the concepts used since the 1980s by historians of technology. It is evident that the Danes delivered technology for the production of cement, but the question is how they stepped in among the other actors in the process and embedded this technology in its new surroundings. Did they assume the role as social carriers of technology? And to what extent did the relative distribution of capital enable them to control the establishment of the technological systems – and thus the development following their initial establishment?

The basis for forming a picture of F.L. Smidth and Co.'s market position is what may be characterised as *inductive hermeneutics*. In concrete terms, this means that the analysis circles around its topic and, by a rather traditional hermeneutically inspired approach drawing on common references to Wilhelm Dilthey (1833–1911) and Hans-Georg Gadamer (1900–2002), it writes itself into an increasingly deeper understanding by explaining about both the entirety and its individual constituents.

Picture and *narrative* are key concepts. Basically, the analysis does not pride itself of discovering, reconstructing or asserting the existence of an overall "Asia strategy" at the time. Rather, based on discoveries of particular elements – concrete conditions and courses of events – it seeks to inductively paint an overall and more universal picture of that which drove and shaped the internationalisation of the company. This means that the analysis does not just progress chronologically, but, as mentioned, somehow writes around and gradually into its topic. In other words, the end product will not be a reconstructed strategy from the past, but indeed a *picture* created at the present time through the narrative which is being established in the process, and which evokes subelements by exploring its main topic from different angles and using different perspectives. In concrete terms, as this is linked to four geographical contexts (Siam, China, Japan and India), places which can be compared and constitute the subjects of analogies. And by letting the narrative, in various ways, bring us close to the actors, their working conditions and their interpretation of these – and thus the background of their choices and actions.

Often, a picture provides better access to understanding, and in some passages, the analysis will therefore draw on the possibility to *show* a picture rather than *analysing it*. It will do so by letting the FLS people themselves be heard. And it will do so by drawing attention to the conditions in which they acted, i.e. the landscapes, factory plans and buildings that constituted the framework of and shaped their lives and everyday routines – and which they themselves were involved in shaping. In this sense too, the exposition is related to a humanist tradition of microhistory, which is seeking to study *the big picture in the small details*, and in which the *narrative*, like a picture, is a key tool to show a story in its entirety and, by doing so, to make it comprehensible to the reader.

Notes

1 Jürgen Osterhammel and Niels P. Petersson: *Globalization: A Short History* (Princeton University Press, 2005).
2 Geoffrey Jones: *Entrepreneurship and Multinationals: Global Business and the Making of the Modern World* (Edward Elgar, 2013).
3 Geoffrey Jones and Harm G. Schröter: "Continental European Multinationals, 1850–1992," in *The Rise of Multinationals in Continental Europe*, ed. Geoffrey Jones and Harm G. Schröter (Edward Elgar, 1993).
4 Geoffrey Jones: *Multinationals and Global Capitalism. From the Nineteenth to the Twenty-First Century* (Oxford: Oxford University Press, 2005), 1–15.
5 Jones, *Multinationals and Global Capitalism*, 5–7.
6 Mark W. Fruin: "Business Groups and Interfirm Networks," in *The Oxford Handbook of Business History*, ed. Geoffrey Jones and Jonathan Zeitlin (Oxford: Oxford University Press, 2007), 244–267. Geoffrey Jones and Asli M. Colpan: "Business Groups in Historical Perspectives," in *The Oxford Handbook of Business Groups* (Oxford: Oxford University Press, 2010).
7 Jan Johanson and Jan-Erik Vahlne: "The internationalization process of the firm – A model of knowledge development and increasing foreign market commitments," in *Journal of International Business Studies*, Vol. 8, No. 1 (1977), 23–32. Jan Johanson and Jan-Erik Vahlne: "The Mechanism of Internationalisation," in *International Marketing Review*, Vol. 7, No. 4 (1990), 11–24.
8 Jones, *Multinationals and Global Capitalism*, 147–148.
9 Jones, *Multinationals and Global Capitalism*, 148.
10 Peter J. Buckley: "Business history and international business," in *Business History*, Vol. 51, No. 3 (2009), 313 and 321.
11 Jan Johanson and Jan-Erik Vahlne: "The Uppsala internationalization process model revisited: From liability of foreignness to liability of outsidership," in *Journal of International Business Studies*, Vol. 40, No. 9 (2009), 1411–1431. Kent Eriksson et al.: "Experiential knowledge and cost in the

internationalization process," in *Journal of International Business Studies*, Vol. 28, No. 2 (1997), 330–360.

12 Johanson, "The Uppsala Internationalization process," 1411.
13 Ivo Zander, Patricia McDougall-Covin and Elizabeth L. Rose: "Born globals and international business: Evolution of a field of research," in *Journal of International Business Studies* 46 (2015), 27–35.
14 M.E. Porter: "Competition in global industries: A conceptual framework," in *Competition in Global Industries*, ed. M. E. Porter (Boston: Harvard Business School Press, 1986).
15 Jones, *Multinationals and Global Capitalism*, 231.
16 Zander, "Born globals," 30.
17 *Innovative Networks: Cooperation in National Innovation Systems* (OECD: Paris, 2001). *Collaborative Innovation Transforming Business, Driving Growth*, World Economic Forum (2015), http://www3.weforum.org/docs/ WEF_Collaborative_Innovation_report_2015.pdf (link ultimo, 2017).
18 Walter W. Powell and Stine Grodal: "Networks of Innovators," in *The Oxford Handbook of Innovation*, ed. Jan Fagerberg, David C. Mowery and Richard R. Nelson (Oxford: Oxford University Press, 2005), 56–86. For a historical overview of the development for enterprise-driven innovation, see Christopher Freeman: *The Economics of Industrial Innovation* (Cambridge, MA: MIT Press, 1982) and others. Nathan Rosenberg: *Inside the Black Box* (New York: Cambridge University Press, 1982).
19 Johann Peter Murmann: *Knowledge and Competitive Advantage. The Coevolution of Firms, Technology, and National Institutions* (Cambridge, 2003), xiv.
20 Jonas Scherner, Jochen Streb and Stephanie Tilly: "Supplier networks in the German aircraft industry during World War II and their long-term effects on West Germany's automobile industry during the Wirtschaftswunder," in *Business History*, Vol. 6, No. 6 (2015).
21 Bruce Kogut: "The network as knowledge: Generative rules and the emergence of structure," in *Strategic Management Journal*, Vol. 21 (2000), 405–425.
22 B. Gomes-Casseres: "Group versus group: How alliance networks compete," in *Harvard Business Review*, Vol. 72 (1994), 62–74.
23 Bruce Kogut, "The Network," 414. R. Burt: *Structural Holes: The Social Structure of Competition* (Cambridge, MA: Harvard University Press, 1992).
24 Joel Mokyr: "Preface: Successful Small Open Economies and the Importance of Good Institutions," in *The Road to Prosperity. An Economic History of Finland*, ed. Jari Ojala, Jari Eloranta and Jukka Jalava (Helsinki, 2006), 8–15. See also Peter A. Hall and David Soskice: *Varieties of Capitalism. The Institutional Foundations of Comparative Advantage* (Oxford, 2001).
25 Mokyr, "Preface," 14–15.
26 Susanna Fellman and Hans Sjögren: "Conclusion," in *Creating Nordic Capitalism: The Business History of a Competitive Periphery*, ed. Susanna Fellman et al. (Palgrave Macmillan, 2008), 568.
27 Wiebe E. Bijker: *Of Bicycles, Bakelites, and Bulbs. Toward a Theory of Sociotechnical Change* (Massachusetts, 1995). Thomas P. Hughes: "The Evolution of Large Technological Systems," in *The Social Construction of Technological Systems: New Directions in the Sociology and History of Technology*, ed. Wiebe E. Bijker, Thomas P. Hughes and Trevor Pinch (Cambridge, MA, Baltimore, 1987), 51.
28 Clifford Geertz: *The Interpretation of Cultures* (New York, 1973).
29 Thomas P. Hughes: *Networks of Power. Electrification in Western Society, 1880-1930* (Baltimore and London: The Johns Hopkins University Press, 1983). Thomas P. Hughes, "The Evolution," 51–82.

30 Jan av Geijerstam: *Landscapes of Technology Transfer. Swedish Ironmakers in India 1860-1864*, Jernkontorets berghistoriska skriftserie 42 (Riga, 2004), 22–25.
31 Daniel R. Headrick: *The Tentacles of Progress. Technology Transfer in the Age of Imperialism, 1850-1940* (Oxford, 1988), 12.
32 Charles Edquist and Olle Edquist: *Social Carriers of Techniques for Development* (Lund, 1979), 42. Hughes, "The Evolution," 52.
33 Michel Foucault: *The History of Sexuality Volume 1: An Introduction* (London: Allen Lane, 1979).
34 Pierre Bourdieu and Loïc J. D. Wacquant: *An Invitation to Reflexive Sociology* (Chicago, 1992), 94.
35 Lorraine Daston, ed.: *Things That Talk* (New York: Zone Books, 2004). Amira Henare, Martin Holbraa and Siri Wastell: *Thinking through Things* (London: Routledge, 2006). Daniel Miller: *Material Culture and Mass Consumption* (Oxford: Blackwell, 1987). Bill Brown: *Things* (Chicago: University of Chicago, 2004). Tine Damsholt and Dorthe Gert Simonsen: "Materialiseringer," in *Processer, Relationer og Performativitet*, ed. Tine Damsholt, Dorthe Gert Simonsen and Camilla Mordhorst: *Materialiseringer. Nye perspektiver på materialitet og kulturanalyse* (Aarhus, 2009), 9.
36 Bruno Latour: *Reassembling the Social: An Introduction to Actor-Network-Theory* (Oxford, 2005), 68.
37 Marilyn Palmer and Peter Neaverson: *Industrial Archaeology. Principles and Practice* (London, 1998), 1–8.
38 Bruno Latour, *Reassembling*, 71.
39 Bruno Latour: *Pandora's Hope. Essays on the Reality of Science Studies* (Harvard, 1999), 179.
40 Geertz, *The Interpretation*, 3–32.
41 Murmann, *Knowledge*, 2003.
42 See Hans Medick: "Mikro-Historie," in *Alltagsgeschichte, Mikrohistorie*, ed. Winfried Schulze (Göttingen, 1994) and others. Carlo Ginzburg: *Clues, Myths and the Historical Method* (Baltimore, MA, 1992). The Formulation regarding the scale of the viewpoint is derived from Giovanni Levi, here quoted from Mikkel Venborg Pedersen: *Luksus. Forbrug og kolonier i Danmark i det 18. Århundrede* (København, 2013), 13.
43 Lawrence Stone: "The revival of narrative. Reflections on a new old History," in *Past and* Present, No. 85 (1979), 19.
44 Bruno Latour: "Why has critique run out of steam," in *Critical Inquiry*, Vol. 30, No. 2 (2004).
45 Troels Troels-Lund: *Dagligt Liv i Norden i det sekstende Aarhundrede* (København, 1914) and others. Palle Ove Christiansen: *De forsvundne. Hedens sidste fortællere* (København, 2011). Bjarne Stoklund: *Hvad er kulturhistorie? Troels-Lund og den kulturhistoriske strid i Tyskland i 1880'erne* (København, 1987). Pedersen, *Luksus*.

References

Amira Henare, Martin Holbraa & Siri Wastell: *Thinking through Things* (London: Routledge, 2006).
B. Gomes-Casseres: "Group versus group: How alliance networks compete," in *Harvard Business Review*, Vol. 72 (1994), 62–74.
Bill Brown: *Things* (Chicago: University of Chicago, 2004).

Bjarne Stoklund: *Hvad er kulturhistorie? Troels-Lund og den kulturhistoriske strid i Tyskland i 1880'erne* (København, 1987).

Bruce Kogut: "The network as knowledge: Generative rules and the emergence of structure," in *Strategic Management Journal*, Vol. 21 (2000), 405–425.

Bruno Latour: *Pandora's Hope. Essays on the Reality of Science Studies* (Harvard, 1999).

Bruno Latour: "Why has critique run out of steam," in *Critical Inquiry*, Vol. 30, No. 2 (2004).

Bruno Latour: *Reassembling the Social: An Introduction to Actor-Network-Theory* (Oxford, 2005).

Charles Edquist & Olle Edquist: *Social Carriers of Techniques for Development* (Lund, 1979).

Christopher Freeman: *The Economics of Industrial Innovation* (Cambridge, MA: MIT Press, 1982).

Clifford Geertz: *The Interpretation of Cultures* (New York, 1973).

Daniel R. Headrick: *The Tentacles of Progress. Technology Transfer in the Age of Imperialism, 1850-1940* (Oxford, 1988).

Daniel Miller: *Material Culture and Mass Consumption* (Oxford: Blackwell, 1987).

Geoffrey Jones: *Multinationals and Global Capitalism. From the Nineteenth to the Twenty-First Century* (Oxford: Oxford University Press, 2005).

Geoffrey Jones: *Entrepreneurship and Multinationals: Global Business and the Making of the Modern World* (Edward Elgar, 2013).

Geoffrey Jones & Asli M. Colpan: "Business Groups in Historical Perspectives," in *The Oxford Handbook of Business Groups* (Oxford: Oxford University Press, 2010).

Geoffrey Jones & Harm G. Schröter: "Continental European Multinationals, 1850-1992," in *The Rise of Multinationals in Continental Europe*, ed. Geoffrey Jones and Harm G. Schröter (Edward Elgar, 1993).

Hans Medick: "Mikro-Historie," in *Alltagsgeschichte, Mikrohistorie*, ed. Winfried Schulze (Göttingen, 1994).

Innovative Networks: Co-operation in National Innovation Systems (Read online oecd-ilibrary.org, OECD: Paris, 2001). *Collaborative Innovation Transforming Business, Driving Growth*. World Economic Forum (2015), http://www3.weforum.org/docs/WEF_Collaborative_Innovation_report_2015.pdf (link ultimo 2021).

Ivo Zander, Patricia McDougall-Covin & Elizabeth L. Rose: "Born globals and international business: Evolution of a field of research," in *Journal of International Business Studies*, Vol. 46 (2015), 27–35.

Jan av Geijerstam: *Landscapes of Technology Transfer. Swedish Ironmakers in India 1860-1864*, Jernkontorets berghistoriska skriftserie 42 (Riga, 2004).

Jan Johanson & Jan-Erik Vahlne: "The internationalization process of the firm – A model of knowledge development and increasing foreign market commitments," in *Journal of International Business Studies*, Vol. 8, No. 1 (1977), 23–32.

Jan Johanson & Jan-Erik Vahlne: "The mechanism of internationalisation," in *International Marketing Review*, Vol. 7, No. 4 (1990), 11–24.

Jan Johanson & Jan-Erik Vahlne: "The Uppsala internationalization process model revisited: From liability of foreignness to liability of outsidership," in *Journal of International Business Studies*, Vol. 40, No. 9 (2009), 1411–1431.

Joel Mokyr: "Preface: Successful Small Open Economies and the Importance of Good Institutions," in *The Road to Prosperity. An Economic History of Finland*, ed. Jari Ojala, Jari Eloranta and Jukka Jalava (Helsinki, 2006), 8–15.

Johann Peter Murmann: *Knowledge and Competitive Advantage. The Coevolution of Firms, Technology, and National Institutions* (Cambridge, 2003).

Jonas Scherner, Jochen Streb & Stephanie Tilly: "Supplier networks in the German aircraft industry during World War II and their long-term effects on West Germany's automobile industry during the Wirtschaftswunder," in *Business History*, Vol. 6, No. 6 (2015), 996–1020.

Jürgen Osterhammel & Niels P. Petersson: *Globalization: A Short History* (Princeton University Press, 2005).

Kent Eriksson et al.: "Experiential Knowledge and cost in the internationalization process," in *Journal of International Business Studies*, Vol. 28, No. 2 (1997), 330–360.

Lawrence Stone: "The revival of narrative. Reflections on a new old history," in *Past and* Present, No. 85 (1979).

Lorraine Daston, ed.: *Things That Talk* (New York: Zone Books, 2004).

Marilyn Palmer & Peter Neaverson: *Industrial Archaeology. Principles and Practice* (London, 1998).

Mark W. Fruin: "Business Groups and Interfirm Networks," in *The Oxford Handbook of Business History*, ed. Geoffrey Jones and Jonathan Zeitlin (Oxford: Oxford University Press, 2007), 244–267.

M. E. Porter: "Competition in Global Industries: A Conceptual Framework," in *Competition in Global Industries*, ed. M. E. Porter (Boston: Harvard Business School Press, 1986).

Michel Foucault: *The History of Sexuality Volume 1: An Introduction* (London: Allen Lane, 1979).

Mikkel Venborg Pedersen: *Luksus. Forbrug og kolonier i Danmark i det 18. Århundrede* (København, 2013).

Nathan Rosenberg: *Inside the Black Box* (New York: Cambridge University Press, 1982).

Palle Ove Christiansen: *De forsvundne. Hedens sidste fortællere* (København, 2011).

R. Burt: *Structural Holes: The Social Structure of Competition* (Cambridge, MA: Harvard University Press, 1992).

Susanna Fellman & Hans Sjögren: "Conclusion," in *Creating Nordic Capitalism: The Business History of a Competitive Periphery*, ed. Susanna Fellman et al. (Palgrave Macmillan, 2008).

Thomas P. Hughes: *Networks of Power. Electrification in Western Society, 1880–1930* (Baltimore and London: The Johns Hopkins University Press, 1983).

Thomas P. Hughes: "The Evolution of Large Technological Systems," in *The Social Construction of Technological Systems: New Directions in the Sociology and History of* Technology, ed. Wiebe E. Bijker, Thomas P. Hughes and Trevor Pinch (Cambridge, MA, Baltimore, 1987).

Tine Damsholt & Dorthe Gert Simonsen: "Materialiseringer," in *Processer, Relationer og Performativitet*, ed. Tine Damsholt, Dorthe Gert Simonsen and Camilla Mordhorst: *Materialiseringer. Nye perspektiver på materialitet og kulturanalyse* (Aarhus, 2009).

Troels Troels-Lund: *Dagligt Liv i Norden i det sekstende Aarhundrede* (København, 1914).

Walter W. Powell & Stine Grodal: "Networks of Innovators," in *The Oxford Handbook of Innovation*, ed. Jan Fagerberg, David C. Mowery and Richard R. Nelson (Oxford: Oxford University Press, 2005), 56–86.

Wiebe E. Bijker: *Of Bicycles, Bakelites, and Bulbs. Toward a Theory of Sociotechnical Change* (Massachusetts, 1995).

2 The Modern Cement Industry: Its Emergence and the Role of F.L. Smidth & Co.

Aiming at a Key Position in the Emerging Global Cement Industry

From the turn of the 20th century, the cement industry became a global phenomenon. Factories were established in all parts of the world, and cement became the preferred building material for housing, business infrastructure, etc. In a very short time, the cement industry grew to become one of the largest and heaviest industries in the world. The volume of the global production speaks for itself, even if no precise figures exist for the first decades of the century. From the 1930s to the 1950s, the annual global production went up from 49 million tonnes to 155 million tonnes, and in the 1970s, this figure grew to almost 300 million tonnes. At the present time, the world's cement production is estimated to amount to 4.2 billion tonnes per year, and the cement industry ranks high among the world's emitters of carbon dioxide.[1] During the first decades of the 20th century, Europe and North America were the centres of gravity, but from the 1960s onwards, Asia accounted for more than 25% of the global cement production. Since then, this percentage has only been growing, with China taking a lead position.

The introduction of a completely new set of production methods during the period 1880–1920 formed the basis of the explosive growth in the world's cement production. The changes in production methods, knowledge base and innovation organisation method that occurred during this period were so radical and happened so rapidly that they may well be characterised as a technological revolution.[2] During the first phases of this revolution, the Danish engineering firm F.L. Smidth & Co. was founded, and from the first years, the strategy of the firm was guided by their attempts to assume the role as an active power in the global development of the industry.

F.L. Smidth & Co. was established in Copenhagen in 1882 by Frederik Læssøe Smidth, who in 1883 was joined by Alexander Foss and Poul Larsen as his partners.[3] Their point of departure was specialisation in the construction of brickworks, but in 1887, F.L. Smidth & Co. received an

DOI: 10.4324/9780429446184-2

order for the establishment of a cement plant at Limhamn in Sweden for the Scanian cement company *Skånska Cement Aktiebolaget*. This provided F.L. Smidth & Co. with their first experience of establishing cement plants, and the following year this was expanded in Norway with the order to construct a plant for the cement company Christiania Portland Cementfabrik.

In 1889 followed the first Danish project when F.L. Smidth & Co., in collaboration with Danish and German investors, proceeded to send out prospectuses for the public issue of shares to finance the establishment of the cement plant *Aalborg Portland Cement Fabrik A/S*. When production at Aalborg Portland began in 1891 near the city of Aalborg in northern Denmark, F.L. Smidth & Co. entered into a new role as a cement manufacturer. This created an opportunity to supplement their experience of establishing plants by solid knowledge of the running of the cement plants and of the new production methods which were about to revolutionise the way in which cement was manufactured.

A Mix of Brickworks, Lime Kilns and Grain Mills

Cement is manufactured by heating a mixture of limestone and other materials, traditionally clay. In the heating process, silicic acid is formed, which, together with water, combines with the limestone, producing in the material the hydraulic, i.e. water-hardening, properties that are absolutely essential when cement is used for building construction.

Lime burning for mortar, which hardens when in contact with carbon dioxide from the air, is known from ancient times, and as naturally occurring mixtures of limestone and clay are quite frequent, we may assume that this would sometimes have resulted in cement-like products. The burning of such "hydraulic mortar" was a method used intentionally by the ancient Romans, but it was not until English cement manufacturers in particular discovered the method around the year 1800 that a basis was established for industrial production on a major scale.[4]

A milestone was reached with John Smeaton's attempts at burning clayey limestone, which resulted in cement of a quality so high that it could be used for the building of a lighthouse at Eddystone, Plymouth, in 1756. However, based on experiments with mixtures of raw materials, Joseph Aspdin was able, in 1824, to take out a patent for the so-called "artificial stone", a mixture of limestone and clay in the proportion of 5:1. Around 1840, Joseph Aspdin's son, William Aspdin, discovered that the cement quality was improved considerably if the burning process reached a temperature high enough (around 1500°C) for the material to undergo a so-called sintering process resulting in clinkers, i.e. fusing together the materials to the point of liquefaction into porcelain-like lumps.

Concurrently, a set of production methods were developed for the five steps in the process: raw material extraction, raw material processing, cement burning, finishing and storing/packing.[5] Raw material extraction was traditional mining, and the other steps proceeded using methods from other industries. The cement industry did not yet have production methods of its own.

The mixing of raw materials took place by adding these to water in slurry basins, i.e. large vessels with rotating agitators, and using other methods which were well-known from the brickworks industry. The final slurry mixture could then be fed into reservoirs, leaving it to pre-cipitate for a period of time before being cut into blocks which, after further drying, could be transported to the kiln for burning. This was a heavy process which was also season dependant and unstable.

Burning took place in shaft kilns of the types known from the lime and mortar industries. The method comprised the stacking of dry raw bricks inside the kilns, followed by the actual burning from the firing holes at the bottom of the kiln before the burnt cement, after cooling, could again be raked out of the kiln. From the 1870s, German engineers in particular developed shaft kiln types that enabled a transfer from batch to flow production. However, the process continued to be labour-intensive and unstable.

The burnt bricks were crushed and ground to cement powder in roller and mill plants with horizontally rotating mill stones, i.e. using techniques derived from traditional grain mills. When the product to be ground was cement, the durability of the millstone was short, however, and the need for repair work and replacement of wearing parts was high. Finally, the cement powder was shovelled into wooden barrels by hand.

A New Innovative Model

The development from the 1880s of new production methods specifically for the cement industry primarily occurred in the context of companies from the American industry, Germany and – via F.L. Smidth & Co. – Denmark. This implied a new way of organising the innovation effort; the technological development work was separated from the actual cement production and now took place in specialised independent industries.

At the same time, this separation meant that highly educated poly-technical engineers took over the development work which had so far been undertaken by the individual manufacturers, who were often self-taught people with roots in the brickworks and lime-burning industries. This was the case, to a large extent, among the workforce at F.L. Smidth & Co. From the time the company was established, the share of engineers among the employees at its head office in Copenhagen remained stable at around

50% – measured in numbers around 200 people in 1920 and 500 around 1930. In other words, whereas further training was up to the company itself, the basic engineering foundation was laid with the opportunities to draw on engineers educated in government-financed institutions.[6]

In overall terms, the Danish version of the new organisation structure reflected a division of labour with specialisations that crossed the dividing lines between industries as well as between private and public actors. Whereas basic engineering skills were secured by the Danish government in the shape of The Polytechnical College, *Den Polytekniske Læreanstalt*, in Copenhagen, the private companies took care of the specialised technology development within the framework of F.L. Smidth & Co, as well as the actual cement production, primarily at the Aalborg Portland Cement Factory from 1889. To this may be added a number of Danish factories, concrete manufacturers and companies and organisations engaged in retail sale of cement. Rather than integrating into a company, the market was split up into a network in which F.L. Smidth & Co. occupied a key position, and where competences and risks were distributed across a number of actors.

At the same time, the development of the Danish cement production became an illustration of the changes made possible by this new organisation structure.

The Danish Breakthrough

With their involvement in Aalborg Portland, it became possible for F.L. Smidth & Co. to experiment with new full-size production plants and to demonstrate the plants in operation to potential buyers. Their work included both their own inventions and the development of inventions made by others, which were purchased and tested in Aalborg with a view to taking out patents.

From the first years, attention was focused on the core of the production process – kilns and milling sections. From 1898, the head office in Copenhagen was supplemented by a machine factory in which a chemical and mechanical research laboratory was set up from 1899 to develop and produce cement technology. Complementary technologies such as electrical installations, engines, boiler and power plants, pumps and packing systems were purchased from sub-suppliers such as Siemens (Germany), Babcock & Wilcox (England), ASEA (Sweden), Fuller Co. and Bates (USA).

The development of new roller and mill types was a characteristic example of the Danish technology research achievements.[7] From the 1890s, work was focused on new horizontal tube mills in which cement clinkers were crushed by rocks or steel balls while the mill rotated slowly. This enabled the manufacturing of very finely ground cement by a small workforce, and the advantages were increased by the fact that the tube mill could be used for both raw material preparation and the manufacture of coal dust as fuel for firing the new cement kiln types. In the first instance, the tube mill was invented by the Danish engineer L.M. Davidsen in 1892, but F.L. Smidth & Co. soon bought up the patent rights and installed their first tube mills at Aalborg Portland in 1893. This created an advantageous basis for a number of further developments of the patent, and by 1914, F.L. Smidth & Co. had mounted and introduced more than 3,000 tube mills around the world.

Precision gear units for the mills became one of the most important selling items as plants grew in size, resulting in power requirements of sometimes far more than 1000 hp in the 1930s, which rendered the previous belt-driven systems insufficient. In 1920, F.L. Smidth & Co. bought the licence for a gear box motor with resilient gear wheels developed in Sweden, and in 1921, the first such motor was mounted at Aalborg Portland, and test runs were commenced to operate the motor.[8] This came to be an example of the importance of being able to collaborate on a full-scale test plant when testing cost-intensive technologies, because two years later, in 1923, they had still not succeeded at making the gear box motor function. However, F.L. Smidth & Co. had acquired so much experience that, in 1922, they could abandon their work with the Swedish gear box motors and instead establish their own gear production in Copenhagen. In 1924, F.L. Smidth & Co. were therefore able to take out a patent for the so-called Symetro gear, which from then on became an integral part of the milling sections they sold.

However, the decisive breakthrough happened with the mounting of the first rotary kilns at Aalborg Portland in 1898–1899. Originally, the Englishman Thomas Russel Crampton had taken out a patent for the rotary kiln in 1877, but he never succeeded in making it operate profitably. This was achieved in the USA, however, where oil was first used as fuel and subsequently coal dust, which turned out to be a much cheaper solution. When FLS managing director Poul Larsen visited Atlas Portland Cement Company in Pennsylvania in 1898 and saw a rotary kiln in operation, he therefore took the initiative to buy two rotary kilns for Aalborg Portland. From then on, developments accelerated fast. At a meeting in 1898, Aalborg Portland's board of directors decided to let F.L. Smidth & Co. install two rotary kilns of 18 metres each bought from the American engineering company Laxhbury & Spackmann in Philadelphia. This agreement made it clear that both close collaboration and a clear formal division of labour existed between the technology supplier F.L. Smidth & Co. and the cement manufacturer Aalborg Portland. The conditions for installing the new kilns implied that six months after the order was placed, the kilns were to deliver 115 barrels of cement per day, and that neither F.L. Smidth & Co. nor Laxhbury &

Spackman were allowed to deliver similar kilns to other Danish factories before 1903. At the same time, Aalborg Portland committed to not buy similar kilns from other suppliers than F.L. Smidth & Co. and to make every effort to keep the construction and operation principles of the kilns secret.[9]

These two kilns were among the first rotary kilns to be put in operation in Europe, and the experience from these became decisive for F.L. Smidth & Co. Until 1921, F.L. Smidth & Co. sold 300 rotary kilns, and according to the company's own calculations, half of the world's cement production in 1950 took place in FLS-manufactured kilns. This was based on a simplified production process with significant increases in both productivity and quality. The previous extensive and season-dependant precipitation and drying processes followed by stacking of raw materials in shaft kilns were abandoned. In the rotary kiln, the suspended raw materials could instead be pumped directly into the upper part of the tilted rotary kiln tubes made of steel. The combination of the tilt of the kiln and the constant rotation enabled the raw materials to slide down towards the firing zone, into which coal dust was being constantly injected. During this process, the raw materials were dried and calcinated before being sintered and falling out of the kiln at the bottom as red-hot cement clinkers. At Aalborg Portland, the two new kilns produced more than 100,000 barrels of cement annually, corresponding to the capacity of eight shaft kilns. The success was accentuated by the fact that the process could be operated by a workforce of four working people and one firing master and completely without the work-intensive and season-dependant raw material handling required when operating the shaft kiln.

In other words, as regards kilns, F.L. Smidth & Co.'s work also involved the purchase of other companies' inventions, which were installed at Aalborg Portland with a view to harvesting experience from the running of the machinery and taking out patents for further developments and combinations cutting across these inventions. An example was that the new precision gear units for the mills could also be utilised in the slow-moving rotary kilns, which soon grew in size to be more than 100 metres long towards 1930. Other examples were systems for cooling of the red-hot cement clinkers. The earliest cooler types consisted of revolving cooling rollers running underneath the rotary kilns, but in 1922, F.L. Smidth & Co. were able to take out a patent for so-called Unax coolers consisting of cooling pipes mounted planetarily around the rotary kilns; the clinkers could then pass through these for cooling, while the heat from the cooling could be fed back into the kiln, thus reducing fuel consumption.

Among F.L. Smidth & Co.'s own inventions was the development of new techniques for storing and packaging of the finished cement, which was based on the discovery that cement dust becomes pumpable by infusion of air. This meant that the unpleasant work of transporting and shovelling the cement could be taken over by air compressors or vacuum pumps, which circulated the cement inside closed systems. In 1909, F.L. Smidth & Co. introduced the so-called Exilor at Aalborg Portland, which automatically fed cement from the silo sections into barrels. In the 1920s, the barrels were replaced by paper bags, following the invention by American William Bates of a bag type with a valve. F.L. Smidth & Co. made use of Bates' patent and in 1925 developed their own so-called *flux-packs*, which permitted the cement to be fed through discharge spouts provided with automatic weighing systems and bag discharge. This was followed by the development of flux transportation, by which the fluid mixture of cement and air was circulated around the factory areas inside closed pipe systems. Now the last step in the production system had become fully automatic.

The Small-Scale State Advantage

The restructuring from the 1880s onwards of the Danish cement industry with F.L. Smidth & Co. holding the position as *research centre* got to be an example of the opportunities that can emerge with the organisation of a market through networks. This situation appeared to be a textbook example of optimal circumstances for the creation of a successful born global. However, it also became an example of the risks that follow when activities are not integrated vertically and therefore cannot be controlled within the company's own framework, and of how such risks may be responded to.

A decisive element in the new organisation of innovation was F.L. Smidth & Co.'s collaboration with Aalborg Portland, which made it possible to spread the considerable costs and risks involved in full-scale tests of the new production techniques – mills, kilns, packing systems, etc. – across more shoulders. The test versions of the new machines were acquired by Aalborg Portland, not by F.L. Smidth & Co., and the development work was integrated into the operating costs of the cement factory. In reality, this meant that the pressure to provide capital for the innovation was solved by imposing the costs involved in prolonged test runs of expensive and heavy machinery on the cement consumers. In other words, the entire innovation model became extremely sensitive to competition on cement prices for the Danish consumers.

To solve this challenge, *generative rules* were introduced, which could be imposed on the Danish market because this was so small that it could be controlled by investments, strategic agreements and personal contacts. This meant that the precondition for the globalisation of F.L. Smidth & Co. was created in the Danish domestic market. Their point of departure in a small-scale economy provided the company with a decisive *small-scale state advantage*, which was challenged on repeated occasions, but which never got out of control.

Since the 1850s, the Danish cement industry has comprised 25 enterprises.[10] The very small factories in the early days were located in the eastern part of Denmark. From the 1870s onwards, the industry moved to the most northern parts of the country where large deposits of limestone and clay are to be found close to the seaborne infrastructure on the two fiords *Mariager Fjord* and *Limfjorden*. With the establishment of Aalborg Portland in 1889, the centre of gravity was placed at the city of Aalborg, where, in the following 25 years, a number of attempts were made to establish more factories, and where F.L. Smidth & Co. therefore had to spend vast resources on maintaining control of the foundation for their on-going innovation activities.

By means of English capital and technology, Isidor Henius, a local and wealthy producer of liquor, made an attempt in 1891 to establish a cement factory south of Aalborg. The new company, *The Danish Portland Cement Company Ltd.,* received much local support as a number of local people subscribed for shares in it, and the Aalborg-based iron foundry *De Smidthske* supplied a number of machines to the factory. However, production did not begin until 1898, following a restructuring process in which the limited company *Portland Cementfabrikken Danmark* had taken over the semi-completed plant in 1896 and concluded the construction works with machinery imported from England. To F.L. Smidth & Co., the factory appeared to be a threat, based as it now was on foreign capital and different suppliers of machinery. There seemed to be a risk that the new competitor, who did not share an interest in the Danish innovation effort, might undersell their products, to the detriment of Aalborg Portland.

The situation became critical when the cement factory *Portland Cementfabrikken Norden* was built a short distance west of Aalborg in 1899. The reason was that not only was this factory financed by local Aalborg citizens, it was also started in 1901 with machinery, e.g. two rotary kilns, purchased from one of F.L. Smidth & Co.'s German competitors in the Hamburg region. In other words, there was a risk that Aalborg Portland's market position might be undermined and that a foreign competitor might gain a foothold and use their new factory as a tool to eliminate F.L. Smidth & Co.'s role as *research centre* for the cement industry.

F.L. Smidth & Co. and Aalborg Portland, therefore, started a fierce price war in the first years of the 20th century, when an economic recession was already putting pressure on the three Aalborg factories.[11] The result was that Aalborg Portland, which had been the only factory with operating profits, took over both *Danmark* and *Norden* in

1904–1905. This meant that both these factories were being controlled by F.L. Smidth & Co. when the market conditions improved again around 1905–1906.

However, another challenge emerged already in 1906 when the effects of the big earthquake in San Francisco on 18 April reached Aalborg in the shape of a big demand for cement and a speculation wave which became known locally as the *Cement fever*. In 1906, four new cement companies were founded in the Aalborg region, and to prevent these from being built, Aalborg Portland had to buy up all the areas with clay and limestone deposits which might constitute the immediate basis for the building of new factories. North of the Limfjorden they did not succeed in preventing a number of Copenhagen investors, led by the Danish shipping company *East Asiatic Company*, from buying up areas for the establishment of *Nørresundby Portland Cementfabrik A/S* in 1906–1908. However, they did succeed in averting the competition threat by entering into cartel-like price, production and sales agreements, which were confirmed by co-owner of FLS Alexander Foss entering EAC's board of directors. At the same time, the order for the factory was placed with F.L. Smidth & Co.

Simultaneously, in 1909, a new factory at Mariagerfjord, *Kongsdal Cement Fabrik*, was forced to join the cartel merger, which had soon become nicknamed *Cementringen* (the Cement Ring). The Kongsdal factory had been established by the master masons and cement factory owners from Copenhagen in 1908, and even though their aim was to undersell the prices of Aalborg Portland, Kongsdal became forced to enter the Cementringen, following a short but fierce price war.

In the following years, a number of companies were formed for the purpose of establishing factories, but it was not until 1911, with the establishment of *Dansk Andels Cement Fabrik* (Danish Cooperative Cement Factory/DAC), that the fifth cement factory at Aalborg became a reality. DAC was established at the initiative of the *Danish cooperative movement* (Forenede Danske Brugsforeninger/FDB), which in 1911 as well had entered into a discount agreement with Cementringen, but felt cheated when the agreement almost immediately resulted in price increases on the part of Cementringen. Moreover, the DAC factory was built using machinery from the Danish machine manufacturer *Frichs Maskinfabrik og Kedelsmedie A/S*, and when production began in 1913, this therefore ignited yet another fierce price war, followed by FDB being summoned for breach of contract. This resulted in the factory being stopped, and it only began operations again in 1917 and, due to lack of fuel during World War I, did not reach full capacity until 1928.

Thus, DAC had been successfully hampered, and as Aalborg Portland had also taken over the two oldest factories at Mariager Fjord in 1919, the Cementringen, led by F.L. Smidth & Co., had efficiently assumed control of the Danish cement industry.

To a wide extent, the members of the board of directors of the cement factories were now leading FLS personalities. It was quite telling for the situation at all the factories that in 1926, for instance, the board of directors of Cementfabrikken Kongsdal was chaired by FLS founder Poul Larsen and also included Aalborg Portland's managing director Ditlev Berg.[12] In a situation like this, buying core machinery from other Danish machinery works was of course completely out of the question, not to mention the purchase of technology from foreign competitors. In 1958, Aalborg Portland established the cement factory *Cementfabrikken Karlstrup* south of Copenhagen, but it remains to be said that all the cement factories were shut down during the course of the 20th century, which meant that as of 1980, Aalborg Portland is the only remaining active Danish manufacturer of cement.

This meant that from the beginning of the 20th century, being formed by national borders was a *generative rule* applying to the networks of the cement industry. This structure might well involve several nations. F.L. Smidth & Co. assumed the role as *research centre* for the Scandinavian cement industry, for instance.[13] However, it was common knowledge in the industry that informal national boundaries existed which could not be crossed in the same manner.

One of the most important of such boundaries was described very precisely in F.L. Smidth & Co.'s 50th-anniversary publication from 1932, summarising the main characteristics of the global development of the industry:

> Although no formal agreement existed, it had become normal practice for the Danish and German cement factories to not enter each other's markets, and this state of affairs had been upheld for a large number of years, ever since F.L. Smidth & Co. succeeded, in the 1890s, through its efforts in the Danish cement industry, to break the dominating position previously held by German cement in the Danish market.[14]

Competitors – Britain and the USA

At the end of the 1930s, the Danish cement industry had become revolutionised. From 1888 to 1913, the total annual production had increased from 17,000 tonnes to 495,000 tonnes.[15] Productivity had increased correspondingly. Whereas in the 19th century, the average cement worker would generate an annual production of 50 tonnes, the figure rose to 100 tonnes in the middle of the 1890s, and further increased to 300 tonnes as early as just after 1910. The consumption of mechanical power had increased from around 1 hp per worker in the 19th century to 3 to 4 hp in the 1910s and 15 hp in the 1920s.

In other words, through collaboration and control of the Danish market, F.L. Smidth & Co. had established itself with a strong foundation for innovation and global technology export. At the same time, competitors had emerged which were among the weightiest actors in the British, American and German industries.

British companies continued their work to deliver machinery to the cement industry, even though they had lost their former leading role. Contrary to the situation in previous times, the innovation process no longer took place within the circle of cement manufacturers. In Great Britain, the development and manufacture of production equipment also became separated from cement production and subjected to division of labour with the engineering industry. This certainly applied to *Vickers Ltd.*, which was the most important British machinery manufacturer of cement equipment in the world market during the first half of the 20th century. However, Vickers never expanded their cement production technology to include more than just one of their products in a product portfolio with a very different focus.[16] Vickers was established in 1828 in the industrial city of Sheffield by Edward Vickers and specialised in the casting of church bells and components for the shipbuilding industry. From the 1880s onwards, their focus became directed towards armament production, including warships and war planes, and during World War I, soldiers in the British trenches were equipped with machine guns from Vickers. Even though Vickers had the capacity to establish cement factories for customers in Asia and elsewhere, activities never grew to a size to be mentioned in the meticulous surveys of the company's history published during the 20th century.[17] To Vickers, the cement technology was a side product that could be offered globally because the company already had at its disposal a large international distribution network created for other purposes.

A similar situation applied to the American competitors F.L. Smidth & Co. encountered in the world market. A clear example was *Allis Chalmers*, established in 1901 by a merger between Edward P. Allis and Co., specialising in steam engines and mill equipment, Fraser & Chalmers, specialising in mining technology, and Gates Iron Works, specialising in machinery for stone and cement mills.[18] Even though their joint competences might suggest specialisation in cement technology, and although this took up some space in Allis Chalmer's early strategy, this was never mentioned as one selected niche on which to focus. From the 1910s onwards, activities were focused on farming machinery – tractors, combine harvesters, etc. Like Vickers, Allis Chalmers could therefore be characterised as a manufacturer of ironware and machines that could deliver equipment to cement factories, but which primarily developed to become one of the world's largest industrial companies based on product lines detached from the cement industry.

Competing Constellation – Germany

If we turn our attention towards the German competitors, it becomes clear that it was no coincidence that it was to the national boundaries towards the networks around the German cement industry that F.L. Smidth & Co. was paying special attention. This originated in Denmark's loss of a considerable part of its territory to Germany in a war in 1864, and from the fact that it was from Germany the strongest *competing constellation* emerged. A grouping of German companies, of which the most prominent were *Polysius, Amme, Giesecke & Konegen, Fellner & Ziegler* and *Humboldt*, developed from the 1890s onwards to become F.L. Smidth & Co.'s biggest unrivalled competitors worldwide. In fact, the organisational structures of the German companies were very similar to those of the Danish cement industry.

The most leading of the German companies towards World War II – and towards the present day, when the company, since 1992, has formed part of the Krupp group – was Polysius, which was founded in 1859 in Dessau by Gottfried Polysius and from 1886 carried on by his sons Otto and Max Polysius. In 1870, the company was expanded to include the unit Polysius Eisengießerei und Maschinenfabrik, which specialised in developing their own mills for the building material industry, and since then, a determined effort was made to further develop mainly crushing machines and preparation sections for the cement factories. The first rotary kiln was mounted by Polysius in 1898 at the factory *Hemmoor* near Hamburg, which served as the German version of a full-scale test plant, i.e. in line with the first kilns at Aalborg Portland.

Not until 1907 did Polysius begin to build their first complete cement plant, i.e. 20 years after F.L. Smidth & Co. built their factory at Linhamn in Sweden. This was not a sign of backwardness, however, but rather of the fact that the German industry had their own suppliers of electrical installations, boiler and power sections, etc. Thus, their projects could be completed around the world by collaboration between German manufacturers of production equipment that was operational on the basis of strong and well-consolidated collaboration with a common national domestic market. F.L. Smidth & Co. did not have this option at their disposal.

Moreover, the German collaboration could be based on strong coordination around the German cement industry that could trace its roots back to 1865, when the collaboration network *Verein für Fabrikation von Ziegeln, Thonwaaren, Kalk und Cement* was established. *Verein Deutscher Cementfabrikanten* was established in 1877 as a joint body for price agreements, quality control and production standards, and this was followed by another number of associations and joint agreements characterised by a strong representation from the German banks which were directly involved in the establishment of several cement factories.

The collaboration manifested itself clearly when, for instance, *Polysius,* together with *Amme, Giesecke & Konegen, Fellner & Ziegler* and

Humboldt, founded an establishment, the so-called *Brennofenbauanstalt*, in Hamburg for the manufacture, development and testing of rotary kilns and further development of these. From 1904 onwards, Polysius ran this Brennofenbauanstalt singlehandedly, and the activity was expanded by the development and building of complete factories. In 1907, 147 rotary kilns had been sold from the establishment, and following the interruption caused by World War I, activities were resumed in the 1920s. The strong coordination by the German activities also involved institutions of higher education, which was reflected at a symbolic level when, in 1928, Otto Polysius was appointed Ehrensenator (Honorary Senator) at the Technische Hochschule Charlottenburg, while Max Polysius was appointed Dr.ing. (Doctor of Engineering) at the Technische Hochschule Braunschweig.

It was in the networks around the German cement industry that F.L. Smidth & Co. found their strongest competitors in the world market. In many ways, the organisation model applying in the German innovation activities corresponded to that in Denmark, and when Polysius was able in 1925 – the year after F.L. Smidth & Co. had taken out a patent for the Symetro gear – to take out a patent for the so-called centro-antrieb and thus secure a competitive gear technology in the product catalogue they offered to the world's cement manufacturers, this was an expression of their equal competition.[19] Like the Danish innovation activities, those in Germany were based on the division of labour, specialisation and coordination, which included state-run research and knowledge institutions, the German bank sector and a strongly organised cement industry.

It was against this backdrop that the German companies became F.L. Smidth & Co.'s main competitors, and outlines thus emerge of the global cement industry as divided into two *competing constellations* with clear national characteristics by virtue of their basis in two *research centres* in Denmark and Germany, respectively.

The Image of F.L. Smidth & Co. as a Born Global

In Denmark, it is a well-known fact that through the export of cement equipment, F.L. Smidth & Co. developed into the country's largest industrial enterprise of the 20th century. Knowledge of the company's globalisation has primarily been compiled on the basis of the company's own anniversary publications from the years leading up to World War II, supplemented by anniversary publications of several of the Danish cement factories. In combination, this has painted a picture of the company as a successful born global.[20]

There was never talk of confining their activities to the small Danish market. Of the 25 Danish cement factories, only a few achieved production figures above a few thousand barrels a year, and only nine of them survived long enough for modern production methods to become relevant. This *small economy effect* rendered export a core activity from the very first years.

As mentioned previously, as early as by 1913, F.L. Smidth & Co.'s sales of tube mills to customers in a large number of countries had surpassed 3,000, and the amount of global activity was also expressed by the fact that by 1930, core components had been delivered to 250 of the world's cement factories, and of these deliveries, the capacity of the 83 plants sold in 1928–1929 accounted for one-tenth of the world's cement production.[21]

On the whole, the lists in the FLS anniversary publications of complete factories that had been established or expansions with new complete production lines – i.e. very large constructions – reflected a significant development in the volume of activities and geographical dispersion.

In the 1890s, the number of large projects was still relatively modest. Thus, before 1900, F.L. Smidth & Co. completed in the vicinity of ten major projects for customers mainly in Europe and Russia, as well as a single project in China and two in the USA. However, after 1900, activities increased rapidly. During the period 1900–1910, 42 major projects were completed, and activities were now in progress in most parts of the world. The majority of activities still took place in Europe and Russia, but a steep increase was seen in the number of projects in Asia and the USA, to which may be added the completion of a few projects in South America. During the period 1910–1920, the total number of major projects increased to at least 135, and in the period 1920–1932 to 250. Of these, the majority were located in Europe, but the least industrialised parts of the world had also attracted so much attention that this had resulted in the establishment of nine major factories and production lines in Africa and 33 in Asia.

Table 2.1 The geographical distribution of F.L. Smidth & Co.'s establishment of new or complete production lines or major reconstructions and expansions of older plants in 1887–1931

Europe and the Near East	Russia	Asia	North America	South America	Australia–New Zealand	Africa
166	7	39	20	3	3	9

At the same time, the anniversary publications provide a rudimentary view of how the company organised itself globally.

They account for the fact that from the 1880s onwards, collaboration was based on agreements with individuals or local companies, but that from 1890, the so-called *affiliate offices* were established. The first of these was opened in London and followed in the 1890s by offices in St. Petersburg (1893), New York (1895) and Paris (1899) and, after 1900, by more offices, in Berlin (1901), for instance.[22] From these offices, knowledge of market conditions could be collected, and information about F.L. Smidth & Co. could be spread to the relevant areas.[23]

The multinational development was further unfolded by the establishment of machinery works in Germany (Lübeck), for a short period in England (Luton), in Russia (Narva), and in the USA (New Jersey/Ohio).[24] Moreover, in 1910, F.L. Smidth & Co. took over *The Tunnel Portland Cement Company Ltd.* near London in order to prevent English cartel formation, which would eliminate Denmark's possibilities to deliver production equipment to England.[25] Furthermore, from 1922, F.L. Smidth & Co. engaged in the Estonian and Norwegian industries with major shareholdings in the cement factories *Port Kunda* and *Nordland Portland Cement Fabrik*. To this were added minor shareholdings in a number of factories, and in 1927, activities were expanded by the construction of the cement factory *Kursachsen* in Germany by Danish capital and with Danish machinery. This was their response to German investment attempts in the Danish cement industry – and the result was a renewed emphasis on the national boundaries between the industries in the two countries.[26]

In the company's own view of itself, globalisation had resulted in sales figures large enough to be a clear sign that they were occupying an extremely strong global position during a multinational development process with foreign direct investments in offices and machinery works and cement factories that were far from being large scale. In other words, a clear picture emerged of an efficient globalisation strategy driven by completely different forces and means than FDI.

A Campaign in the East

F.L. Smidth & Co.'s globalisation effort seems to have been particularly efficient in Asia. In their anniversary publications, the company itself highlighted a "Campaign in the East" in 1922 with the establishment of a "sales organisation" for China and Japan and the posting of individuals at offices in Tokyo and Beijing.[27] However, the sales figures from the company archives disclose that a targeted and comprehensive effort aiming at all of Asia was initiated as early as from the 1890s onwards.

Assessed by their sale of production capacity – measured by rotary kiln capacity – Asia accounted for more than one-third of the company's global turnover in the 1930s. At this time, the Asian market segment accounted for the second-largest part of the company's sales – only a few percentage points below that in Western Europe. Following a decline in the 1940s, sales to customers in Asia rose again, and towards the 1970s, the levels fluctuated between 20% and 30% of global sales. Asia's ranking as the second-largest market segment now became challenged by North and Latin America, but they maintained their position as one of the core market segments.

Table 2.2 The different market segments' purchase in percentages of the FLS capacity (rotary kiln capacity) sold during the years 1932–1981. The market segments are based on F.L. Smidth & Co.'s own geographic understanding of the global market ca. 1980

	1932–1938	1939–1946	1947–1951	1952–1956	1957–1961	1962–966	1967–1971	1972–1976
Western Europe	47		36	35	32	32	31	28
Eastern Europe	4		6	6	7	7	8	9
USSR	7		7	10	14	16	17	16
North America	24		34	27	21	18	14	11
Latin America	3		5	5	5	5	5	7
Asia	12		8	13	17	18	21	25
Africa	2		3	3	3	3	3	3
Australia	1		1	1	1	1	1	1
Sum	100		100	100	100	100	100	100
Sum mio. tons pr. year	49		84	123	155	207	255	286

Source: FLSA.

Table 2.3 Survey of the distribution of the 87 rotary kilns in total delivered by F.L. Smidth & Co. to countries in Asia in 1904–1938. The country names are those appearing in the company's lists

Year	China	Hong Kong	British India (India)	Dutch East India (Indonesia/Sumatra)	Siam (Thailand)	Siberia (Turkestan)	French Indochina (Vietnam)	Japan (incl. Manchukuo)	Burma
1904	2		1						
1905									
1906	2								
1907									
1908									
1909									
1910	2								
1911									
1912			2		1				
1913						1			
1914			1			1			
1915									
1916									
1917				1					
1918			2						
1919									
1920	2		4	1					
1921					1				
1922			2						
1923									
1924	1								
1925									
1926			1	1			1		

(Continued)

Table 2.3 (Continued)

Year	China Hong Kong	British India (India)	Dutch East India (Indonesia/Sumatra)	Siam (Thailand)	Siberia (Turkestan)	French Indochina (Vietnam)	Japan (incl. Manchukuo)	Burma
1927				1			4	
1928		3					7	
1929	1					1		
1930						1	1	
1931							2	
1932		1					2	
1933	1	1					4	
1934		2					1	
1935	2	4	1				1	1
1936	2	2					5	
1937		4	1					
1938							1	
1939								
1940								
Number of 13 kilns	2	30	5	3	2	3	28	1

Source: FLSA.

Among the Asian countries, activities before World War I were focused around China, Japan and India. This is reflected in particular in the figures regarding the sale of rotary kilns, which was synonymous with the delivery of either production lines (including facilities for raw material processing, cement mills, packing facilities, etc.) or complete *turn key* factories.[28] In 1896–1897, a shaft kiln factory with prototypes developed at Aalborg Portland was sold to Macao, and in 1904, F.L. Smidth & Co. was able to ship the first three rotary kilns to Hong Kong and India, respectively. In 1906 and 1910, a further four rotary kilns were shipped to China.

In the following years, the Chinese factories continued to take delivery of a large part of the Danish machines, but from 1913, the Indian market in particular grew steadily and stably, while, at the same time, F.L. Smidth & Co. sold plants to be erected in Dutch East India, Siam and Siberia. From the middle of the 1920s, rotary kilns were also delivered to French Indochina, and from 1927, sales to Japan began to accelerate. During the following 13 years, almost as many rotary kilns were delivered to Japanese plants – including some to the puppet state Manchukuo – as had been delivered twice this time to India, which, however, came to be F.L. Smidth & Co.'s largest Asian market for rotary kilns by 1940. Thus, in the 1930s, Japan was, beyond comparison, the most important Asian buyer of the rotary kilns produced in Denmark.

Of the total number of rotary kiln lines delivered to Asia in 1939, China, incl. Hong Kong, had bought 17%, Japan 32% and India 34%, while customers in Dutch East India and Siam had bought 6% and 3%, respectively.

Following the Actors – in Siam, China, Japan and India

The case study below focuses on F.L. Smidth & Co.'s globalisation during the period 1890–1938 in Siam, China, Japan and India, which – measured by the number of rotary kilns – accounted for 85% of their total sales to the Asian markets.

For each market, my point of departure is general reflections concerning the context in which F.L. Smidth & Co. first sought to establish themselves, and the conditions for their *market entry*. From this starting point, I follow the actors in descriptions and analyses of the positions they were occupying, their relations and their reaction patterns. By alternating between detail-oriented observations of people at an everyday level and more overall reflections, the case study draws an increasingly detailed and more nuanced picture of how and to what extent F.L. Smidth & Co. were able to exercise control of the Asian cement manufacturers by other means than FDI.

The precondition for this inductive hermeneutic method is the possibility to draw on the material in *the company archives* in Copenhagen.

Comprehensive collections (approx. 15,000 pages) of correspondence at both management level and of a more personal character in particular permit micro-historical network analyses in which the actors with and against whom the FLS people acted are pointed out by the Danes themselves and by a number of their Asian business partners by virtue of the descriptions of their relations they exchanged with one another. The correspondence material consists mainly of reports and discussions between the management at the head office in Copenhagen, Danish staff at the factories and offices (in Beijing, Shanghai, Tokyo and Bombay) and customers concerning market conditions, market and collaborative relations and political, social and cultural conditions. The company archive also comprises comprehensive collections of drawings and photographs, which when juxtaposed with statements in the correspondence may provide and insight into the physical frameworks that existed and were created around the activities of the Danes and which – in Bruno Latour's terminology – might lend their steely quality to the interhuman relations.

Outside of the company archive, it is possible to draw on a few private exchanges of letters between a small number of the Danish expatriates and their families and friends in Denmark. In certain cases, the private correspondence provides particular possibilities for *close descriptions* of issues in the intimate proximity of the individuals themselves, e.g. their everyday lives and relations, thus contributing with particularly valuable circumstantial evidence for piecing together an overall assessment of the Danish possibilities to exert influence and control.

One of the best possibilities to study closely the Danish expatriates' experience of their room for manoeuvre as well as how this was closely entwined with a conscious design of the physical framework surrounding the social relations derives from Siam, which was one of the company's minor markets in Asia during the period leading up to World War II. The analysis of F.L. Smidth & Co.'s activities in Siam may thus draw an exemplary picture of a general understanding of the tools available and of the control they enabled the Danes to potentially achieve in the Asian markets.

Notes

1 *FLS i 100 år, forarbejde* (FLSA). Robbie M. Andrew: "Global CO2 emissions from cement production, 1928-2018" (Oslo: CICERO Center for International Climate Research, 2019), https://www.earth-syst-sci-data.net/11/1675/2019/essd-11-1675-2019.pdf. M. Garside: "Global cement production 1995-2019," https://www.statista.com/statistics/1087115/global-cement-production-volume/
2 Carlota Perez: *Technological Revolutions and Financial Capital. The Dynamics of Bubbles and Golden Ages* (Edward Elgar, 2002), 8, 9.
3 Povl Drachmann: *Aktieselskabet Aalborg Portland Cementfabrik 1889-1914* (Copenhagen, 1915). Povl Drachmann: *F.L. Smidth & Co. 1922-1932* (Copenhagen, 1932). Knudaage Riisager: *F.L. Smidth & Co. 1882-1922*

(Copenhagen, 1921). Steen Andersen and Kurt Jacobsen: *Foss* (Copenhagen, 2008). Søren Ellemose: *FLSmidth – et eventyr i cement* (Aarhus: Jyllands-Postens Forlag, 2005).

4 Gerd Meier: *Entstehung, Entwicklung und Strukturwandel der Portland-Zementindustrie im Raum Hannover vom 1878 bis 1989*, Dissertation (Fakultät für Geistes- und Sozialwissenschaften der Universität Hannover, 2001), 1, 2, 15, 16. Friedrich Quietmeiyer: *Zur Geschichte der Erfindung des Portlandszements* (Berlin, 1912). A. J. Francis: *The Cement Industry 1796-1914: A History* (London, 1978). Gustav Haegermann: *Vom Caementum zum Zement* (Wiesbaden & Berlin, 1964). Robert Whitman Lesley: *History of the Portland Cement Industry in the United States* (New York, 1924). *A History of Technology*, Vol. V, 483–487.

5 Francis: *The Cement Industry.*

6 Jesper B. Larsen: *F.L. Smidth & Co.'s teknologiske udvikling gennem det tyvende århundrede*, unpublished thesis (University of Southern Denmark, Odense, Center for Historie, 2001), 76–77.

7 Morten Pedersen: *De danske cementfabrikkers bebyggelsesmiljø. Forandringer i en branches industrielle miljø ved den anden industrielle revolution* (Odense: University Press of Southern Denmark, 2008), 33–46.

8 Larsen, *F.L. Smidth & Co.*, 41.

9 Aalborg Portland Cement Factory, minutes of the board of directors, 15 November 1898, *Aalborg Portland Company Archives*, Aalborg.

10 Pedersen, *De Danske*, 51–75.

11 Henning Bender: *Aalborgs industrielle udvikling 1735-1940. Aalborgs historie vol. 4* (Aalborg, 1987), 379–383.

12 *Green's Danske Fonds og Aktier* (Copenhagen: Dagbladet Børsens Forlag, 1926), 132.

13 Malin Dahlström: "Dansk-svenskt samarbete inom kalkstens- och ce-mentindustrin. 1880-tal till 1970-tal," in *Fabrik & Bolig. The Industrial Heritage of the Nordic Countries* (2019), 3–31.

14 Drachmann, *F.L. Smidth & Co. 1922-1932*, 52.

15 Pedersen, *De danske*, 61–67.

16 J. D. Scott: *Vickers: A History* (London, 1962). Clive Trebil Coch: *The Vickers Brothers. Armaments and Entreprise 1854-1914* (London, 1977).

17 See, for instance, J. D. Scott, *Vickers.*

18 Walter Geist: *Allis-Chalmers: A Brief History of 103 Years of Production*, Newcomen Society Address Series (Short Monographs on Industrial Firms), (Newcomen Society in North America, 1950).

19 Larsen, *F.L. Smidth & Co.*, 41.

20 Examples are Drachmann, *Aktieselskabet Aalborg Portland.* Drachmann, *F.L. Smidth & Co. 1922-1932.* Riisager, *F.L. Smidth & Co. 1882-1922.* A more recent contribution is Steen Andersen and Kurt Jacobsen: *Foss* (Copenhagen, 2008).

21 Drachmann, *F.L. Smidth & Co.*, 68. Larsen, *F.L. Smidth & Co.* Ole Hyldtoft: *Teknologiske forandringer i dansk industri 1870-1896* (Odense, 1996), 126–131. Ole Hyldtoft and Hans Chr. Johansen: *Teknologiske forandringer i dansk industri 1896-1970* (Viborg, 2005), 75, 299 and 352.

22 Riisager, *F.L. Smidth & Co.*, 85–112. For more recent accounts of the multinational development, drawing on information in the anniversary publications, see for instance Hans Chr. Johansen: *Industriens vækst og vilkår 1870-1973. Dansk industri efter 1870*, bd. 1 (Odense, 1987), 284. Andersen, *Foss*, passim.

23 Riisager, *F.L. Smidth & Co.*, 253.
24 Riisager, *F.L. Smidth & Co.*, 119–123.
25 Riisager, *F.L. Smidth & Co.*, 140–141.
26 Drachmann, *F.L. Smidth & Co. 1922-1932*, 32–34, 49 and 51–55.
27 Drachmann, *F.L. Smidth & Co. 1922-1932*, 25 and 91–93.
28 *Rotary Kilns Supplied by F.L. Smidth & Co., 1938* (FLSA).

References

Steen Andersen & Kurt Jacobsen: *Foss* (Copenhagen, 2008).

Robbie M. Andrew: "Global CO2 emissions from cement production, 1928-2018" (Oslo: CICERO Center for International Climate Research, 2019), https://www.earth-syst-sci-data.net/11/1675/2019/essd-11-1675-2019.pdf

Henning Bender: *Aalborgs industrielle udvikling 1735-1940. Aalborgs historie vol. 4* (Aalborg, 1987).

Clive Trebil Coch: *The Vickers Brothers. Armaments and Entreprise 1854-1914* (London, 1977).

Malin Dahlström: "Dansk-svenskt samarbete inom kalkstens- och cementindustrin. 1880-tal till 1970-tal," in *Fabrik & Bolig. The Industrial Heritage of the Nordic Countries* (2019), 3–31.

Povl Drachmann: *Aktieselskabet Aalborg Portland Cementfabrik 1889-1914* (Copenhagen, 1915).

Povl Drachmann: *F.L. Smidth & Co. 1922-1932* (Copenhagen, 1932).

Søren Ellemose: *FLSmidth – et eventyr i cement* (Aarhus: Jyllands-Postens Forlag, 2005).

A. J. Francis: *The Cement Industry 1796-1914: A History* (London, 1978).

M. Garside: "Global cement production 1995-2019," https://www.statista.com/statistics/1087115/global-cement-production-volume/

Walter Geist: *Allis-Chalmers: A Brief History of 103 Years of Production*, Newcomen Society Address Series (Short Monographs on Industrial Firms) (Newcomen Society in North America, 1950).

H. Green and H. Stein: *Green's Danske Fonds og Aktier* (Copenhagen: Dagbladet Børsens Forlag, 1926).

Gustav Haegermann: *Vom Caementum zum Zement* (Wiesbaden & Berlin, 1964).

Ole Hyldtoft: *Teknologiske forandringer i dansk industri 1870-1896* (Odense, 1996).

Ole Hyldtoft & Hans Chr. Johansen: *Teknologiske forandringer i dansk industri 1896-1970* (Viborg, 2005).

Hans Chr. Johansen: *Industriens vækst og vilkår 1870-1973. Dansk industri efter 1870*, bd. 1 (Odense, 1987).

Jesper B. Larsen: *F.L. Smidth & Co.'s teknologiske udvikling gennem det tyvende århundrede*, unpublished thesis (University of Southern Denmark, Odense, Center for Historie, 2001).

Robert Whitman Lesley: *History of the Portland Cement Industry in the United States* (New York, 1924).

Gerd Meier: *Entstehung, Entwicklung und Strukturwandel der Portland-Zementindustrie im Raum Hannover vom 1878 bis 1989*, Dissertation (Fakultät für Geistes- und Sozialwissenschaften der Universität Hannover, 2001).

Morten Pedersen: *De danske cementfabrikkers bebyggelsesmiljø. Forandringer i en branches industrielle miljø ved den anden industrielle revolution* (Odense: University Press of Southern Denmark, 2008).

Carlota Perez: *Technological Revolutions and Financial Capital. The Dynamics of Bubbles and Golden Ages* (Cheltenham: Edward Elgar, 2002).

Friedrich Quietmeiyer: *Zur Geschichte der Erfindung des Portlandszements* (Berlin, 1912).

Knudaage Riisager: F.L. Smidth & Co. *1882-1922* (Copenhagen, 1921).

John Dick Scott: *Vickers: A History* (London, 1962).

3 Like Living on an Island ... Siam and Southeast Asia 1913–1925

Machinery for a Cement Plant

The *Siam Cement Co.* (today the cornerstone of the Siam Cement Group) was founded in 1913 at the initiative of His Majesty King Vajiravudh (Rama VI). The first meeting of the founding group took place on 14 June, and the company was officially registered on 13 December with an authorised share capital of one million baht. According to the articles of the company, a minimum of three quarters of the shares were to be Siamese owned. The starting capital was provided by the Majesty himself and from the royal Privy Purse.[1] The founding of the Siam Cement Co. clearly took place in an atmosphere of Siamese/ Thai national interests.[2]

F.L. Smidth & Co. were introduced to the founding process at an early stage. On 2 September, the management in Copenhagen announced their acceptance of the terms of the purchase of machinery for the construction of a cement plant in the small village of Bangsue a short distance north of Bangkok.[3] Thus, only a little more than two months after their first meeting, the Siamese founders were ready to sign a contract for an extensive transfer of technology from Denmark.

The contract included the delivery and construction of all necessary production lines and buildings at a total cost of £12,400. Shipments from Copenhagen were planned to be dispatched in June and July 1914, and production was to commence on 15 January 1915. F.L. Smidth & Co. guaranteed a daily production of 400 barrels, equivalent to a yearly production of approximately 25,000 tonnes. Moreover, the contract obliged F.L. Smidth & Co. to deliver to the Siam Cement Co. a well-qualified construction engineer, a chemical engineer, a burner master and a first-class machine fitter to manage the construction and start-up of the plant.

The pace of the process was remarkably high. Before signing the contract with the Danes, the Siamese founders had even had the time to send a delegation to Europe to inspect several cement plants and to call on the British and German competitors of F.L. Smidth & Co. and evaluate

DOI: 10.4324/9780429446184-3

propositions from them.[4] The design and production of the machinery in Copenhagen and the construction and start-up of the plant – on the other side of the globe – were to take place in a time interval of less than 18 months after the signing of the contract.

However, in the summer of 1913, the Siamese-Danish cooperation had seemingly already entered an advanced stage. Simultaneously to accepting the contract in September, F.L. Smidth & Co. asked for more samples of raw materials for chemical analysis in Copenhagen in addition to those previously sent. And when looking towards the political context, it becomes obvious that it was no coincidence that the first cement plant in Siam was to be constructed in the early 1910s by a Danish machine supplier.

Independent Siam in a Colonial World

By the early 20th century, Siam had been working constantly for decades to stay independent and retain its position as the only non-colonised area of Southeast Asia.[5] At the time, modern Indonesia, Vietnam and India were known among westerners as Dutch India, French Indochina and British India. During the 19th century, immigration caused the Chinese population in Siam to increase to 370,000 in 1910, and from the 1820s onwards, Myanmar served as a base for British endeavours to increase their influence on and control of the Siamese territories.

The Opium Wars in China in 1842 made obvious the consequences of opposition to the British requests for advantageous trading conditions. In 1855, King Rama IV (Mongkut) therefore signed the first Siamese-British trade treaty – the Bowring treaty – that assigned to the Brits their own administration of justice in Siam. In the following years, similar trade treaties were signed with more western countries. Mongkut (1851–1868) and later Chulalongkorn (1868–1910) worked energetically for an opening and modernisation of Siam in order to prevent further western influence and ensure Siamese independence. The success of this strategy was promoted by the fact that Siam served as a buffer area between the British in Myanmar to the west and the French in Vietnam to the east. However, Siam had been forced to surrender territories to Britain and France on several occasions between 1888 and 1909.

The Siamese reforms were thus initiated and coordinated by the monarchy, but they relied heavily on western models and counsellors. Among the major contributions were the construction of an infrastructure to supplement the previously weather-dependent river transportation. A network of roads and canals was constructed, and after a period of private railway construction, the *Royal Siamese Railways* were founded in 1892. In 1930, the royal railway system consisted of more than 3,000 km tracks connected by bridges across the river Menam.

From 1881, the infrastructure included postal services, and the construction of power supply systems began – starting with the royal palaces and from 1897 the Danish-driven *Siam Electricity Company Ltd.* and in 1912 the *Samsen Power Station.*[6]

Parallel to this, the royal army was modernised following western models from the 1860s, and from the 1880s markedly expanded. Between 1898 and 1913, military budgets rose from 1 million bahts to 13 million bahts. In the war with France in 1893, the Siamese navy was unable to muster any notable resistance, but by 1910, its strength had increased to 60 vessels, including two armoured cruisers imported from Scotland and Hong Kong and a marine corps of 15,000 men – all of whom were under the command of admiral Andreas du Plessis des Richelieu, a seafaring Dane who had become Chulalongkorn's entrusted advisor during the 1880s.[7] According to western standards, this was maybe a relatively modest-sized navy, but its presence clearly signalled the Siamese intentions of future independence. At the same time, it provided an effective instrument for internal enforcement of sovereignty, in particular towards the former independent city states in Lanna centred around Chiang Mai.[8]

At the beginning of the 20th century, Siam's business structure was still dominated by the agrarian sector, in particular the rice- and sugar-producing farmers. From the 1880s onwards, British and German logging companies had been trading teak to the European markets, and several western companies exploited the country's resources of tin and rubber. Bangkok was beyond comparison the largest city with a population of approximately 360,000, and during the 1910s, it became, in the eyes of western and Chinese entrepreneurs, a potential site for substantial industrial development. The city experienced the gradual rise of industries in the fields of iron and metal, chemicals and textiles, and the building sector slowly started a modernisation process with the first use of bricks and imported cement as replacements of the traditional use of wood and bamboo as building materials for housing, infrastructure and commerce.[9]

When Chulalongkorn died in 1910, he was succeeded by Vajiravudh, who had been out of Siam for several years to be educated at Cambridge and in the British army – and to spend time in Copenhagen. After being appointed as king, Vajiravudh continued the reform work. In 1912, slavery was finally abolished, and in 1917 Bangkok's first university was founded. In 1921, elementary schooling was introduced.

The founding of the Siam Cement Co. in 1913 took place as part of this constant series of initiatives from the Siamese monarchy to modernise Siam and keep the country stable and independent from western colonial forces. The supply of cement was crucial to the process, and as long as Siam continued to rely on imports from cement plants in Europe, cement delivery remained a strong potential tool for westerners to enforce their influence on internal Siamese affairs.

The Siamese decision to import Danish technology in order to establish the cement plant in Bangsue could, in other words, be perceived as the launch of a *development project* on both a national and an international political level. The Bangsue plant was supposed to play a key role in the ongoing modernisation process aimed at building a strong and independent Siam. This particular starting point was formative for the introduction of Danes – and F.L. Smidth & Co. – to the scene.

Two Small Economies Cooperating

Denmark had achieved its first trade treaty with Siam in 1858.[10] During the following decades, the presence of Danes in Siam's political and commercial spheres had grown steadily. Danish sailors entered the Bangkok-based commercial fleet, and in 1879 at least 65 of them served as captains or mates. In the 1870s, Danish companies were founded in Siam, and Danish-Siamese relations expanded significantly, including networks up to the highest political and business levels of the two countries.

Essential to the network-building was the foundation of the shipping company Andersen & Co. at the initiative of the Dane H.N. Andersen in 1884. Andersen had arrived as an ordinary sailor in Bangkok in 1879, but – probably assisted by his countryman Richelieu – he became mate on board Chulalongkorn's sailing ship Thoon Cramon and soon established himself as a leading figure in Danish and Siamese business circles.[11] The base for Andersen & Co. was the *Oriental Hotel* in the centre of Bangkok, but soon after the founding, the activities of the company within trade and shipping expanded considerably. The Siamese navy became a major customer, and during the 1890s, Andersen developed a strong personal relationship with the Siamese royal family. He even became an important intermediary to the increasingly stronger links between the Siamese and Danish monarchies. In 1890, Andersen acted as a guide to the grandson of the Danish king Christian X – Russian grand duke heir Nikolai – on his visit to Siam.

Andersen's importance grew as, in 1897, Andersen & Co. became part of the *East Asiatic Company* (EAC), recently founded on his initiative, and as the royal connections continued. The EAC established shuttle services on a regular basis between Copenhagen, Bangkok and the East China coast, and the company invested heavily in Siam, in teak woodlands in the northern territories and sawmills in Bangkok. The EAC-vessel *Siam* carried Chulalongkorn as a passenger on a journey in 1900 to Copenhagen, where several of the Siamese princes stayed for a number of years to study and experience western civilisation. As mentioned, one of the princes spending time in Copenhagen was Vajiravudh, who had lent his name to one of the EAC ocean-going steamers in 1899.[12]

From the 1890s, Andersen's activities linked the Siamese consumers – and the Siamese royal family – directly to the Danish cement industry. During the 1890s, the ships of Andersen & Co. that transported teak to Denmark returned to Siam heavily loaded with cement from the Danish plants. After the founding of the EAC, cement imports from Denmark rose considerably and became a strong argument for the initiative to establish *Nørresundby Portland Cement Fabrik A/S* 1906–1908.[13] Of more than 400,000 barrels produced at the plant each year during the 1910s, a major part was exported to Siam, and as late as the 1920s – when the Siam Cement Company was fully functional – the EAC vessels still transported approximately 4,000 tonnes of cement to Siam every year.[14]

Moreover, even though it was founded as a direct challenge to the Danish market monopoly by Aalborg Portland Cement Fabrik, *Nørresundby Portland Cement Fabrik A/S* was constructed by F.L. Smidth & Co., and their part-ownership of the plant meant that the EAC became part of the Danish *Cementringen*. From 1910, the export purpose of the Nørresundby plant was formalised by a contract with *Cementringen*, which secured the base for F.L. Smidth & Co.'s research and development activities at the other Danish plants. The personal relationships between the tycoons were sealed in 1912 when FLS founder Alexander Foss entered the EAC board after having resisted for years due to a strong outspoken distrust towards especially Andersen's accounting methods. The entrance of Foss to the EAC board thus occurred shortly before the order from the Siam Cement Co. for the Bangsue plant and was probably a price Andersen demanded to be paid by Foss in order to secure F.L. Smidth & Co. a foothold in Siam.[15]

Above the level of personal and company networks, developments in national politics worked strongly in favour of Danish business opportunities in Siam. The Siamese were constantly searching for partners whose primary interest was to do business and not to promote a process of colonisation. Especially as regards an important strategic resource such as cement, this was a conclusive argument which was of clear disadvantage to British partners in particular, such as machinegun-producing Vickers. In contrast, F.L. Smidth & Co., coming from a small and politically insignificant nation, could not be seen as an extension of a dominating colonial power. Since 1864, when 20% of Denmark's territories had been lost in a war with Germany, Danish politicians had kept a very low profile in international politics and pursued a neutrality-seeking line in an attempt to balance between British, German and Russian interests. Generally, for Danish companies, this was another aspect of the *small-scale advantage* at hand, from which it seemed particularly relevant to benefit in Asia.[16]

When the construction of the Bangsue plant began in 1914, it was therefore obvious to the Danes that their work on the site would be shaped by a larger political context which placed them in a position as the apparently most harmless and reliable business partner obtainable. However, it was beyond doubt that the Siamese wanted controllable modern cement production without having to fear the formation of a western bridgehead as a side effect. The extent to which the Danes could enter a position as *social carriers of technology* and gain control of the technological system therefore still remained to be seen.

Transfer of Machinery and Men

From the outset, the prospects of a strong Danish position seemed promising. The agreement entered in the autumn of 1913 that F.L. Smidth & Co. would provide staff for key positions in the future running of the Siam Cement Co. seemingly demonstrated a far-reaching acceptance of Danish influence. Nevertheless, several months passed before F.L. Smidth & Co. announced, in February 1914, to the Siam Cement Co. that their search for a future manager, a chemist and an accountant was well underway, but that this was a difficult task.[17] It was no doubt true that great efforts were being made to identify the best suited people for the jobs in Siam. At the same time, emphasising the serious considerations that were taking place in Copenhagen also reflected the thorough considerations that were needed from the perspective of the Danes in cases where the transfer of technology included machinery as well as personnel.

These considerations originated primarily from the fact that F.L. Smidth & Co. generally shared interests with their customers. This was no different in Siam than in Denmark, even though the partnership in Aalborg was closer than that in Bangsue. The fruitful installation and successful running of the delivered cement plant were the prerequisites for a happy and thriving customer. This was also a prerequisite for winning orders for the future continuous work on maintenance, plant extensions, etc. It was F.L. Smidth & Co.'s ability to make the transfer of technology successful that could pave the way for their future chance to continually benefit from their customer's successful and thriving business operations. If the technology transfer included personnel, it was therefore of utmost importance for F.L. Smidth & Co.'s future business opportunities that highly competent candidates were identified. Such considerations became even more important in cases where management skills were in demand. On the one hand, it was imperative to provide candidates with top qualifications in order to satisfy the customers. On the other hand, this would result in a drain of the key competences in the ranks of F.L. Smidth & Co., which formed the basis of the company's very existence.

Regarding management skills, considerations were made even harder by the fact that such competences were not necessarily a part of the personal profiles of the engineers trained at *Den Polytekniske Læreanstalt* in Copenhagen. This was a matter of consideration in general, but it was even more relevant when search for personnel for a cement plant in a, from a Danish perspective, remote and different market such as Siam. It would require a certain set of characteristics of a future manager to overcome the personal challenges of everyday life far from home in a cultural, political and social context that would be difficult to comprehend and navigate, and at the same time successfully run a big and complicated undertaking such as a cement plant. The group of likely candidates consequently narrowed even further.

Other matters of concern were the risks connected to handing over personnel to manage key positions in the customer's organisation. This implied supplying ambitious candidates to partners who might potentially expand significantly and develop into substantial future buyers of machinery and services from F.L. Smidth & Co. The staff supplied by F.L. Smidth & Co. would in a sense be "serving two masters", which, in effect, might cause a vulnerable flank to be exposed. The risk of opportunism was obvious. Facing highly qualified individuals supplied by F.L. Smidth & Co. and in possession of detailed knowledge of the internal affairs of their old parent company, i.e. products, prices, negotiation procedures, etc., on the other side of the negotiation table was not necessarily a desirable situation. The position of the customer would be extremely strong, and the basis for attracting F.L. Smidth & Co.'s competitors could turn out to be even stronger. The worst-case scenario was that the knowhow developed and paid for by F.L. Smidth & Co. and their Danish partners would fall into the hands of German competitors. Consequently, loyalty became a matter of utmost importance. It was essential to identify candidates who could effectively enter the payrolls of the customer and who could, at the same time, be assumed to remain loyal towards their Danish parent company.

Along with the risks came, however, a significant potential for building strong and intimate business relations and potential tools to control the customers' operations. Appointing trusted and loyal employees to fill key positions in the organisation of future major customers was a golden opportunity. Especially, candidates in possession of the required cultural and social capitals required to fill managing positions might become important tools in order to gain knowledge of the internal affairs of the customers, as well as of their different markets, and to exercise an influence on vital decisions regarding the running and development of the customers' cement plants. The concept of a Trojan Horse does not fully cover this situation because it was not F.L. Smidth & Co.'s aim to eliminate their business partner, rather the opposite. But the situation opened a potential for exchanging cultural and social capital into cash and earnings in Copenhagen.

The question of loyalty was thus a matter of utmost importance and could be perceived as a risk as well as an opportunity. It was essential to spot candidates with significant diplomatic skills that would enable them to manage the art of balancing on a knife's edge. In theory, complete Danish control of the customers' dispositions might seem to be a top priority, but not in reality. In everyday situations, a Danish appointed manager would have to exercise great sensitivity in order to balance the interests of his parent company and those of the owners, boards, co-managers, etc. of the contracting company paying his salary. Customers, such as the Siam Cement Co., were of course very aware of the Danish bonds of loyalty and would probably accept their influence to some degree in order to keep up good relations. But if an appointed manager turned out to become a single-minded Danish protagonist, the risk of a collapse of good relations was imminent. In the worst case, the effect could be a bad reputation effecting F.L. Smidth & Co., not only with this single customer but also on the global market in general.

In the best of all cases, the appointment of employees from the ranks of F.L. Smidth & Co. to key positions in the customer companies could result in a close and trusting relationship aimed at promoting their shared interest in a thriving cement-producing business. In real life, the presence of the underlying potential conflicts of interests was to be expected regularly, if not on an almost daily basis.

Spotting Skilled Personnel

The thoroughness of the considerations taking place in Copenhagen in 1913–1914 as regards the Siam Cement Co. reflected how the process of spotting skilled personnel could open a potential for influence and control of the investments of the cement-producing companies. It also reflected how an important part of the internationalisation effort was made in the offices in Copenhagen, where the best candidates could be spotted and recruited, and where fundamental engineering skills could be supplemented by basic preparations for life as expatriates. Subsequently, the appointment of the first manager of the Siam Cement Co., the Dane Oscar Schultz, came to reflect how such considerations could lead to certain deliberate choices. The company based their trust in Oscar Schultz on close family relations, his previous experience and his ambitions and ability to cope with difficult and changing situations.

Oscar Schultz was born in 1884 on a small Danish island, the son of lighthouse keeper William Schultz.[18] As a boy, he showed a strong wish to experience the world, maybe inspired by the life of his grandfather, Johan Philip Schultz, who had served as a Danish admiral and director in the marine ministry.[19] As a young man, Oscar Schultz planned for a career as a naval officer.[20] Nevertheless, he graduated as a construction engineer in 1909, and in 1910 was employed by F.L. Smidth & Co.

His employment at F.L. Smidth & Co. did not come about out of the blue. In 1891, when Oscar Schultz was seven years old, his aunt, Margrethe Schultz, had married the FLS-founder Alexander Foss. Shortly after their marriage, it was agreed among the three owners – Frederik Læssøe Smidth, Poul Larsen and Alexander Foss – how the company assets should be distributed among the families in case of death.[21] Thus, family relations linked young Oscar Schultz directly to the fastest growing fortune in Denmark at the time.

As early as in 1911, Oscar Schultz was sent to Austria to partake in the construction of a cement plant and later the same year, he travelled to Sctschurowo, near Moscow, where another new plant had been commissioned. His letters home often reflected strong excitement over the opportunity of adventure in a new and unknown part of the world, as one example from December 191 clearly illustrates:

> Schtschurowo 19 December 1911:
> Unfortunately, nor wolf or bear is to be traced for miles, so I cannot enjoy the pleasure of spending my Russian holydays hunting.
>
> Every factory in Russia has a saint, and a big party is held on his name day and initiated by a service followed by heavy eating and drinking. This factory threw such a party a couple of days ago, and this was quite interesting to witness. As soon as a worker had had too much to drink, he was transported home. In the end, only some of the managers and us Danes stayed put, and we finished off the leftovers.[22]

In 1912, Oscar Schultz was stationed at the Czech city of Brno, and in the autumn he left for New York to work at F.L. Smidth & Co's office there. Everyday life was quieter at the office in New York, and Oscar Schultz soon became bored and took time to write to Alexander Foss on several technical matters and probably to remind his uncle of his existence and high ambitions.

Oscar Schultz's ambitions and loyalty towards F.L. Smidth & Co. were further reflected when, in December 1913, he announced to his parents that two life-changing developments were about to happen; first, that he had been suggested by F.L. Smidth & Co. as manager of the first cement plant in Siam, and secondly, that he was about to marry a young woman, Emily Passano, before leaving New York. The contract for his position as manager of the Siam Cement Co. was signed in January 1914, and shortly after their wedding in February, the young couple left for Denmark on their way to Siam.

The journey from Denmark to Bangkok began in April 1914, and in the meantime, Oscar Schultz had the opportunity to spend time at the head offices of F.L. Smidth & Co. and to study and discuss the layout of the plant. At the same time, the physical framework for Emily Passano's and his own lives was being tailored just as carefully as Schultz's future presence at the site.

Tailor-Making a Danish Domain

The decision to place the cement plant in Bangsue was based on a number of logistical considerations.[23] The site was located 5–7 km from the main cement market in Bangkok, but it was close to a railway line connecting the capital with the northern provinces. An additional vital supplement to the infrastructure could be provided by canals and small rivers connecting the marshy landscape with the river Menam. Coal and cement could thus be transported to and from the plant from the Bangkok harbour a relatively short distance away, while limestone had to be supplied by rail from quarries at Cong Kae in the province of Changwat Lopburi, approximately 170 km to the north.[24]

This meant that the Bangsue location of the plant was not ideal for cement production, which uses large amounts of limestone, but it was an acceptable compromise which gave priority to the proximity to Bangkok. However, considering the means of transport available in the area at the time, the Danes who were to be employed at the Siam Cement Co.'s site in Bangsue could look forward to leading their everyday lives in a relatively remote location surrounded by the local rural population. In the beginning, travel between Bangsue and Bangkok would be limited to slow connections by boat, requiring almost half a day each way, or the few and irregular train services carrying passengers.

The physical framework of daily life at the quite isolated factory en-clave was designed in Copenhagen in the summer of 1913. At a meeting in Turin in Italy in October 1913, the plans were presented to and ap-proved by E.G. Gollo, who was chief engineer at the Siamese state office for public works and appointed as a member of the board of the Siam Cement Co.[25] This included general plans for the entire site as well as more detailed drawings of the layout of infrastructure, production lines, building constructions, architectural details, etc.

In order to build sufficient infrastructure, the existing network of rivers and canals connecting the factory location to the river Menam had to be expanded by excavation and the construction of a connecting track to the railway station in Bangsue. This strengthened the appearance of the plant as an enclave.

At the factory, the limestone would thus be unloaded from railway wagons coming from the north and entering the area at a storage site close to the slurry basins sited at the top end (in the general plan) of the rotary kiln. The new railway track would then continue to the east of the plant towards the south and arrive at the cement packing and storing facilities, from where the commodity could be transported away from the plant and delivered to the market in Bangkok. At the opposite side of the plant, towards the south and the west, canals would run past the storage facilities and constitute a southern perimeter around the factory area. A newly excavated 200-m long canal would be connected to the system and enable transportation of clay by boat on the western side of the plant area towards the slurry basins, where it would be mixed with limestone before entering the kilns. The clay would be unloaded in an open storage site connected to a rectangular basin covering most of the area between the canal and the railway track, thus more or less fencing off the entire plant towards the north.

All in all, this would create a factory core area defined by canals, railway tracks and uncrossable raw material deposits and further out by the surrounding marshy rice fields of the local famers, and forests. A road was planned to be constructed at the top of a dam along the southern canal, but human access to the plant was primarily designed to take place by boat.

The production line could be characterised as a standard package. The key component would be a 34-m-long rotary kiln located on an elevated base, and below this, a clinker cooler constructed as an air-cooled rotating steel cylinder. Raw materials would be prepared by mixing with water in slurry basins and milling in a tube mill. They would then be kept in two basins before entering the kiln. The clinker would be pulverised in tube mills, and the packing of cement in wooden barrels and handsewn jute bags would take place in a combined silo and packing building. The design of the production machinery thus encompassed two parallel lines – the rotary kiln and the clinker storage flanked by slurry basins, cement mills and cement storage facilities. In between these two lines, the supply of energy for the rotation of the machinery was supplied by electric motors powered by Siam Electricity Company Ltd.'s power plant in Bangkok.

Besides a production line layout designed to secure a rational production flow, the planning that was taking place in Copenhagen during the summer of 1913 also included an even more detailed design of future social relations at the cement plant. This was not done by organisation charts or descriptions of management hierarchies, but by adding a third parallel staff quarters section into the design of the industrial landscape and building design. The main idea was to incorporate the presence of the Danish key personnel into the structure of the plant while at the same time keeping the Siamese daily influence at a distance, and this materialised in a number of details.

Next to the canal on the western side of the plant, the built environment would include housing facilities for the future Danish plant manager, chemist and accountant, who were to be provided by F.L. Smidth

& Co. during the preparation phase in 1914–1915. The Danes would reside in the three identical stately bungalows facing the canals and the landscape of rice fields and forests and with their backs fairly close to the machinery.

Thus, the physical layout deliberately prepared the ground for a future in which the site might appear to be a Danish domain showing clear similarities with manors and older industrial estates in Denmark as well as in Western Europe in general.[26] The manager – and his assisting staff – would take residence in a central position, at a location which would mark the entrance of the area and which offered optimal general views of the plant. In this way, the physical design of the plant in Bangsue marked a clear social structuring of the future operations of the plant. However, in contrast to traditional European rural manors, the central position would not be filled by the owners of the plant, but by selected employees – that is, the future Danish workforce.

The bungalows designed for the Danes would be two-storey buildings with open galleries towards the landscape and large porches that could be shielded from the sun by bamboo curtains. Trees would be planted on the dam towards the canal, but there would be an open view towards the rice-cultivating peasants and the forests. The interior would consist of living rooms on the ground floor and bedrooms on the first floor, where the potential for a cooling breeze during the warm tropical nights would be best.[27] The first floor could also be shielded from any intruding animals, even though bats and cobra snakes might be expected to occasionally enter the sleeping rooms. In order to provide the Danes, who were accustomed to a much cooler climate in Denmark, with the best possible living conditions, the floors would be coated with polished teak. This would make it pleasant to move around the house barefoot.

The prospect of living on polished floors behind open windows – next to a cement plant operating around the clock and spewing coal and cement dust up through its chimneys – made the question of cleaning urgently. Dust would be cleaned from the floors at short intervals (twice daily would be the necessary solution after the startup of production in 1915). In general, the needs of the households of the future managers and high-ranking white-collar employees in the bungalows called for the proximity of servants. The spaces between the bungalows were therefore laid out for housing for cooks, cleaners, etc. connected to the Danish living quarters by covered corridors to provide shelter during the rainy season.

Behind the housing facilities, a gap was left open towards the cement plant for private gardens fenced off by hedges and trees. It would, predictably, be difficult to maintain an atmosphere of privacy and of a green oasis in the gardens – right next to the busy work life around the dust-spewing and noisy cement plant. Nevertheless, the reservation of some of the area for gardens opened a potential for creating an environment for leisure and recreation.

Looking at the planning of the layout of the factory in combination with photos in 1913–1915, when the construction work had just been completed, one easily gets the impression that the cement plant was to be constructed in the backyard of the Danish expatriates and would come to occupy a de facto status as part of their dominion. Apart from the locally hired servants, the presence of the future workforce of the cement plant was not included in the design, nor was there any sign of the presence of the Siamese founder of the Siam Cement Co.

Consequently, the plant would be constructed as an enclave-resembling area where the workforce – as well as everyone else – would enter from the outside to experience the everyday presence of the Danish management. The Danes would be the residents of stately villas, and they would have a full overview of the production activities and any other daily routines from their gardens and bedroom windows and, accordingly, optimal possibilities to intervene and control operations whenever needed – day or night.

Michel Foucault's use of the panopticon structures of penitentiaries as a metaphor of the disciplining force of modern society may well spring to mind.[28] The question is, however, how daily life would come to be. How far-reaching would the control assigned to the Danes by their Siamese employers be? Would they be subjected to strict surveillance in their daily routines with only minimal influence on matters beyond daily operations?

Such questions were probably on the mind of Oscar Schultz as he and Emily approached Bangkok in May 1914 after more than a month's travel from Copenhagen. The young couple had travelled by train to Genoa, Italy, and from there by ship to Port Said and the Suez Canal. Their journey continued by steamer to Singapore, where they changed to a smaller vessel that carried them to Bangkok. In Port Said their warm Danish clothing had been replaced by lighter outfits appropriate for the unfamiliar warm tropical climate in Siam – and as they approached Bangkok, Oscar Schultz noticed how the heat started to rise.[29]

Among Europeans and Orientals in Bangkok

The arrival of Oscar Schultz in Siam in 1914 came to demonstrate how the transfer of technology to an unacquainted and distant world can imply significant barriers. It did, however, also demonstrate how such challenges could in fact reduce F.L. Smidth & Co.'s potential worries about opportunism in cases where the transferred technological systems implied key personnel. Even for the bold Oscar Schultz, the move to Siam was an abrupt change, and his urge for adventure was immediately tainted by disdain for parts of his and Emily's new way of life.

Construction works in Bangsue were only at a preliminary phase, and Oscar and Emily Schultz therefore spent their first four months in Siam in Bangkok as residents at H.N. Andersen's Oriental Hotel. This offered good living conditions, but in his letters to family in Denmark, Oscar immediately complained about the high temperatures and humidity in Bangkok.

An important job task for Oscar Schultz was to meet up with relevant business connections and make acquaintances among the other Danes and westerners in the Siamese capital in general. Oscar Schultz was thus introduced to the board of the Siam Cement Co., chaired by William Lennart Grut, who was the Swedish Consul General in Bangkok and director of Siam Electric as well as chairman of the Scandinavian owned company United Plantations Ltd., whose main activity was the production of palm oil in Siam and Malaysia.[30] Besides a few other westerners – including Italian E.G. Gollo – the board consisted of Siamese members from the upper echelons of society, socially and politically. Among the Siamese was Chao Phraya Yomaraj, who had led the first meeting of the founding group in 1913 and now held a prominent position in the Chulalongkorn administration of the country. In 1907, he had become minister of public works and later on minister of the interior and had earned the right to carry the highest non-noble rank, expressed by the excellency title *Chao Phraya*.[31] The board consisted of other prominent Siamese members as well, including Chulalongkorn's brother Prince Luang Svasti Wiengchai.

Among the European population in Bangkok, the acquaintance was made with Danish engineer Hugo Zachariae, director of the Bangkok tramways owned by Siam Electric, and Kay Ingerslev-Jensen, who was director of EAC operations in Bangkok.[32] Moreover, several friendships were formed with people of British origin. After very long working hours, time was spent on tennis courts and at coffee and dinner parties with other members of the community of expatriates. A considerable effort was put into forming a mixed network of personal contacts that would be of potential use for Oscar Schultz in his future operations in the world of business. At the same time, these personal contacts offered a comforting social context that would help keep at bay the ever-present troublesome feelings of isolation and homesickness.

Connections of a personal nature with the Siamese are completely absent in Oscar Schultz's letters to his family in Denmark, probably because they were never formed. In general, his perception of the local population, whom he referred to as *orientals*, was not characterised by enthusiasm, but rather by elements of disrespect. This became especially significant following the outbreak of World War I on 1 August 1914. In a letter to his parents, Oscar Schultz thus described how the news of the war had caused substantial outbreaks of anti-German sentiments among the Siamese, and in particular in Vajiravudh:

Bangkok 4 October 1914:

The king of Siam is very concerned about the war and gives one patriotic speech after the other. But patriotism is not a matter of concern among the Siamese, because they are Orientals, too lazy and too uncaring. All the king achieves is to become unpopular, and I would not be surprised if he will get himself murdered someday and the crown prince will be elected as king. And this would take place without any consequence or notice of any of us Europeans, nor would the majority of the working population care much about it.

So far, Oscar Schultz lived among westerners in Bangkok, at a distance from the daily routines of the ordinary Siamese population. His one-sided views on the *orientals* were to change in the following months after the startup of the plant in Bangsue, but a strong feeling of detachment towards the Siamese context would prevail.

Arrival in Bangsue

In October 1914, Emily and Oscar Schultz embarked on their life at the cement plant in Bangsue, where construction works and the fitting of machinery were entering their final stages. This implied another abrupt change in the young couple's way of life.

The construction of the bungalow was completed in October, and in the eyes of Oscar Schultz, the house was big and solid. He found the scenery beautiful and the air considerably better than in Bangkok. The domestic staff was a very pleasant feature of life in Bangsue, which also offered the chance to go hunting. So far, Oscar Schultz was very content:

Bangsue 18 October 1914:

Our domestic staff consists of a cook, a boy and a coolie. So far, they have only caused us joy, but for how long that will prevail one can never tell. The cook is excellent and seems to possess a sense of economy.

A moment ago, and Italian friend of mine returned from a hunting trip and offered us four snipes. We shared a glass of beer, and he then hurried to catch the train. For my part, I have been hunting snipes several times and managed to hit 14, which is a poor result in these conditions. A success is at least 30 per day. ...

Life is certainly very different in the tropics, and it has its downsides, but at the same time, many pleasant things as well, and if one gets used to them, it will become difficult to live without them later on.

The acquaintances in Bangkok could still be reached by the infra-structure provided by the railway and canals, but from the end of 1914, Oscar and Emily would have to settle into a daily routine with the company of each other in their bungalow, the few other Danes at the plant and the locally hired workforce of Siamese and Chinese origin. Eventually, this implied a change with far-reaching consequences for their intimate relationship – and for the strategic potential for F.L. Smidth & Co. to place Oscar Schultz in a key position in the running of the Siam Cement Co.

During the daytime, Oscar was heavily occupied with the fitting and later running of the cement plant. The task could be of an overwhelming nature to him, but at the same time, it kept his mind focused on the challenging circumstances in which he and Emily were now living. When the news of his father's sudden death reached him in a letter from Alexander Foss in November 1914, he described the job at the cement plant as a way to overcome grief and regain confidence in the future.

Emily's primary occupation, however, was a white fox terrier, which she had been given by the English vicar in Bangkok. Even though life was busy around the plant, her part in it was limited, and without the close presence of friends and social life in Bangkok, feelings of boredom and loneliness loomed. Emily therefore soon began to work on the layout of the garden between the bungalow and the cement kiln, which was still under construction. The garden became an image of her effort to combat feelings of isolation in the Siamese context in an introvert manner, and not by seeking ways of integration. This tendency was also seen in Oscar's description of his encounter with employees and superiors.

The mentioning in his letters to his family in Denmark of the domestic staff in Bangsue was the first time Oscar described his relations to or-dinary Siamese – after five months in Siam. The local population was seemingly not a matter of great concern in his many letters to Denmark. Nevertheless, at the end of 1914, he found it relevant to sketch the character of the workforce at the plant:

Bangsue 1 December 1914:

I am becoming increasingly fond of my Siamese workers. They are hard-working good-natured children who, as you know, do what-ever they are told. They have a reputation of being very thievish, but so far, I have no experience of this nature.

It is now six o clock, so work has finished for today, and all my workers are bathing joyfully in the canal below my window and enjoying life.

Oscar Schultz's first description of the *orientals* as lazy and uncaring was thus replaced by a more positive description, but clearly, his perception of the relationship between him and the local population was that it was strongly unequal.

The Chinese members of the workforce seem to have been a particular source of resentment to him, and, especially, their tendency to constantly commence strikes. In most cases, Oscar wrote to his family, they could be made pliable by refusing to pay them for their work or offering them a small extra sum to buy rice. But the greatest cause of frustration was his suspicion that the Chinese were the wire-pullers behind thefts from the construction site. It had not yet been possible for him to stop this, even though he had hired and organised an energetic police force to patrol the plant.

Oscar's indulgent perception of the local population as *orientals* fundamentally collided with the fact that his presence in Bangsue was owing to leading figures in Siamese society, and that he was under Siamese superiority. This became clear on several occasions, for instance, one Sunday in December 1914, when Chao Phraya Yomaraj suddenly appeared at the construction site accompanied by his wife and a considerable number of children. Chao Phraya Yomaraj wished to inspect the fitting of the machinery, and suddenly the Danish manager and his American wife had to take on the roles of servant and nanny to the prominent Siamese family. Nevertheless, Oscar Schultz described the unusual afternoon in a positive tone. Apparently, the relationship with Chao Phraya Yomaraj was characterised by mutual trust.

The relationship between Oscar Schultz and other members of the high-ranking Siamese population, however, was characterised by a strong sense of mistrust. This became particularly clear in April 1915, when strong anti-western feelings among the Siamese tainted the work of the board of the Siam Cement Co. At that time, Oscar Schultz had noticed how Vajiravudh acted as a strong instigator of Siamese discontent with the European influence in Siam in general. On several occasions, the king had requested his subjects to seek to improve their qualifications in order to eliminate the European presence in Siam. In April 1915, sentiments came to a head, however, as the Swedish king Gustav, following a visit to the court of Vajiravudh the previous year, had published a book with – as Oscar described it – "strongly disrespectful" descriptions of Siamese society and government. Even though the wrath this provoked in Vajiravudh seemed ridiculous in the eyes of the Dane, Oscar found it quite understandable, and on the board of the Siam Cement Co. – which counted several members of government and of the royal family – the Swedish chairman, commander W.L. Grut, came under strong pressure.

This made it very obvious to Oscar Schultz that he was part of a European presence in Siam which was in essence considered a necessary evil to the Siamese, and how this affected the minds of his superiors.

Meanwhile, he had to keep his mind focused on completing the construction of the cement plant as the final parts had arrived from Copenhagen in February 1915. In the middle of April, when heat made work unbearable, the final preparations for production start were being finalised. At that time, three other Danes had arrived in Bangsue; the chemist Uldall-Jørgensen, whom Oscar Schultz instantly disliked, the 21-year-old accountant Erik Thune, and the 28-year-old engineer Svend Aage Valdemar Andreasen.[33] The three bungalows were now being lived in, and after many months of construction and fitting work, life at the factory-island could enter a new phase.

Like Living on an Island ...

When the cement production began, the pressure on the Danes in Bangsue increased. Very soon, however, it became clear that the startup was successful and that the expectations from the Siam Cement Co. as well as from F.L. Smidth & Co. could be met. In June 1915, Oscar Schultz concluded to his family that the machinery was running well, and the cement was of good quality. During the summer, cement was piling up in the storage buildings, but soon sales increased, and in November, working profits were being made. In April 1916, the profits amounted to 14,000 ticals (baht) and at the end of the first year of production, Oscar Schultz received a large bonus.

Despite the successful running of production, life in Siam was still a challenge to Oscar Schultz. In particular, the great distance to the limestone pit in Cong Kae, 170 km to the north, caused quite a lot of concern. Several days each month had to be spent on regular visits to the pit, and when extraordinary circumstances occurred, additional trips had to be made – for example, in April 1916, the factory's stocks of dynamite had been raided. Oscar Schultz soon commenced a search for a suitable supply of limestone at shorter distances from Bangsue, and during 1916, he undertook several journeys to different parts of Siam for that purpose. Visiting the countryside and especially the Buddhist temples was encouraging to the adventurous Dane. At the same time, the journeys offered a much-needed interruption of daily life at Bangsue, which was becoming increasingly marked by the conflicts and personal challenges that had instantly revealed themselves after his arrival at the site in late 1914.

When production began, the workforce at the cement plant consisted of approximately 100 workers, among whom more or less half were Chinese *coolies*. The latter were a source of constant frustration to Oscar Schultz, due to their nationalistic sentiments.[34]

Bangsue 15 June 1915:

> Working conditions are not that easy in the East, and the Chinese in
> particular are very difficult to deal with as they are stubborn, lazy
> and unwilling to take orders from anybody other than foremen of
> their own nationality. Unfortunately, I have not yet been able to hire
> a suitable Chinese foreman. One has to keep on trying until a
> satisfactory staff is created.
>
> The coming month is going to be busy as well, but I am planning on
> taking a small vacation and maybe travel to the northern parts of
> Siam where I have some Danish acquaintances.

Racism was mutual at the plant, and the Chinese determination to
maintain a command structure of their own was a local expression of a
general phenomenon in Siam at the time. The Chinese community in
Siam had increased extensively in size during the 19th Century, and
growing concern regarding their expressions of national identity had
caused the Siamese government to issue several regulations during the
first years of the 20th century. In 1905, a special police force had been
formed in order to maintain law and order in the Chinese-populated
areas of Bangkok, and in 1910, riots had broken out as the Chinese had
been ordered to pay personal income tax. In 1913, the use of Thai first
names had been instructed by law. Following these events, the Chinese
turned their backs on Siamese society and settled in separate commu-
nities. This also led to the foundation of a series of Chinese institutions –
schools, newspapers, hospitals, etc.[35]

The Chinese determination to exercise self-control was a constant
source of frustration to Oscar Schultz, and this feeling was further ag-
gravated by the fact that the resentment between the Chinese and the
Siamese caused unrest at the plant for several months during the summer
of 1915. In June and July, the situation escalated to outspoken violence,
and Oscar Schultz had to expand the local police force he had already
organised at the plant. Probably due to the language barrier, the cause of
the riots remained a bit of a mystery to Oscar Schultz, but starting in
June 1915, his ability to exercise social control came to imply a self-
proclaimed monopoly of violence.

As months passed, the continuing quarrels and incidents of violence
among the workforce started to get to Oscar Schultz's nerves. In
September 1915, he expressed his bad temper in a letter to his mother:

Bangsue 24 September 1915.

> The production of cement is slowly progressing. Due to many
> difficulties and annoyances, my mood goes up and down. One day

everything seems to be in perfectly good order, and the next, there are a hundred complaints and difficulties to be dealt with.

During the autumn of 1915, temperatures were rising, and the ever-present mosquitoes were a constant bother, and in the end, Oscar Schultz's mood had reached boiling point. Among the workers he now became feared for his violent temper and outbursts, and he was soon nicknamed *The Tiger*. Not surprisingly, Oscar Schultz never described his corporal punishments of the workforce in his writings to his family in Denmark. But they came to be remembered among the workers. At the 50th anniversary of the Siam Cement Co. in 1963, one of them, Nai Kim Ou Chianpradit, described vividly how Emily had tried to make Oscar bite his knuckles or punch his fist against the wall in order to cool down, but despite the effort of the no-doubt emotionally affected wife, the anger of the hot-tempered Danish manager often led to physical punishment of his subordinates.[36]

Towards his Siamese superiors – and in particular king Vajiravudh – good relations were essential, and in this case, Emily proved a great help to Oscar on several occasions when prominent members of the board appeared in Bangsue to inspect the plant. Chao Phraya Yomaraj was often a guest in the Danish bungalows, and even though the board never managed to make Vajiravudh himself pay a visit to Bangsue, his younger brother, prince Prajadiphok, inspected the plant in March 1916. Prajadhipok was accompanied by several other princes. Nevertheless, his visit left the Danish manager worried about his relationship with his Siamese superiors:

Bangsue 6 February 1916:

The crown prince and his madam, a Russian duchess, were here a couple of days ago to inspect the plant. Afterwards we took tea at our place. He is very intelligent and vividly interested in every step forward for his country, but he is certainly not very friendly to Europeans. Yesterday I spent the day waiting for another prince who had announced a visit, but the fellow never showed up.

The visit by Prajadiphok had obviously been marked by animosity, which left Oscar Schultz wondering how things would turn out when, one day, the prince would succeed Vajiravudh as king.

Gradually, the hardships left Oscar Schultz with a feeling of being victimised, which he expressed in his letters to his mother in Denmark. Oscar felt a strong longing to be closer to his European associates in Bangkok, and his everyday life at the factory enclave left him with an increasing feeling of living on an island:

Bangsue 6 February 1916:

> We have constructed a tennis court and normally play three times a
> week. This is a welcome break; I mean, it takes one's mind off the
> plant and cement. Sometimes when the plant causes too much
> trouble, you need to get away a little from the company. But due to
> the lousy communication with Bangkok, it is more or less like living
> on an island.

1916 had offered a constant stream of annoyances, and Oscar Schultz's
distaste of his life in Bangsue had grown accordingly. In May, Emily and
Oscar's cook had suddenly died of the plague, and the bungalow had had
to be washed with phenol. The Danes and their servants had been vac-
cinated, but more than two weeks had elapsed before the incubation
period had passed and everybody could breathe more easily again.

The plague was of course an unpleasant phenomenon, but Oscar's
greatest worries now originated from his marriage. During 1916, it was a
returning subject in Oscar's letters how he and Emily were planning her
departure from Bangsue in order for her to undergo medical examina-
tions in Denmark and convalescence in Switzerland. In December, it was
decided that she would depart for America in February 1917. Slowly
Oscar started to reveal the true cause of her departure, and finally, in
May, the lid came off:

Bangsue 2 May 1917:

> Even though I should like to spare you from any more worries, I can
> no longer hide the fact that the marriage between Emily and myself
> has run aground, and that we are now negotiating the terms for a
> divorce. Emily was never satisfied in Siam. Everything was wrong.
> My home was not suitable, my salary not sufficient for her liking etc.
> So the last three years have not been easy for me.
>
> Two years ago, she made acquaintance with a young Russian envoi
> who madly paid court to her. When matters went too far approxi-
> mately a year ago, I had to make things clear and give her the choice
> of either terminating the affair or facing a divorce immediately. She
> chose to give up on the Russion and they did not meet after that, but
> still they must have been in contact behind my back since two days
> ago, I received a letter from Helsinki saying that Emily was now
> living at the Russian's mother's house, and that they will marry
> immediately after our divorce has been finalised.

Life as the wife of an almost always absent, choleric and brutal cement
plant manager on a dusty and noisy cement plant site in a remote and

isolated corner of Southeast Asia had been too much for Emily to handle. The role as social carrier of technology had taken its toll on the young couple's private life. In the eyes of F.L. Smidth & Co., however, the situation was not necessarily unambiguous as from early 1917, Oscar Schultz was left alone in the manager-bungalow with a strong longing for his family, friends and Denmark. He immediately started planning for a vacation in Denmark in order to get away from Siam and the "total failurfe" of his private life. By then, he had been trying for months to get in touch with his uncle, Alexander Foss, but had been left without a reply, he even asked his mother to help him reach the FLS founder – still without success.

In August 1917, when the time had come to renew his employment contract with the Siam Cement Co., Oscar was basically left with no alternative – as he later briefly remarked:

Bangsue 31 December 1917:

I am not happy about Siam … .

The Danish Base

To sum up, the design of social relations in Bangsue through staffing and the careful design of the physical environment had created a strongly asymmetrical knowledge base in favour of the Danes when production commenced during 1915. In everyday life, the Danes were always present at the factory enclave to run the machinery, which required expertise that only they fully possessed, while the presence of the Siamese owners and board members for primarily social visits only happened occasionally. Oscar Schultz and his associates took care of every aspect of management in the running of the plant – from technical considerations to sales and a forceful control of social relations.

Events in the following years became a demonstration of how this base could be exploited to gain extensive control of key dispositions of the Siam Cement Co., including the supply and maintenance of machinery, and even of schemes for new plants elsewhere in Southeast Asia. The tool was cheap – it was paid for by the payrolls of the Siam Cement Co. – and the events taking place in Oscar Schultz's life, in business matters as well as in his private life, had strongly facilitated the maintenance of his loyalty. This may appear as a colourful coincidence, but the physical context in general – the heat, humidity, mosquitoes, danger of diseases, etc. – in combination with the social and cultural barriers between the Danish and the Siamese members of the workforce acted as a strong driving force to prevent the Danes from turning away from their old parent company. The long geographical distance between Denmark and

Siam could act in favour of F.L. Smidth & Co.'s strategy, which could be strengthened by the deliberate design of the plant as an enclave, ensuring daily isolation of the Danish employees and their families.

Even though the situation resembled a Danish fifth column inside the Siam Cement Co., such characterisation would be misleading in the overall picture since here was a shared interest in making the plant in Bangsue a profitable investment. Nevertheless, as things progressed, they did in fact develop strongly towards resembling a fifth column, or maybe even a Trojan horse, when the question of new schemes in Southeast Asia started to emerge.

On the Malayan Peninsula 1917–1924

Communication with Alexander Foss was finally resumed when Oscar Schultz received a letter from his uncle in October 1917. The letter was not, however, written out of concern for Oscar's personal wellbeing but originated from pure business reasons as while the young Danish manager was deeply engaged in preparations for extensions of the production capacity of the Siam Cement Co. in order to meet the demand from markets further down the Malayan Peninsula. As a part of these preparations, he commenced a reconnaissance travel in August 1917 that took him to the areas around the Malacca Strait near Singapore and close to Kuala Lumpur in the British-controlled Federated Malay States, presently Malaysia. Apart from inspection of limestone deposits, the purpose of his travel was negotiations with British missionaries and Chinese businessmen on the possibility to take over two small cement plants, based on old shaft kilns, at Batu Arang and at a location near Singapore.

The project was, however, postponed until the summer of 1919, when Oscar Schultz finally managed to return to Denmark for vacation – combined with discussions in Copenhagen with Alexander Foss on the potential of establishing a modern cement plant on the Malayan Peninsula. Immediately on his return from Copenhagen, Oscar therefore stopped over in Singapore to negotiate the purchase of the old cement plant at Batu Arang near Kuala Lumpur.[37] His negotiation position was of course as manager of the Siam Cement Co. – the only modern cement company in Southeast Asia – with a powerful backing from the Siamese monarchy. Nevertheless, he acted as an arbitrator between the different parties showing interest in the scheme. And judging from his position in the centre of this constellation, there seems to have been no doubt in his mind of keeping his loyalty primarily towards F.L. Smidth & Co. and only as a second priority towards the Siam Cement Co.

When Oscar Schultz arrived in Singapore in December 1919, it thus turned out that the plant at the Batu Arang had already been bought by the British owned tin and coal-producing company J.A. Russel & Co., managed by the founder J.A. Russel, who had also taken over the mining concessions in the area. Oscar Schultz therefore had to advocate the idea of collaboration with the Siam Cement Co. as well as with F.L. Smidth & Co., even though he considered the effort to be more or less futile. J.A. Russel & Co. was a successful company which would presumably undertake the installation of a cement plant by itself, with the help of British machine suppliers. Nevertheless, Oscar Schultz tried to convince F.L. Smidth & Co. to gain initiative and establish contacts directly to J.A. Russel & Co. and further to suggest a collaboration, with reference to the construction of the plant in Bangsue. F.L. Smidth & Co. abstained from such an initiative, but the suggestion from Oscar Schultz was a clear sign of his self-perception as an agent for the interests of his old parent company. His clear-cut loyalty, based on family bonds and strengthened by the fact that he considered F.L. Smidth & Co. his only possible career option – or way out of Siam – was clearly expressed in his letters to his family:

Bangsue 30 May 1920:

At the moment I am busy making great and promising plans. If things turn out right, my position will be markedly improved in every way during the next two years. ... If successful, the result will be a major contract for F.L. Smidth, and you will probably understand how it will be of great satisfaction to me to appear as a big client in that manner. But keep silent on this to anybody but our family as it may all still come to nothing.

Oscar Schultz's operations on behalf of F.L. Smidth & Co. were thus of an informal nature as no employment or contract on services were involved. Still, there was no reason to doubt in Copenhagen that measures could be taken with the direct help of a highly loyal contact who could take action from a key position in the Siam Cement Co. and act on behalf of the Siamese.

There was, however, a limit to Oscar Schultz's ability to control the dispositions of the Siam Cement Co. Despite initial pessimism, it had surprisingly been possible, in the spring of 1920, to convince J.A. Russel to enter into collaboration. The planning of a scheme consequently started to materialise. The plan was to form a new company led by J.A. Russel and with the Siam Cement Co. only as a potential participant. As was expressed by Russel in a letter to F.L. Smidth & Co. – "the Siam Cement Co. probably will be partners". Despite the fact that the future planning would be based on an extensive report which was being prepared by Oscar Schultz, it was, in the eyes of Russel, an evident option that the scheme would be a future competitor to the Siam Cement Co. This was, however, not only an option created in Russel's imagination but also a plausible outcome in the eyes of Oscar Schultz, who apparently had not been able to exchange his control of the plant in Bangsue into influence on a decision by the board of the Siam Cement Co. to further engage in the Kuala Lumpur scheme. In a letter to F.L. Smidth & Co., Oscar Schultz thus listed the participants in the preparation of the scheme during the summer of 1920, and at that moment in time, the Siam Cement Co. apparently was no longer among them:

Bangsue 25 June 1920:

Promotors of the scheme will be J.A. Russel and party Kuala Lumpur and E. G. Gollo, O. Schultz and party Bangkok.

Oscar Schultz even added that it was his plan to relocate to Kuala Lumpur to lead the construction of the plant in collaboration with the engineers from F.L. Smidth & Co. His mind seemed to be fixed on the Danish business potential, not least to himself as he now counted himself as a member of the group of initiators along with the Italian board member of the Siam Cement Co. E.G. Gollo. Of his own accord, he even wrote to Alexander Foss and FLS co-founder Poul Larsen, trying to persuade them to make direct investments in the Kuala Lumpur scheme. In response, Poul Larsen suggested that half of the payment for machinery would be effected by giving F.L. Smidth & Co. shares in the future plant.

However, optimistic things may have appeared during the summer of 1920, the project soon faced major obstacles. Analyses of raw materials from the Batu Arang area did not turn out as expected. In combination with the effects of the world economic crisis in 1920–1921, this caused a halt to further work on the scheme, and Russel announced that it would not be possible on his part to resume preparations until 1924. Meanwhile, on his own initiative and at his own expense, Oscar Schultz nevertheless kept trying to restart preparations by attempting to raise funding from F.L. Smidth & Co. and by searching for better raw material deposits. His effort continued relentlessly until June 1924, when J.A. Russel finally retracted from the project. This put a preliminary end to the Danish dreams of an extended involvement in the cement industry in Southeast Asia. However, by then it had been possible for more than seven years for F.L. Smidth & Co. to use the manager of the Siam Cement Co. as a trusted spearhead in the region, even though it had not been possible to secure the support from his employer and Siamese superiors towards the final stages of the project, and despite the fact that he was actually participating in the establishment of a future competitor.

Danish Control in Bangsue 1920–1925

The withdrawal of the Siam Cement Co. from the Kuala Lumpur scheme in 1920 happened simultaneously with – and was probably closely related to – the decision to extend the plant in Bangsue for the purpose of securing a strong position in the Siamese home market and the commencement of exports to the rising cement market in Singapore.[38] Thus, the extensions in Bangsue were aimed at a market of utmost importance to a future cement producer in Kuala Lumpur. F.L. Smidth & Co. were, in other words, gambling on two horses in the same race.

The danger of negative consequences from this double-dealing does not, however, appear to have been of a very serious nature. The extension in Bangsue was effected by F.L. Smidth & Co. in 1921–1922 by yet another vast purchase of a 25-m-long rotary kiln and adherent machinery from Copenhagen, doubling the capacity of the plant.[39] The potential advantage of having Danes located at both sides of the negotiation table was thus being fully exploited. The new kiln was even installed in parallel to the existing machinery with no modifications of the location of the entire plant just behind the hedges of the Danish gardens. So far, Danish control at Bangsue remained unaltered, and in 1922, the Danish legation in Bangkok could sum up the situation in a report to the foreign ministry in Copenhagen:

Bangkok 21 March 1922:

The Siam Cement Co. is under Danish control, and there has so far been no considerations from the Siamese to take over the management. At the plant, a Danish construction engineer and chemist are employed as well, and under the present management, these positions will expectedly always be occupied by Danish engineers.[40]

From the Danish point of view, the Siamese seemed content with the fact that the plant was under Danish control. In the Danish newspapers, the report was paraphrased into the description that "all important positions at the plant" were occupied by six Danes; however, it had been necessary, as one newspaper explained, to place a few high-ranking Siamese on the board of the company in order to satisfy the emotions of the owners.[41]

Despite his partaking in the preparations for the Kuala Lumpur scheme, the personal position of Oscar Schultz was so far unaltered as well. In 1922, it therefore made sense to the Danish legation to appoint him vice-consul in Bangkok. The solidity of his position was probably to a great extent due to his close friendship with Chao Phraya Yomaraj.[42] In 1922, the influential Siamese was appointed minister of the interior and, in the eyes of the Danish legation, became one of the most influential people in Siam.[43] In general, the Danish officials praised Yomaraj for the continuing and out-spoken policy of choosing Danish partners instead of British.[44] Among the Siamese, the Bangsue plant was considered a close sphere of interest, almost the private property, of the ever more powerful Yomaraj, who consequently was an extremely important associate of Oscar Schultz.[45] In general, the Danes considered Yomaraj to be Siam's upper hand.[46] It was therefore a matter of grave concern when Vajiravudh died at the age of 44 in November 1925 and was succeeded by Prajadiphok, which resulted in the voluntary resignation of Yomaraj as minister of the interior. In Bangsue, Oscar Schultz had been well acquainted with the newly elected king's hostile attitude towards westerners in general since he paid a visit to Emily and Oscar Schultz in 1916. The risk of losing their position in the Siam Cement Co. as a strong foothold in the Southeast Asian cement industry as a consequence of the accession of the new king could seem imminent to F.L. Smidth & Co.

In November 1925, the situation in Bangsue had changed in one de-cisive aspect, however: the departure of Oscar Schultz from Siam in early 1925. To the knowledge of the FLS headquarters in Copenhagen, this had been – on the surface – the consequence of a voluntary agreement caused by disagreements with the chairman, Lennart Grut, on matters connected to the running of the plant in Bangsue. Below the surface, it seemed evident that Oscar Schultz had lost some sort of internal power struggle. Considering the timing of Oscar Schultz's exit, the obvious conclusion was that this was probably a side effect of the double-sided activities of the Danish manager in the previous years. However, the nature of what had really happened remained blurred in Copenhagen.[47]

In any case, Oscar Schultz had apparently felt obliged to depart from Siam shortly after the collapse of his grand scheme to extend the East Asian cement industry with a competitor to Siam Cement Co. Chao Phraya Yomaraj's closest associate was therefore already gone at the time when Prajadiphok succeeded to the throne. During the summer of 1925, Oscar Schultz could be smoothly replaced by the former ac-countant Erik Thune, and the Danish control in Bangsue thus remained intact and more or less undisturbed by any former personal distrust.

Controlling the Investments of the Siam Cement Co.

Erik Thune became the second in an uninterrupted line of Danish FLS general managers of the Siam Cement Co., starting with Oscar Schultz and ending with Viggo Frederik Hemmingsen in 1974. During the 20th Century, the company expanded to become one of the largest con-glomerates in Southeast Asia and one of the most profitable enterprises of the Siamese/Thai monarchy. The plant in Bangsue was extended several times, and from 1957 more cement plants were added, the first of these in Ta Luang. In 2006, the Siam Cement Co. was renamed The Siam Cement Group in order to modernise the brand, which now covered several branches from cement plants to petrochemicals and building materials.[48]

The strong Danish influence on the Siam Cement Co. during the 20th Century was not the result of a gradual multinational establishment chain developing over many years. Even before their own employees set foot on Siamese soil, F.L. Smidth & Co. had been able to make their interest felt due to their personal and professional relations with a wide range of business contacts and officials back home in Denmark – most importantly H.N. Andersen and the EAC. The close-knit Danish network at the outset made it easy, so to speak, for F.L Smidth & Co. to be a born global in Siam and, without any further direct investments, to enter directly into a position of deep entanglement with the Siam Cement Co. The close tailormade relationship between the two companies did not lead to the formation of a new multinational enterprise in the common understanding of the term. A formal bond was never established between the Siam Cement Co. and F.L. Smidth & Co. However, one could easily be forgiven for suggesting that the relationship between the two bore a close resemblance to a vertical integration which, due to a strong asymmetrical knowledge base and strongly helped by the physical design of social relations in Bangsue, enabled F.L. Smidth & Co. to exploit the potential for influence and control of the dispositions of the Siam Cement Co.

The case from Siam thus gives a very clear insight into the character of the control towards which F.L. Smidth & Co. could aim their strategy. It shows how a set of decisive comparative advantages could be gained from installing a local Danish plant management, enhanced by various types of cultural capital in particular and solidified by the physical world of things.

If focus were to remain fixed on the consensus-definition of multinational enterprise as the *ability to control income generating assets in foreign countries,* it would be tempting to characterise F.L. Smidth & Co. as an *informal multinational* in Siam from the start-up of activities in Siam Cement Co. in 1914/15. Activities were never based on direct investments from Denmark to Siam or any formalised command structure or flow of payments. But from Copenhagen, there was never any reason to fear that the ex-patriate Danes would stop acting as reliable and controllable partners inside The Siam Cement Co. and that, to any wide extent, they would no longer be able to exercise far-reaching influence on their Siamese superiors to the benefit of their Danish parent company.

Notes

1 *SCG 100 Years of Innovation for Sustainability* (Bangkok: The Siam Cement Public Company Limited, 2013), 22. M.R. Kukrit Pramoj: *In Commemoration of the 50th* (Bangkok: The Siam Cement Co., Ltd., 1963), 125.

2 The official use of *Thailand* was introduced in 1939. In the following, I use the former country name *Siam* which is still widely used to denote Thailand's present population as *Siamese*.

3 *The Letter from F.L. Smidth & Co. to The Siam Cement Company, Ltd,* 2 September 1913 (FLSA).

4 *SCG 100 Years of Innovation for Sustainability,* 24. *The Siam Cement Company Ltd.* 1957 (Bangkok: The Siam Cement Co., 1957), 6.

5 D.G.E. Hall: *A History of South-East Asia,* 4 ed. (New York, 1995). Chris Baker and Pasuk Phongpaichit: *A History of Thailand,* 2 ed. (Cambridge, 2009). Stephen Lyon Wakeman Greene: *Absolute Dreams. Thai Government under Rama VI, 1910-25* (Bangkok: White Lotus Press, 1999).

6 A. Kann Rasmussen: *Danske i Siam 1858-1942* (København: Dansk Historisk Håndbogsforlag, 1986), 39–49.

7 Tage Kaarsted: *Admiralen. Andreas de Richelieu. Forretningsmand og politiker i Siam og Danmark* (Odense, 1990), 40ff and 162ff.

8 Greene, *Absolute Dreams,* 48.

9 Pramoj, *In Commemoration,* 126.

10 Ole Lange 1986: *Den hvide elefant. H. N. Andersens eventyr og ØK 1852-1914* (København: Gyldendal, 1986). Rasmussen, *Danske.* Kaarsted, *Admiralen.* Martin Iversen: *Udsyn. ØK, Danmark og verden* (København: Lindhardt & Ringhof, 2016).

11 On Richelieu in Siam, see Kaarsted, *Admiralen.*

12 Kaarsted, *Admiralen,* 126.

13 Lange, *Den hvide,* 179; Henning Bender: *Aalborgs industrielle udvikling 1735-1940. Aalborgs historie bd. 4* (Aalborg, 1987), 380.

14 "Oversigter over dansk import til Bangkok 1920-1924"; "Siams Handel," *Udenrigsministeriets Tidsskrift, hefte 75, Aarg. 4.* Danish National Archives, Copenhagen (Rigsarkivet): Udenrigsministeriet, Oplysningsbureauet for Erhvervene, Gruppeordnede sager 1922-28: Siam.

15 Nils Foss: *Efter min bedste overbevisning. Om iværksætteri, ledelse og samfundsansvar* (København, 2014).

16 Lange, *Den hvide.*

17 *The letter from F.L. Smidth & Co. to The Siam Cement Company, Ltd., dated 10 February* (FLSA).

18 Rasmussen, *Danske,* 216.

19 Povl Vinding: "Oscar Schultz 24/8 1884 – 25/2 1929," in *Ingeniøren,* nr. 10 (København, 1929), 121–122. Steen Andersen and Kurt Jacobsen: *Foss* (København: Børsens forlag, 2008), 88.

20 Vinding, "Oscar Schultz," 121.

21 Andersen, *Foss,* 88.

22 *Oscar Schultz til familien 19 December 1911.* Oscar Schultz, privatarkiv, Rigsarkivet. Unless otherwise indicated, the description of the travels and activities of Oscar Schultz in the following is based on the letters in his personal archive, today kept in the Danish National Archives in Copenhagen (Rigsarkivet).

23 Pramoj, *In Commemoration,* 126.

24 Pramoj, *In Commemoration,* 127.

25 The drawings are still kept in the archives of FLSmidth (FLSA).

26 Caspar Jørgensen: "Carlsbergs bebyggelseshistorie 1847-2008. En industriarkæologisk skitse," in *Architectura 31* (2009), 54.

27 The descriptions of the villas and the daily life are based on photos from the archives of FLSmidth (FLSA) and the memoirs in the private collections of Anne-Marie Ganner (Rigsarkivet).

28 Michel Foucault: *Discipline and Punish. The Birth of the Prison* (New York, 1975).

29 The descriptions in the following on the life of Oscar Schultz are based on his letter to his family in Denmark, today kept in the Danish National Archives in Copenhagen (Rigsarkivet).

30 Pramoj, *In Commemoration*, 11–17. Maurizio Peleggi: *Lords of Things: The Fashioning of the Siamese Monarchy's Modern Image* (University of Hawai'i Press, 2002), 192. Susan M. Martin: *The UP Saga* (København: Nordic Institute of Asian Studies, 2003), 45ff.

31 Greene, *Absolute Dreams*, 22 and 27.

32 *Oscar Schultz til Bertha og William Schultz 10 June 1914*. Oscar Schultz, privat arkiv (Rigsarkivet). Rasmussen, *Danske*, 160, 172 and 186.

33 *Oscar Schultz til Bertha Schultz 23 April 1915*. Oscar Schultz, privat arkiv (Rigsarkivet). Rasmussen, *Danske*, 212.

34 Pramoj, *In Commemoration*, 136.

35 Baker, *A History*, 95–96.

36 Pramoj, *In Commemoration*, 137.

37 *Oscar Schultz til Alexander Foss 27 June 1920*. Oscar Schultz, privatarkiv, Rigsarkivet. *Oscar Schultz til F.L. Smidth & Co. København 2 April 1920* (FLSA). Unless otherwise indicated, the descriptions of the process on the scheme in Kuala Lumpur are based on the letters in "Kuala Lumpur 1920-1932" (FLSA).

38 "Siams Handel," *Udenrigsministeriets Tidsskrift, hefte 75, Aargang 4*; "Siams Handel og Søfart," Ges. No. 151 af 19 September 1923. Udenrigsministeriet. Oplysningsbureauet for Erhvervene. 1922-28, gruppeordnede sager, Siam (Rigsarkivet). "Siamesiske Erhvervsforhold," in *Børsen* (København, 15 June 1922).

39 The information on buildings and machinery in the following are based on the drawings kept in the drawing archive of FLSmidth (FLSA).

40 "Oversigt over Muligheder for ansættelse af Danske Ingeniører i Siam," 21 March 1922. Udenrigsministeriet. Oplysningsbureauet for Erhvervene. 1922-28. Gruppeordnede sager, Siam (Rigsarkivet).

41 "Siamesiske Erhvervsforhold," in *Børsen* (København, 15 June 1922).

42 "In memoriam. Ingeniør Oscar Schultz," Obituary in a Danish newspaper. Oscar Schultz, privatarkiv (Rigsarkivet).

43 Depeche No. XII, 19 August 1922. Udenrigsministeriet, Depecher 1848–1972, Bangkok 1922–1941 (Rigsarkivet).

44 Depeche No. IV, 16 April 1923. Udenrigsministeriet, Depecher 1848–1972, Bangkok 1922–1941 (Rigsarkivet).

45 Greene, *Absolute Dreams*, 80.

46 Depeche No. VIII, 18 November 1926; Depeche No. VI, 11 March 1926. Udenrigsministeriet, Depecher 1848–1972, Bangkok 1922–1941 (Rigsarkivet).

47 *A.V. Jensen til T. Stig-Nielsen 15 January 1925*. Japan-Kina 1923-1932 (FLSA).

48 https://www.scg.com/en/01corporate_profile/03_milstone.html

Literature

Steen Andersen & Kurt Jacobsen: *Foss* (København: Børsens forlag, 2008).

Chris Baker & Pasuk Phongpaichit: *A History of Thailand*, 2nd ed. (Cambridge, 2009).

Henning Bender: *Aalborgs industrielle udvikling 1735–1940. Aalborgs historie bd. 4* (Aalborg, 1987).

Nils Foss: *Efter min bedste overbevisning. Om iværksætteri, ledelse og samfundsansvar* (København, 2014).

Michel Foucault: *Discipline and Punish. The Birth of the Prison* (New York, 1975).

Stephen Lyon Wakeman Greene: *Absolute Dreams. Thai Government under Rama VI, 1910-25* (Bangkok: White Lotus Press, 1999).

D.G.E. Hall: *A History of South-East Asia*, 4th ed. (New York, 1995).

Martin Iversen: *Udsyn. ØK, Danmark og verden* (København: Lindhardt & Ringhof, 2016).

Caspar Jørgensen: "Carlsbergs bebyggelseshistorie 1847–2008. En industriarkæologisk skitse," in *Architectura*, Vol. 31 (2009), 46–90.

Tage Kaarsted: *Admiralen. Andreas de Richelieu. Forretningsmand og politiker i Siam og Danmark* (Odense, 1990).

Ole Lange: *Den hvide elefant. H. N. Andersens eventyr og ØK 1852–1914* (København: Gyldendal, 1986).

Susan M. Martin: *The UP Saga* (København: Nordic Institute of Asian Studies, 2003).

Maurizio Peleggi: *Lords of Things: The Fashioning of the Siamese Monarchy's Modern Image* (Honolulu: University of Hawai'i Press, 2002).

M.R. Kukrit Pramoj: *In Commemoration of the 50th* (Bangkok: The Siam Cement Co., Ltd., 1963).

A. Kann Rasmussen: *Danske i Siam 1858–1942* (København: Dansk Historisk Håndbogsforlag, 1986).

SCG 100 Years of Innovation for Sustainability (Bangkok: The Siam Cement Public Company Limited, 2013).

The Siam Cement Company Ltd (Bangkok: The Siam Cement Co., 1957), 6.

4 *When China Awakens* ... China 1890–1938

The Chinese Context at the Turn of the 20th Century

F.L. Smidth & Co. could not expect the conditions for stepping directly into a strong market position with far-reaching control of the dispositions of the cement industry to be present everywhere. It was not necessarily as easy to become a born global in all other contexts as had been the case in Siam, where a substantial willingness to let the Danes be fully in charge of everyday life and the running of the plant in Bangsue was seen, even maybe to a surprising degree. The Siamese setting was small and simple compared to other much larger and complex contexts such as China, Japan or India. The strategy applied in Siam could therefore be perceived as an ideal that could be implemented when conditions were particularly favourable. In other areas, such as China, the need for adjustments of such a strategy was foreseeable, not least considering how, at the turn of the 20th century, the Chinese were struggling with the ambition to regain their former position as inhabitants of the Middle Kingdom.

During the 19th century, the balance between China and the West had tipped over in favour of the latter.[1] China was constantly losing strength due to internal political unrest following declining social and economic circumstances which have later been characterised by some historians as *involution,* to denounce that the growth of the population was not matched by the evolution of new means of production and technology in the mainly feudal agrarian country.[2] Consequently, the Malthusian limit was being felt to an increasing extent. The Taiping rebellion during the 1850s was only one major incident in a continuous series of riots and uprisings effectively eroding the power of the Qing emperor. In the period from the 1850s to the 1870s, the emperor lost control of coastal areas stretching from Beijing towards Shanghai, and enormous territories from Xi'an towards western Xinjian came under Muslim authority. The existence of the Qing dynasty was threatened, and in a number of provinces, the power monopoly was in effect taken over by incremental regional governments and large landowners.

DOI: 10.4324/9780429446184-4

Meanwhile, the rise of the industrialised West was accompanied by aggressive military power and colonialism. The humiliating Chinese defeat in the Opium wars and the treaty of Nanjing in 1842 not only secured the British their continuous export of opium to China, but also the surrender of Hongkong and the establishment of a number of treaty ports, including Shanghai, where westerners could conduct business protected from Chinese law and encouraged by certain trade benefits. The treaty ports soon developed into commercial centres, which were controlled by western actors who were able to do business relatively protected from the unrest in imperial China. The treaty of Tientsin in 1858, following a war with British and French military forces, added more cities to the list of treaty ports as well as the surrender to Russia of large territories in north-western China. In 1876–1877, more treaty ports were added as a consequence of yet another war with Great Britain, and in 1884, the French protectorate in Vietnam was established after a conflict with France.

Finally, in 1894, the Chinese suffered total humiliation following their devastating defeat in the war with Japan, traditionally perceived as China's little brother to the east. The treaty of Shimonoseki meant the freeing of Korea from Chinese rule and the surrender of Taiwan and several islands in the East Chinese Sea to Japan, as well as heavy indemnities. It also dictated the possibility for westerners to establish industries in the treaty ports and led to a process in the following years that became known as *splitting the melon*. To the north, Japanese influence grew, while the Yangtze valley became a sphere of British interests. The French strengthened their position in the southeast, and Qingdao turned into the centre of Bismarck's plans to establish a German province in China.

China's defeat in 1894 made the need for economic development painfully evident to the Chinese rulers. The severe situation had, however, been acknowledged for decades by several of the local power-holders, who had become important drivers of Chinese development since the 1850s. One of the most notable of these was Hunan-based Li Hongzhang, the governor of the Beijing province Zhili and the advocate of the notion that modernisation should take place within the imperial context as a movement of *self-strengthening* – not without parallels to the simultaneous initiatives of Chulalongkorn to modernise Siam. The idea was often expressed by the motto: "Chinese learning for substance and Western learning for application", and starting in the 1860s, western technology was introduced.[3] Progress was however extremely slow. In the decade 1885–1895, no more than a dozen major corporations were established.[4] From 1894, the modernisation process was supported by the emperor Guangxu, however, and a series of reforms and initiatives were introduced to encourage a growing business life, including a more efficient postal service, the financial sector and ambitious plans for the Chinese railroad system.

The railroad was of particular importance, not only from a commercial point of view but also from a strategic perspective, which had become evident during the war with Japan. In 1895 and 1898, western entrepreneurs were given concessions to establish railroads through Manchuria, Shandong and a rail connection to Vietnam, while Russian, British and French contractors took care of the construction of connecting port facilities, warehouses, etc.[5] The control of the railway system was of course of utmost interest to the Chinese, but due to the lack of financial resources, the government was forced to engage foreign contractors. In effect, a door was opened for foreign governments to fight each other over concessions and benefits from the operation of the railways.[6]

Despite the political turbulence, the reform process continued through the following decades with the support of the weakened Qing dynasty and, from 1912, the Kuomintang party. The ideas of the self-strengtheners became the basis for the establishment of new industries at the initiative of the government administration, and this was accompanied by an increase in Chinese and foreign private investments. Extensions of the railway system were highly prioritised. Sun Yat-sen, leader of the Kuomintang, planned for the construction of a further 160,000 km stretch of tracks, and the Chinese became increasingly successful in their efforts to ensure that the control of concessions and the operation of the railway remained in their own hands.[7]

Entry to the Chinese Market and Consolidation (1890–1922)

To a foreign company like F.L. Smidth & Co., it was a precondition that the reforms of the Chinese administration and business life in the first decades of the 20th century took form in an anti-western atmosphere. In the mind of Sun Yat-sen, the purpose of the Kuomintang was the formation of a political system that would enable China to exploit the technological progress of the West so as to free itself from foreign domination and regain its position as the Middle Kingdom. This setting implied a potential for foreign partners but also the need for strategic adjustments regarding an explicit Chinese ambition for independence and control. In this context, which showed clear parallels to the Siamese setting, being based in a neutrality-seeking, small and insignificant nation, in terms of political and military power, such as Denmark was no disadvantage.

In Denmark, the potential of the small-scale-state advantage in China was well known. It had been exploited with great success by one of the most successful Danish business tycoons, C.F. Tietgen, during the

1870–1880s. Based on close collaboration with Li Hongzhang, he had succeeded in winning the Great Northern Telegraph Company's (Store Nordiske Telegraf-selskab) concessions for the first telegraph connections between Europe and China/Japan and the construction of China's telegraph system.[8]

In 1908, the politically based Danish business advantage in China was emphasised again in a report on the Danish delegations abroad presented by the Ministry of Foreign Affairs and produced by a working group including FLS founder Alexander Foss. The report concluded that the present Chinese reform process would probably result in a substantial potential for foreign business partners and that "... the fact that Denmark is a small nation is in this matter to be perceived as an advantage, as the [Chinese] fear of foreign political dominance will only be present to a minor degree".[9] The small-scale-state advantage would be particularly relevant in matters of strategic interest to the Chinese, and central among these were the construction and control of the telegraph and also the railway system. During the 1880s, C.F. Tietgen had tried without success to expand the activities of the Great Northern Telegraph Company by winning concessions for the construction of a national railway system under Chinese control.[10] However, the matter was clearly not closed from a Danish point of view.

From the start, F.L. Smidth & Co. could thus aim its strategy at the vast Chinese potential and build it on a political advantage that had already proved itself successful to other Danish companies working in China. A further advantage was the possibility to make use of the market knowledge and business contacts they had already built when approaching the new market. In particular, the close relationship between C.F. Tietgen and Li Hongzhang turned out to be of utmost importance to F.L. Smidth & Co. From 1870, C.F. Tietgen himself owned a small cement plant, Rødvig Cement Fabrik, in a small seaport a short distance to the south of Copenhagen, and when in 1882, he personally hosted the German Gustav Dietring, special advisor to Li Hongzhang on industrial matters, this created a direct link between the Danish cement industry and China's leading industrialists.[11] On this background, the leading engineer at Rødvig Cement Fabrik, Danish V. Uldall, left his position in 1890 to take on a similar position at the Green Island Cement Co., established in 1887 and owned by the Hong Kong-based company Shewan Tomes Co.[12] At the time, the company was operating its first cement plant at Hokun Macao, and V. Uldall moved quickly towards a powerful position. In 1899, he carried the title as *assistant manager* among a group of four managers, while in 1908, he was listed as an influential *General Manager* in a British list of China's most important industries:

> The general manager of the factory, Mr. V. Uldall, a man of great experience in the trade, has been in the service of the Company for

15 years. He has under him a staff of nearly two thousand men; but if the persons indirectly concerned are taken into account the probability is that the enterprise gives employment to upwards of three thousand.[13]

Being the first cement producing company built on western technology in – a colonised part of – China ensured the Green Island Cement Co. a lucrative market position. At Hokun, production capacity soon became insufficient, and when the decision was made in 1896 to build a large extension to the plant, this was certainly not a disadvantage seen from a Danish perspective, with V. Uldall in a key position. Despite the British dominance in the Green Island Company, the order for the extension went to Copenhagen, which meant that in 1897, F.L. Smidth & Co. delivered a completely new plant constructed around 12 shaft kilns of a type that had just been developed at Aalborg Portland.[14] In order to ensure the successful operation of the plant, workers from Aalborg accompanied the transferred technology. Central among these was burner master Jens Marinus Jensen, who had been involved in the kiln development at Aalborg Portland and was employed by the Green Island Cement Company. In 1897, he left Denmark together with his wife, Ellen Jensen, and their two children to live at the plant in Macao. The office building next to the extremely dusty cement packing facility became the home of the Danish family. The Danish position in the centre of the Green Island Cement Company's operations had thus been strengthened significantly, even though conditions for living in China were far from easy. The change in climate and living conditions was overwhelming to Ellen Jensen, and she died just before Christmas 1897.[15]

In 1903, yet another extension of the Green Island Cement Company was ordered from F.L. Smidth & Co. to be built at Gin Drinkers Bay, Hong Kong.[16] This time, the technology transfer included two rotary kilns as well as tube mills. Again, the machinery was accompanied by men from Aalborg. This time two burner masters, Jens Peter Kristensen and Thomas Ch. J. Christensen, were sent to China together with a number of cement workers who were all experts in the running of the machinery from their previous employment at Aalborg Portland.[17] Spread across two locations, the Green Island Cement Company had turned into a Danish-dominated enclave in China's developing world of business.

The Chee Hsin Cement Company

Outside of the treaty ports, the eyes of F.L. Smidth & Co. had to be fixed on the potential emanating from an even more politically coloured context. This potential emerged from 1906 from the Chee Hsin Cement

Company, which was to become central to almost everything that took place in China's cement industry during the first half of the 20th century.

The incremental need for cement had led to the construction in 1889 of a cement plant at Tangshan, next to the railway connection to Beijing as well as to coal supplies at Shenyang and shipment in the ports at Qinhuangdao. Initiators were the British-controlled company Chinese Engineering and Mining Company.[18] However, in the early years of the plant, production numbers never rose beyond an insignificant level. The use of cement for construction of Chinese bridges, harbour facilities, housing, etc. thus continued to rely on imports from Europe, Japan and the Green Island Cement Company's plants in Macao and Hong Kong.

Import dependence in a field of strategic importance was not what the Chinese wanted at all. In 1906–1907, the Qing administration therefore commenced a modernisation process at the Tangshan plant and a procedure to convert into a limited company. Private ownership was thus maintained, but the reconstruction was strongly aimed at gaining political control of a key component for the establishment of an efficient railway-based Chinese infrastructure. A new name was introduced, *the Chee Hsin Cement Company* (Qixin Yanghui Gongsi – "The New Cement Company"), and reconstruction took place under the leadership of Zhou Xuexi, manager of the *Peiyang Bureau of Industry* in the province of Zhili.[19] Zhou Xiexi had been a close associate to Yuan Shikai since his time as governor of Shandong in 1899–1901. When the army leader had been appointed governor superior of Zhili, Zhou Xiexi had been placed in charge of economic reforms of the province. As the right hand of Yuan Shikai, Zhou Xiexi was not only influential in the reconstruction and management of the Chee Hsin Cement Company; this was only one of many companies in which he was involved. In the Chee Hsin Cement Company, he was regarded as manager from 1907 to 1925, while the main shareholders counted four of Yuan Shikai's sons and more than a dozen officials from his administration. When Yuan Shikai entered the self-pronounced post as emperor in 1912, eight of his appointed ministers were shareholders of the Chee Hsin Cement Company. After Yuan Shikai's resignation in 1916 and through the chaotic years of civil wars and until the 1930s, the ownership of the Chee Hsin Cement Company remained in the hands of leading politicians. Large amounts of the earnings had to be spent on payments in cash of the so-called "pao-hsiao" – that is return offers for stately benefits, i.e. bribes. In return for this, the company received a *de facto* monopoly in the Chinese cement market. Tax exemption was accompanied in 1908 by a monopoly on the delivery of cement to Manchuria, Zhili and the entire Yangtze valley. This position was further secured by long-term contracts on cement deliveries needed in connection with the construction of the railway lines between Beijing and Suiyuan, Beijing and Hankou, Longhai, Tianjin-Pukou, among others. Even though the formalised monopoly ceased to exist with the resignation of the Manchu emperors in 1912, the tax exemptions and a constant flow of long-term contracts connected to state-driven railway construction continued as a solid base for the Chee Hsin Cement Company.

For more than two decades, the large majority of all cement production in non-colonised China was thus controlled by the Chee Hsin Cement Company, which operated from the plant in Tangshan and, following a takeover in 1914, from a second plant in Hubei. From the early 1920s, a handful of competitors entered the scene, primarily in the Shanghai area. Nevertheless, the Chee Hsin Cement Company remained in charge of more than 50% the total production in China.[20] In 1936, the number, including the Hubei plant, was still as high as 37%.

In the Safe Space of a Monopoly

Following the construction of the Green Island Cement Company in Macao and Hong Kong, F.L. Smidth & Co. had become highly visible to Chinese industrialists from the years around 1900, and in 1906 the Danes won the order for the reconstruction of the Tangshan plant. During the following year, machinery and equipment were shipped from Copenhagen to Tianjin to be transported the remaining distance to Tangshan by rail and installed in an entirely new factory layout designed by F.L. Smidth & Co. Construction works were led by Danish engineers, and the start-up of production was managed by burner masters and cement workers shipped out from Denmark.[21] Nonetheless, under the guidance of Zhou Xiexi, the Chinese appointed a German, H. Günther, as chief engineer – probably because of the strong links from the 1890s between Yuan Shikai and the German military advisors.[22]

The presence of H. Günther inside the organisation of the Chee Hsin Cement Company did not, however, stop the Danes from trying to gain a foothold in Tangshan. In 1910, they succeeded when the order for an extension of the plant went to Copenhagen. This time, the rotary kilns and tube mills were accompanied by 27-year-old Harry Schrøder, who had graduated as an engineer in 1906 and since then had worked as a trainee at the head office in Copenhagen.[23] Having completed the construction work, he entered the payrolls of the Chee Hsin Cement Company in 1911 to fill in a position as chemical engineer, which was a situation loaded with potential for disagreements. Whether the sudden appearance of Harry Schrøder happened as a result of pressure from F.L. Smidth & Co. or, even worse, as a consequence of a lack of work management by H. Günther, the situation was destined to be complicated. In reality, Harry Schrøder's position at the plant thus took on a rather fluent nature, and in Copenhagen it was often difficult to establish his influence. Formally, he was a chemical engineer under the management of H. Günther, but from time to time – and often during long time intervals – it seemed as if the German only managed his job in a pro forma manner, and that Harry Schrøder filled the position as chief engineer and was, in reality, the plant manager.[24]

Whatever the situation, Harry Schrøder's strong influence was still evident when the Tangshan plant was extended once more in 1920, again based on deliveries of machinery from Copenhagen.[25] By then, the plant ran seven rotary kilns with a workforce of approximately 2,000 and an annual production of 1,200,000 barrels. All the important machinery had been delivered from Copenhagen, and in combination with the fact that most work management was placed in the hands of a former employee, which greatly resembled the situation in Siam/Bangsue, the future for F.L. Smidth & Co. in China seemed bright. With strong relations to the monopoly holder in the Chinese cement market, the Danish prospects for becoming the only supplier of technology to the entire industry in China were promising.

A Campaign in the East (1922–1926)

From 1922, the Danish everyday presence at the plants in Macao, Hong Kong and Tangshan/Hubei was supplemented by an official company representation of F.L. Smidth & Co. in China. In the company's historical literature, the initiative became known as *A Campaign in the East* – coined at a combined China-Japan office in Tokyo led by engineer Kai Neergaard until, in 1923, operations were split into two offices in Tokyo and Beijing, the latter to be led for years by the young engineer Thorkild Stig-Nielsen, who succeeded Neergaard after his death in late 1923.[26]

At a time when the Danish influence at the Chee Hsin Cement Company, which was by far China's most dominating cement producer, seemed stronger than ever, it was apparently necessary to extend the Danish platform in the country. The background soon became clear, however, when the staff at the new office – in particular Stig-Nielsen and a secretary – engaged in their activities in the following years. The opening of a China office came as a consequence of a very urgent need to adjust and augment the tools previously used. This need followed as a response to both internal and external factors that were threatening the ability to control the key dispositions of the cement-producing companies and potential future customers. These threats emanated from cases of death, incompetence and opportunism among Danes employed at the Chinese cement plants as well as from the inability of these individuals to facilitate the development of a position in leading Chinese political and business networks and thereby gain an influence on new schemes for establishing cement plants.

Decline by Death

Unless the first platforms were expanded, death was a foreseeable threat to the ability to control the cement producing companies through the tool of expatriate Danes first used by F.L. Smidth & Co. in China – as well as in Siam. This became very clear when the question of new machinery for the Green Island Cement Company arose again after years of stagnation.[27]

With its old machinery from 1897 and 1904, the company had grown very rich due to its lucrative position as the only in-land cement supplier to the South China market. In the years after 1920, it therefore seemed obvious to launch a plan to build a new plant in Hong Kong. Ambitions were high. It was considered realistic to build an extension which in size would equal the Tangshan plant. Winning the order for such a scheme would be another big achievement for F.L. Smidth & Co., whose advantage was that they had successfully delivered not only the old plants of the Green Island Cement Company but also the technological basis for the Chee Hsin Cement Company. Since the early 1900s, the Danish presence in the circles of the Green Island Cement Company had slowly diminished, however, mainly due to the fact that the Danes had grown older and died. Eventually, in the spring of 1924, the last remaining Dane, burner master Jens Peter Christensen, died, and the risk of competing machine suppliers entering the scene suddenly became very imminent.[28] In a situation like this, the ability to collect and spread information through channels outside of the company was of utmost importance. Stig-Nielsen and his staff at the office in Beijing therefore had an important task ahead of them.

As early as in July 1924, Stig-Nielsen had travelled from Beijing to Hong Kong to inspect the old plant there and to prepare a report for Copenhagen on possible improvements which could be suggested to the owners. During his stay at the plant, he made personal acquaintance with key employees and plant owners. As he reported to Copenhagen, this caused a great deal of optimism:

> ... knowing now personally Keith [*secretary of the board*], Mendham [*board member*] and old Shewan [*chairman of the board*], I hope to be able to secure valuable private information from time to time, which will help us later when we are ready to make the final quotation.[29]

The invitation to make suggestions for future improvements was a positive sign, even though the Danish control of the Green Island Cement Company was clearly beginning to weaken. This happened while Stig-Nielsen was working on his report on the Hong Kong project and became evident when F.L. Smidth & Co. lost the competition to fill in the available position as assistant manager at the plant. In August, the head office in Copenhagen received an enquiry for potential candidates, and a similar enquiry was sent at the same time to German Polysius, which suggested Henry Pooley, a young English engineer, for the position. This caused some anxiety in Copenhagen, of course, as was ironically expressed by the leading engineer O.V. Mørch: "... we wouldn't be too pleased to have him placed at Green Island, and we are therefore making an extra effort to secure our own man for the position as 'Assistant Manager'".[30] Whatever the extra effort was, the effect of this was not what was hoped for. At the end of August, Henry Pooley was offered the job. Consequently, F.L. Smidth & Co. had to face the risk of losing one of its strongest footholds in China to their worst competitor – even though, as Stig-Nielsen perceived the situation, the hope for future orders from the Green Island Cement Company should not be ruled out:

> Of course it would have been an advantage had we got in our man as assistant manager, but I imagine the company must have considered it a kind of commitment to actually take on one of our men for the purpose of working out details in connection with the new plant.[31]

The real winner was the Green Island Cement Company, however, which had achieved the possibility to play off the Danes and the Germans against each other.

Incompetence and Opportunism

Too long intervals between fresh supplies of Danish engineers did not only imply the risk of elimination of the informal presence of F.L. Smidth & Co. at the plants; the consequences of growing incompetence among the Danes were an even greater risk as these might cause them to potentially end up in very difficult situations that could eventually lead to inappropriate or opportunistic behaviour. In effect, the result could be a total loss of control, combined with a bad reputation for F.L. Smidth & Co. It was almost unavoidable that the running of the most recent types of machinery would be negatively affected by the rusty knowledge and skills that inevitably followed from long periods of stay at remote cement plants – measured from the headquarters in Copenhagen – with expensive, laconic telegraph communication and an extremely slow postal service as the only means of communication with the Danish centre for developing and testing new and improved production techniques. If no further action was taken, the asymmetrical distribution of knowledge between the expatriate Danes and their employers could consequently lose its former power as a tool to influence and control the running and development of the plants. After more than ten years at Tangshan, the seriousness of the situation was being strongly felt by Harry Schrøder in the early 1920s. The situation was made even worse by the fact that he had to run the newly delivered extension of the plant, which had been constructed of the most modern kilns and mills based on techniques developed a long time after his own departure from Copenhagen. Again, intervention by the FLS office in Beijing was sorely needed.

In 1923, continuous complaints from the Chee Hsin Cement Company of the quality of the cement from the new kilns led to a visit in Tangshan by Kai Neergaard and his assistant engineer Nygaard to inspect the machinery. Their report on the matter did not, however, focus on the hardware but was, in essence, a reprimand aimed at Harry Schrøder. For a start, the report referred to previous efforts by the Chinese to keep the European presence in Tangshan at a minimum and explained how they had been strongly opposed to the idea of receiving updated engineers from Denmark. Despite this, the report concluded, after 1920, Harry Schrøder had failed to inform F.L. Smidth & Co. that the problems with the cement quality were not due to failing machinery, but "... a lack of management in the running of your plant".[32] In other words, from a Danish point of view, the actual problem was the unclarity of the situation. It was obvious that Harry Schrøder had been unable to make the machinery run successfully, but it was unclear why he had not revealed his lack of competence to Copenhagen. Either he was not aware of it, or, even worse, he had been trying to hide the actual reason for the problems in order to secure his own position in Tangshan – and, as a part of this manipulation, had blamed the situation on the technology delivered from Denmark.

In Copenhagen, the situation was evaluated in light of the effort made by Harry Schrøder the previous years to be re-employed by F.L. Smidth & Co. and to leave Tangshan. As he had explained to FLS founder Poul Larsen, his situation was becoming increasingly bad. However, his request to leave his position at the Chee Hsin Cement Company had been flatly turned down by Poul Larsen, who had a very clear interest in keeping the Dane in the position in Tangshan.[33] The conclusion in Copenhagen in 1924 was therefore that, during these events, Harry Schrøder had turned into a loose cannon, and that, since then, the situation in Tangshan had in reality been getting out of control. The need for intervention towards Harry Schrøder was urgent. The question was how to intervene towards a person who was clearly acting on his own behalf while being formally employed by another company.

During the summer of 1924, the situation moved from bad to worse. In July, Stig-Nielsen described to Copenhagen: "... how dangerous the entire position at Tangshan has been in the last three or four months ...".[34] A week earlier, he had arrived in Tangshan, assisted by engineer Axel V. Jensen, who had hastily travelled out from Copenhagen. In Tangshan, the two of them were to discover that new machinery had already been bought from Amme Gieseke & Konegen in Germany. The man behind this was, of course, H. Günther, and, according to Stig-Nielsen, a swarm of Germans were seen in and around the plant. He also learnt that an order for turbo generators was about to be placed at a German company without even giving F.L. Smidth & Co. the opportunity to quote their price for the job. Immediate action was required.

During the night of their arrival in Tangshan, Stig-Nielsen and Axel V. Jensen were able to organise a meeting with Li Shi Ming, the managing director of the Chee Hsin Cement Company, who briefly informed the Danes that all that remained to be decided was whether the order should be given to A.E.G. or Siemens. After giving up the usual consulting fee and offering an advance discount of 5%, the two Danes were allowed, however, to hand in a quotation. In the eyes of Stig-Nielsen, the whole thing was a direct consequence of German influence on the dispositions of Li Shi Ming: "Evidently the Germans have been telling him a lot of tales ...", as he described the situation in his report to Copenhagen. As the meeting had progressed, it had turned into: "... pure childishness, as Li Shi Ming was all the time too erratic for anybody to follow". By allowing the Germans to have one foot in the door in a situation without the previous Danish doorkeeper Harry Schrøder in place, Li Shi Ming was slowly beginning to liberate himself and the Chee Hsin Cement Company from the domination by F.L. Smidth & Co. So far, the Danes were getting nowhere.

Stig-Nielsen attuned his strategy with the head office in Copenhagen. Apparently, until this moment, it had never occurred to him that F.L. Smidth & Co. might have overexploited the trust placed in the Danes and that they might have gone too far in pricing the machinery delivered to the Chinese during recent years. Instead, he exclusively blamed the nature of Li Shi Ming, whom he considered "an extraordinarily difficult man to negotiate with" due to a personality he described as "a mixture of a mere child and a rather shrewd businessman". In Stig-Nielsen's eyes, the Germans had succeeded in speaking to the childish side of Li Shi Ming. This was made particularly obvious by the fact that Li Shi Ming, as Stig-Nielsen perceived the situation, had felt obliged to let the Germans make their quotations because of the free consulting services they had offered him. Fortunately, the Danish leader of the repair workshop at the plant, Peter Carlsson, had been able to persuade the Chinese that the situation would be uncontrollable if everyone waiting at the factory doorstep were to receive orders. Stig-Nielsen concluded that the future of F.L. Smidth & Co. in Tangshan depended on the ability to uphold a parallel organisation:

> Summing this up, you will see that what is more desirable for us than anything else is to keep a very strong man at Tangshan, who should be able at all times to steer Li Shi Ming in the direction wanted by us. A visit from Peking now and then is not nearly enough, and although Carlsson ... is doing very capable work and is, in fact, as we see it,

doing his best to steer Li Shi Ming in the wanted direction, more support from F.L. Smidth is urgently requested.

The everyday Danish presence at the plant was essential to F.L. Smidth & Co., and having the incompetent Harry Schrøder placed at the centre of this was clearly a major problem.

Despite the non-flattering evaluation by Stig-Nielsen, Li Shi Ming was probably handling the situation in a very competent and deliberate manner. By letting the Germans make their quotations he had placed F.L. Smidth & Co. under serious pressure and made it obvious that the everyday contribution of Harry Schrøder was highly insufficient. The Danes were forced to try to improve their situation by lowering their prices and by investing in a more competent and balanced tool than Harry Schrøder to make sure the Chee Hsin Cement Company remained a technologically updated and competitive cement producer.

During the summer of 1924, Li Shi Ming was therefore free to set the terms for the future cooperation between the Chee Hsin Cement Company and F.L. Smidth & Co., and his proposal was to introduce a three-year stationing of Danish chemical engineers at Tangshan. As Li Shi Ming remarked, such a hiring-out arrangement would not only ensure a continually updated knowledge base in Tangshan, but also a stronger Danish delegation at the plant. It was obvious to F.L. Smidth & Co. that this was a take-it-or-leave-it offer, as expressed by Stig-Nielsen to his superiors in Copenhagen:

> We hope you will realise how urgent it is for us to fully re-establish our connection with Chee Hsin. This will have a considerable bearing on our future success in China, the reason being that if we become more or less outclassed at Chee Hsin, this will provide our competitors with a very strong weapon against us ... .

To Li Shi Ming it was clearly very useful to be able to place F.L. Smidth & Co. under such pressure, thus regaining some control of the price level of the supply of machinery and services from Copenhagen. But on the other hand, it was not a desirable position to be constantly shifting between the Danes and the Germans. Maintaining balanced and close collaboration was so far not only the primary goal for F.L. Smidt & Co., but also for Li Shi Ming and the Chee Hsin Cement Company. The smooth replacement of Harry Schrøder by a Danish chemical engineer – without exposing the previous Danish incompetence – was therefore a joint task. This was not, however, a wish shared by Harry Schrøder himself. Li Shi Ming could thus inform Stig-Nielsen that the hiring-out arrangement had been discussed several times during the 1910s, but that Harry Schrøder had ardently opposed the idea. To Stig-Nielsen, this was new information brought forth by his Chinese counterpart and not by Harry Schrøder's supposedly loyal channel of information from Tangshan. His conclusion was therefore clear: "Altogether we are under the definite impression that Mr. Schrøder has not worked in our interest as he ought to have done, and mostly for the reason that he has been afraid to lose his own position". It was obvious that Li Shi Ming was very well aware of the incompetence of Harry Schrøder, and that his "gentleman"-like manners had made him an even more annoying element in Tangshan. Stig-Nielsen drew the general conclusion "... that any man sitting in the same place and dealing with the same Chinese for 15 years is bound to gradually come more and more under their influence and to increasingly adopt the Chinese way of thinking".

In light of these events, it is no wonder that Harry Schrøder's visit to Denmark during the summer of 1924 developed into a veritable nightmare. When entering F.L. Smidth & Co.'s head office for the first time in 14 years, Schrøder was immediately informed that his replacement by a young engineer, Emil Schmit-Jensen, had already been prepared.[35] He was further informed that orders for German machinery to Tangshan had only been stopped due to the British influence on the Chee Hsin Cement Company emanating from the coal supplying company, the Kalian Mining Administration, which had no interest in a strengthened German position. When Schrøder proceeded to enter the office of FLS-founder Poul Larsen, he received a fierce reprimand. As Poul Larsen remarked, it would have been in his own interest to safeguard those of his parent company.[36]

Driven into a corner, Harry Schrøder now moved even further in his own direction – and away from being controlled by F.L. Smidth & Co. In a desperate search for alliances, he telegraphed H. Günther saying that he now supported orders for German machinery. He then travelled to Berlin to pay a visit to Dr. Kühl, who was closely associated with the cooperating German machine suppliers and offered him information which, shortly afterwards, enabled Amme Gieseke & Konegen to make suggestions for improved production methods in Tangshan.[37]

However, Harry Schrøder's state of panic was now obvious to everyone involved, and as a consequence, nobody was interested in engaging into further cooperation with him. In October 1924, he therefore returned to F.L. Smidth & Co.'s offices in Copenhagen to do penance. He was informed that the purpose of sending out Emil Schmit-Jensen was to ensure the presence of a person in Tangshan who could "Patiently stay there and study the men responsible for operating the plant and in that way support us in winning their confidence and take action at every right moment".[38] After being offered a position at the headquarters in Copenhagen, in November 1924, Harry Schrøder finally gave in and openly expressed his support for Emil Schmit-Jensen as his successor in Tangshan.[39]

Thus, from early 1925, the situation in Tangshan again looked bright from a Danish perspective. The daily presence at the plant had been reinforced by an arrangement that was more balanced towards the Chinese and more controllable to the Danes as their new envoy, Emil Schmit-Jensen, maintained his formal position as an employee of F.L. Smidth & Co. It had even been possible to strengthen the personal relationship with Li Shi Ming by making an agreement on how to solve the shared problem concerning Harry Schrøder. In the spring of 1925, Li Shi Ming openly described to Stig-Nielsen how it had been a strong wish to get rid of Schrøder who had "... grown a little too big, wanting to sit in the administration office most of the time", while what was needed was "... a foreigner who can fully control the chemical part of our manufacture". And Li Shi Ming expressed confidence in Emil Schmit-Jensen's ability to fulfill the latter.[40] So far, a strong position for exercising influence and control of the operations of the Chee Hsin Cement Company had been regained.

New Tools for Influencing Chinese Cement Producers

As regards matters connected to new arrivals among the group of Chinese cement producers, the Danish employees at the existing plants were of almost no use to F.L. Smidth & Co. In Siam, the dominance of Danish managers and plant engineers had in some cases been strong enough to enable them to act as extensions of the FLS organisation towards new customers. But this was not the case in China, when new competing companies and schemes for cement plants began to appear at the beginning of the 1920s. If any part of this new market potential were to be won, this would require the action of an – at least on paper – independent representation of F.L. Smidth & Co. in China. Moreover, when work began on approaching the new schemes, it was an open question whether the previous 30 years of successful work in the country would be a hindrance to the future Danish position. While everybody would no doubt be well informed of the existing close links between F.L. Smidth & Co. and the old actors on the Chinese cement production scene, the ability to balance on a knife's edge towards new customers would in any case be absolutely essential.

During the first 15 years after the reconstruction of the Tangshan plant in 1906, almost no threats had appeared towards the de facto monopoly of the Chee Hsin Cement Company.[41] In 1908, the local government in the province of Guandong had opened a small plant at Canton, and in 1909, Hua-Feng Cement Company, led by Shanghai-based investors, had established a plant in Hubei at the Yangtze river approximately 100 km from Hankou. The Hubei plant was constructed on the basis of machinery from Germany, but in 1914 it was taken over by the Chee Hsin Cement Company, which meant that it entered the Danish sphere of influence. In 1909, the Japanese Onoda Cement Company established a plant at Dairen, which was soon extended significantly, while German investors in

1915 built a small plant close to Qingdao in Shandong, which was taken over by Onoda after a very short time. A considerable share of the Chinese need for cement was continuously covered by imports from Europe and Japan. The Chee Hsin Cement Company could rest assured of its state-secured market position.

However, during World War I, the supplies of cement from Europe came to an end, while the Chinese need for cement continued to rise. This made conditions promising for new schemes for cement plants based solely on commercial – and not political – considerations. At the initiative of Shanghai-based merchant Liu Hong-sheng, the Shanghai Portland Cement Company was thus established in 1923 with a plant at Longhua between the Huangpu river and the Shanghai-Hangzhou-Ningbo railway. Simultaneously, financed by one of Shanghai's largest building entrepreneurs, Yao-Hsi-chou, and the banker Ch'en Kuang-fu, production commenced in 1924 at the China Portland Cement Company at Longtan close to the Nanjing-Shanghai railway. And, at this time also, the support of local business people in Jinan, the main city of the province of Shandong, formed the base of beginning the production in 1923 at the Chihching Cement Company.

Seen from F.L. Smidth & Co.'s perspective, the situation during only one year in 1923–1924 had caused things to develop in the wrong direction. Increasing numbers of potential customers were generally a desirable situation. But the way things turned out in 1923–1924, an increasing amount of the Chinese machinery for cement production was now delivered by the German competitors. Shanghai Portland Cement bought its machinery from Polysius and entrusted a German engineer, Mollitor, with the responsibility for running the plant. Something very similar happened at the China Cement Company, which placed its order for machinery with the Nagel & Kemp and Fellner & Ziegler consortium and proceeded to let German P. Kretzmann run the plant afterwards. And finally, machinery for the Jinan plant was delivered by the Hamburg-based trading company Carlowitz & Company. Measured by production capacity, the plants delivered or controlled by the Danes in 1924 accounted for no more than 56% of the total Chinese cement production. In contrast, in only two years, the new German-controlled plants had acquired a share of 21%. It was evident that the previous tools for influence and control of the Chinese cement market had become obsolete and that the appearance of new companies and plants would be a major concern for the newly established FLS office in Beijing.

The potential for acquiring knowledge of the existence of new schemes and for establishing and maintaining the most important business relations weighed heavily among the arguments for placing the new office in Beijing.[42] First and foremost, the location of the head offices of the Chee Hsin Cement Company in the capital city as well as the proximity of the Danes in Tangshan made Beijing an obvious choice. At the same time,

Table 4.1 F.L. Smidth & Co.'s own list of active cement producers in China and neighbouring areas in 1924, leaving out Japan and Japanese-owned factories in China

Company	Capacity – Annual Production 1924 (Barrels)	Established	Technology/Machine Supplier
China:			
Green Island Portland Cement Company	600,000	Macao: 1887 Macao reconstruction 1896	Macao: Unknown Reconstruction: F.L. Smidth & Co.
The Chee Hsin Cement Company	1,200,000	Hong Kong: 1904 1889 Reconstructed 1906 Extensions 1910, 1920	Hong Kong: F.L. Smidth & Co. 1889: British 1906: F.L. Smidth & Co.
Hupeh Portland Cement Company (after 1914 operated by the Chee Hsin Cement Company)	250,000	1909	Extensions: F.L. Smidth & Co. German machinery
Shanghai Portland Cement Works	360,000	1922–1923	Polysius
China Portland Cement Company	120,000	1922–1923	Nagel & Kemp, Fellner & Ziegel
Tsinan Portland Cement Company	60,000	Ca. 1927	Carlowitz & Company
Liu-Ho-Kou not yet started in 1924	300,000	1924	F.L. Smidth & Company
In total (without Liu Ho Kou's prod)	2,590,000		

(*Continued*)

Table 4.1 (Continued)

Company	Capacity – Annual Production 1924 (Barrels)	Established	Technology/Machine Supplier
Local region:			
Dutch East Indies (Indonesia) – Sumatra, Padang Works	300,000	1911 Reconstruction 1917, extensions 1924 and 1928	German machinery Reconstructions and extensions by F.L. Smidth & Co.
Siam – Bangsue	300,000	1913	F.L. Smidth & Co.
The Phillippines – Cebu Works	400,000	1923	Allis Chalmers
Indochina (Vietnam) – Haiphong	600,000	Unknown Reconstruction 1926 & extensions 1929 & 1930	Originally built by the French Reconstructions and extensions by F.L. Smidth & Co.
Straits (Malaysia) – Ho Hong	300,000	Unknown	Unknown
F.M.S. (Malaysia) – Batu Caves	6,000	Unknown	Unknown
In total	1,906,000		

Source: FLSA.

Beijing was the ideal location for establishing contact with future customers and their surrounding networks. At regular intervals, the managers of the largest Chinese companies visited the capital city to tend to their political networks. Potential investors for schemes were also close at hand due to the proximity to the harbour city Tianjin, where China's richest people were investing large sums in order to avoid confiscations effected by the warlords of the on-going civil war. In addition to the prestigiousness of Beijing, Stig-Nielsen also emphasised more cultural arguments. According to him, Beijing's western ex-patriates were not as isolated from the Chinese as was the case in Shanghai. This created certain opportunities: "In Peking one much easier gets in direct contact with the Chinese people whereby one stands a better chance of getting into a position of better understanding their often, for us, very funny ways of reasoning".[43]

Establishing and managing contacts with existing as well as potential customers were demanding jobs. The language barrier was enormous, and travelling activities soon absorbed all of Stig-Nielsen's available time. In the spring of 1924, he had to call for help from Copenhagen and was accompanied by Axel V. Jensen before travelling to Tangshan for the difficult negotiations with Li Shi Ming.[44] At the end of 1924, he felt quite well-grounded in China, however, and at this time, he was bragging to his colleagues in Denmark about how it had become a colourful everyday pastime for him to walk the streets of the civil-war-torn country and witnessing decapitated heads on spikes. Such conditions were of course difficult, but at the same time "... from the point of view of offering experience, I can hardly think of anything better", Stig-Nielsen concluded.[45] According to him, the name of F.L. Smidth & Co. had by now become so well known that he no longer had to use "all sorts of tricks to even get in contact with prospective clients".

In a more formal tone, Stig-Nielsen described in a thorough report in November 1924 to FLS founder Poul Larsen how he took great comfort from the foreignness of the Chinese context, and how a network reaching into the circles of new potential customers was beginning to take shape.[46] During the previous year, he had been in contact with at least 17 schemes of a nature solid enough to deserve a follow-up. One of these, the so-called *Liu-Ho-Kou* project, had even placed an order for machinery with F.L. Smidth & Co. Most of the schemes were in the northern parts of China, at manageable distances from the office in Beijing, and contacts were handled by Stig-Nielsen personally. Some were located further away, however, and Stig-Nielsen had therefore made arrangements with local partners for "... the purpose of establishing ourselves" as he described this to Poul Larsen. These arrangements were, as Stig-Nielsen continued, "purely friendly or on commission", and resembled a patchwork of what was possible locally. However, a decisive factor seems to have been the complex Chinese political context and the effort to navigate in this through careful selection of partners of certain nationalities.

Table 4.2 List of cement factory projects in China in 1923–1924 with potential order placements with F.L. Smidth & Co., prepared by T. Stig-Nielsen 1924

Ho Hong
Hsing Yu (Peking scheme)
Chiang Hua (Mukden scheme)
C.F. Wang (Mukden)
Chun Hsin Coal Mining Company
Mills & Manning
China Portland Cement Works
Sintoon scheme
Da Fung (Nielsen & Winther)
Mills & Manning
Lincheng
Overgaard, Hankow
Szechuan scheme
Harbin, Jacobsen
Canton Municipality
Chen Kwang Ceramics Company
Frank Oakden (Shanghai-Nanjing Railway)
Cheefu (Rosenberg)

Source: FLSA.

Table 4.3 List of F.L. Smidth & Co.'s business partners in China in 1924, prepared by T. Stig-Nielsen 1924

Babock & Wilcox
Sintoon Overseas Trading Company
General Electric Company
Chinese Engineering & Development Company
Arnold & Company
Jacobsen, Harbin
Witt, Mukden [Shenyang]
Hankow Chemical Laboratory
Skodawerke
Far Eastern Review
Journal & Proceedings of the China Society for Chemical Industry
Nielsen & Winther
Great Northern Company

Source: FLSA.

First of all, Stig-Nielsen had been able to make arrangements with Danes scattered across different parts of China. This included single individuals such as a certain Rosenberg (first name unknown), who lived in Shanghai and kept his eye on the so-called *Cheefu* project and, in Hankou, V. Overgaard. The arrangements also included other Danish companies operating in China, such as the trading company Nielsen & Winther, which maintained contacts with the *Da Fung* project. In Harbin, the contact to a developing scheme was handled by the representative of The Danish East Asiatic Company Henrik V. Jacobsen, who was also a Danish honorary consul. At the time of writing in 1924, Stig-Nielsen was planning to engage another Danish individual in Harbin, Ibsen (first name unknown), as well.

The use of arrangements with Danish actors – single individuals as well as companies – maintained the political advantages. This was a top priority. Stig-Nielsen did not include arrangements with western partners of non-Danish origin unless he was forced to because of their close association – or direct involvement – with the developers of the schemes. Contact with the so-called *Szechuan-scheme* was made only via mail correspondence through the Shanghai-based firms Fraser & Chalmer and the General Electric Company of China, both of which were directly involved in the project. Similarly, relations to the so-called *Frank Oakden* project included British Jardine Matheson & Company.

Whenever possible, contact was established directly with Chinese key figures, without western interference. This included single Chinese individuals as well as firms and leading political networks.

In some cases, relations with project developers had to be based on personal contacts of an informal nature. One example was the scheme originating from the *Chung Hsin Coal Mining Company*, which was based on close collaboration with German Siemens Company and, consequently, Polysius. Stig-Nielsen explained to Poul Larsen that the only possible way to approach this project would be through personal contact to single individuals inside the company – but that he was pessimistic of the options. A similar situation existed at *China Portland Cement Works*, which had only recently been built by German Nagel & Keamp. Rumours had it in 1924 that the German machinery was not working to the satisfaction of the Chinese plant managers and investors. This potentially opened a door to F.L. Smidth & Co., and Stig-Nielsen was therefore trying to get acquainted with a high-ranking employee at the Liu-Ho Kou-project, a Mr. Wang, whose father-in-law was one of the key financial supporters of China Portland Cement Company.

Business contacts of a more open nature involved the *Chen Kwang Ceramics Company*, which was planning the construction of a cement plant and therefore had made a request for a quotation from F.L. Smidth & Co. in 1923. In 1924, Stig-Nielsen visited the Hong Kong-based project and discussed it personally with the managing director Y.Y. Wang, who guided the Dane on a visit to the company's limestone pit. Another example was the relations with the so-called *Ho-Hong* project near Singapore, which caused Stig-Nielsen and F.L. Smidth & Co. to become involved in a much wider network of investors and business contacts. Only a few years earlier, Oscar Schultz had paid a visit to the old Ho-Hong plant owned by the

Xiamen-based Lim Peng Siang, who was in charge of one of the old Chinese *Hong* trading companies.[47] In 1904, he had expanded the family business to include shipping, rice mills, oil mills and cement, and specialised in trading between China, Hong Kong and Malaysia-Singapore. In other words, Lim Peng Siang was a prestigious acquaintance from the established business circles in China and South East Asia; he had been president of the *Singapore Chinese Chamber of Commerce* (1913–1916) and was a long-time member of the so-called *Chinese Advisory Board* (1921–1941). Stig-Nielsen concluded to Poul Larsen at the end of 1924 that several personal meetings in Xiamen had led to promising prospects: "The company and Lim Peng Siang have absolute confidence in us, and I think it is safe to say that in case they go ahead with the scheme we shall get the job".[48]

A considerable share of Stig-Nielsen's efforts had, however, been directed towards key figures from China's leading political circles, which were busily engaged in the on-going chaotic civil war. Evidently, it had been necessary for him to enter a complex minefield of constantly changing alliances and strategical political considerations. As he explained to Poul Larsen, it had nevertheless been possible for him to navigate across some of the worst lines of conflict.

In northern China, Stig-Nielsen had succeeded in making contact to the Manchu-*Fu* family, who under the leadership of the Zhili-based warlord Wu Pei-Fu – nicknamed *The Philosopher General* – stood behind the so-called *Hsing-Yu* scheme. Stig-Nielsen concluded to Poul Larsen: "... the Fu familiy ... I think trust us completely now". The Hsing-Yu project had been temporarily halted by the war in 1920–1923, in which Beijing had been seized by the de-facto ruler of Manchuria, *The Old Marshal* Zhang Zuolin, and also by the successful attack on Wu Pei-Fu by the *Christian General* Feng Yu-xiang in the Zhili-Anhui war in 1922. In 1924, it was Stig-Nielsen's impression that Wu Pei-Fu had successfully reorganised and acquired the necessary financial support for building the planned cement plant – which would secure him the possession of an important source that could provide the building materials needed for the construction of infrastructure and fortifications.

Even if Stig-Nielsen supported one side of the civil war, this did not stop him from approaching the other side as well. Parallel to his negotiations with Wu Pei-Fu, he had thus established direct contacts with the leading circles of Zhang Zuolin, *The Old Marshal*, who stood behind the Shenyang-based scheme which Stig-Nielsen named *C.F. Wang*. The latter was the brother of Dr. C.T. Wang (Chengting Thomas Wang) who had been educated in Japan and the USA and was, in 1924, one of China's most prominent political figures.[49] In 1912, C.T. Wang had entered the first republican government and later the opposition government of Sun Yat-sen in Canton. After World War I, he was appointed the minister of foreign affairs and minister of finance parallel to several positions as chairman of textile, mining and railroad-related companies. In 1922–1923 and 1924, C.T. Wang assumed the position as prime minister of China.[50] C.F. Wang himself was managing director of the coal mining company Fengtien Mining in southern Manchuria. More importantly, he was a puppet of Zang Zuolin and even though, as Stig-Nielsen described it, "Chang Tso-lin ... of course can now think of nothing but ammunition", this could be expected to change.[51] In his evaluation to Poul Larsen in November 1924, Stig-Nielsen concluded how this could potentially affect the business opportunities for F.L. Smidth & Co.: "... having won the present war, we should have every chance of great developments in Manchuria".[52]

Stig-Nielsen's optimism regarding the potential gained from his friendly relations with the Wang brothers was based on prior experiences in 1922–1923 during the construction work of the cement plant for Liu-Ho Kou in the province of Hunan. F.L. Smidth & Co. had delivered all the necessary machinery, and the construction work had been led by Danish engineer Aage Friis, who was expected to take on the position as plant manager as soon as production began.[53] This was in itself an optimal outcome, but in 1924 the civil war had obstructed the planned plant start-up – and consequently stopped the final payments to F.L. Smidth & Co.[54] The prospects of a start-up in the near future did not seem promising either, and in his report to Poul Larsen, Stig-Nielsen focused on the network potential of the Liu-Ho-Kou project.[55] It was Stig-Nielsen's clear assessment that the real figure behind the company was the former minister of communications and finance of the Chinese republic *Tsao-Ju-Lin* [Cao-rulin], who, as he described him to Poul Larsen, was "... one of the biggest squeezers China has ever known". In 1924, C.H. Li was managing director of the company, but the post had earlier been held by C.T. Wang, whom Stig-Nielsen had therefore met several times. While dark clouds hung over the question of receiving full payment from Liu-Ho-Kou, Stig-Nielsen could still add an optimistic tone to his report to Poul Larsen. C.T. Wang was, Stig-Nielsen explained, "a very nice man to talk with", and due to his influential political network, he would be of great value to F.L. Smidth & Co.

Stig-Nielsen's optimism regarding the near future was limited, however, when it came to the question of business prospects in China in general. An end to the destructive civil war could be the beginning of a golden era, a time "When *China awakens*", as he described this with a clear reference to Napoléon Bonaparte. Predicting when this would happen was impossible, however: "I do not think the man has yet been born who has been able to prophesy future events in China".[56]

During 1925, the German competition at Tangshan kept Stig-Nielsen busy, but the reestablishment of the Danish control of the plant combined with the negative impact of the civil war on developing schemes eliminated the urgent need for his presence in China. In June 1926, Stig-Nielsen therefore left the office in Beijing and headed for Tokyo. In

China, the future still looked bright to him, in particular in light of his good relations to the Fu family with "General Chiang" as the "top figure".[57] But for the moment it did not seem realistic that any of the planned schemes would materialise in the middle of a war zone.

Reorganisation (1926–1930)

Stig-Nielsen's departure from the FLS office in Beijing in 1926 was a sign of downward adjustment but with the clear awareness that new opportunities for harvesting the enormous market potential in China might eventually open up. In 1926, he expressed this as follows: "I feel sorry for poor China, but have not given up hope yet".[58] As a matter of fact, full withdrawal from China was not the case at all.

Since 1922, Stig-Nielsen had had the opportunity to make an assessment of the loosely attached contacts in various parts of China. This had sparked new possibilities. As a collaboration with the Beijing-based company Leth-Møller & Co. on the Liu-Ho Kou project had proceeded particularly smoothly, the FLS people felt, in 1926, that it would be safe to establish a firmer agreement with them. Leth-Møller & Co. was owned by Danish V. Leth-Møller and engaged in projects within the construction sector and consulting assignments in the Beijing region in particular.[59] In 1929, this firm won the commission to build the National Beiping Library in Beijing, which resulted in plans to open a branch office in Chiang kai-Shek's new government city Nanjing – and enhanced the firm's reputation among the Chinese. The key figures in the firm were V. Leth-Møller himself and co-owner Erik Nyholm, both of whom, according to Stig-Nielsen in 1929, were "working quite hard and steadily, and both are liked and respected by the Chinese".[60] In other words, Leth-Møller & Co. was a useful tool for maintaining contact with the different Chinese business partners and networks. Moreover, the agreement stated that an official FLS office was to remain at Leth-Møller & Co.'s premises in Beijing, where it would also be possible for Stig-Nielsen and other FLS people to stay when visiting. Finally, regular reports were to be submitted on major issues requiring follow-up action by F.L. Smidth & Co. The collaboration agreement was not formalised in detail, but was, as phrased by Stig-Nielsen in 1929, "... half based on friendly understanding".[61]

Throughout their collaboration with Leth-Møller & Co., F.L. Smidth & Co. succeeded in maintaining contact with the factory projects in northern China as these were beginning to show signs of life following Chiang kai-Shek's seizure of power in 1928. Leth-Møller & Co. followed the Ching Hua project in Shenyang directly, for instance, whereas contact to a number of factory projects in Harbin was maintained through consul Jacobsen. Moreover, they continued to follow the attempts to revive the Liu Ho Kou project, and the technical aspects of the planning of a factory at Wusi, near Kiangsu, were transferred by means of Leth-Møller & Co.'s preliminary negotiations to F.L. Smidth & Co., who were able to submit their proposal for a complete factory in 1929. A watchful eye was also kept on the mainly preliminary factory plans, particularly around Beijing and in Shansi.[62]

Once the worst civil war riots subsided, Stig-Nielsen's life came to include long-term travels to China. During the years 1928–1929, he was travelling almost constantly on business, and in 1930, his wife and children chose to leave for Denmark because Stig-Nielsen hardly ever stayed in Japan anyway.[63] Generally, contact to the new factory projects required his attention, and particularly in south China where the first major Chinese order for almost ten years was brewing.

When Stig-Nielsen went back to China in 1928, it was to begin negotiations regarding the order for a cement factory at Sai Chuen near Canton, which was to deliver cement for the reconstruction of the civil war-torn Canton province. The project was to be managed by a newly established commission under the provincial government, and it was essential to the Danes to give a high priority to the preparatory negotiations. The Canton province was far from the only part of China in which the new government was facing an enormous task of restoring the country to a sound condition following more than ten years of civil war. Generally, the work was entrusted to similar reconstruction commissions in the provinces, and a possibility therefore began to emerge that factories for government-guaranteed cement supplies might be established in a number of locations.[64] It was therefore on the cards that the Danish small-state advantage might again become useful in a context where the political conditions were decisive, and where the possibilities for influence as a result of Stig-Nielsen's personal network effort in the early 1920s would hopefully present themselves.

At the same time, it was helpful that targeted efforts were being made in the high politics sphere to establish high-ranking diplomatic relations between the new nationalist government in Nanjing and Denmark. Taking into account the large amount of personal overlap between leading Chinese political and business circles, enhanced diplomatic relations were almost synonymous with an increase in the possibilities for collaboration in the very heart of China's cement industry. One example of this was Dr. C.T. Wang, managing director of Liu Ho Kou in 1923–1924, who in 1928 assumed the role of minister of foreign affairs in the Chiang kai-Shek government. Thus, their old relation with the powerful Wang family created a favourable negotiation climate for F.L. Smidth & Co. The positive prospects were further enhanced by the fact that C.T. Wang was, at the same time, personally acquainted with the Danish envoy in China, the diplomate Henrik Kauffmann, and that the latter in August 1928, as the first official representative from abroad, paid an official visit to Nanjing and thus afforded a welcome recognition of the legitimacy of the new regime. During Henrik Kauffmann's visit, the Chinese regime's negotiations with Stig-Nielsen – who was also one of the envoy's close personal acquaintances – were indeed the main topic in the discussions with the nationalist leaders, for instance, at a six-hour-long meeting with the deputy foreign minister Chu Chao-hsin [Zhu Zhaoxin].[65]

In February 1929, Stig-Nielsen informed Poul Larsen that the order for a cement factory for the Canton government had been settled, and that he was very optimistic as to the possibilities of more orders in the future:

> Apart from the order itself the whole thing will be of very great advertising value for us, as it is the <u>first</u> order ever settle with a Chinese Government on proper business lines. The Government itself has already started advertising for us, they on their part being very proud of the "equal treaty" entered into with them. As a first result it seems that the Kwangsi Government will also build a works soon. If conditions in China, therefore, keep on improving – which is by no means certain – the consequence of the Canton order may mean very large business for us.[66]

From 1929 to 1930, a promising picture began to emerge of the re-establishment of F.L. Smidth & Co.'s strong position in Chinese cement production ten years earlier. Thus, in November 1929, Stig-Nielsen travelled to Beijing for negotiations concerning an order from Hsing Yi Cement Co. and discussions with a north Chinese general, Dzau, about the establishment of a factory in Shenyang – however, both without result.[67] At the beginning of 1930, he took a longer trip to Southeast Asia, one purpose being to enter into negotiations regarding resumption of the old project at Kuala Lumpur.[68] As the Chinese market was beginning to show signs of increasing activity, this effort had to be supplemented by colleagues from the Japan office. One of these, engineer Bernhard Olsen, set out for China in 1930 to take part in the work, and in both June and October of the same year, engineer Tyge Møller went to Harbin and Huludao to analyse possible factory projects.[69]

The Informal Platform (1926–1930)

In addition to their collaboration with Leth-Møller & Co. and visiting FLS representatives, a method for F.L. Smidth & Co. to maintain their strong position in the Chinese market was the use of their oldest tools available, namely the Danes employed by the Chinese to run the existing cement factories. In the course of time, this informal FLS platform had been very thoroughly tested. However, in light of the difficulties it had caused in China around 1920, it was an open question to what extent the old tool was still operational at this time when the 1926 support function of the China office had even been phased out. However, with the Canton order followed a test as to whether it was still safe to count on the establishment of tools for informal control deeply within the customers' organisation. As a point of departure, the order did not include managing or administrative personnel, but only deliveries of machinery, buildings and start-up of the plant. For the successful employment of Danes in positions with an influence on the running of the factory, the soil therefore had to be prepared, and for this reason, it became crucial to organise a careful personal profiling of the FLS people who were to operate closest to the Chinese during the building phase.

In light of this, the head office in Copenhagen suggested, in February 1929, to let the experienced engineer Harald Hardvendel lead the establishment of the factory. Harald Hardvendel had just completed the establishment of a cement factory at Haiphong in Indochina. For Stig-Nielsen, who did not know the 39-year-old engineer and was uncertain of his skills, it was nevertheless crucial to make sure that Hardvendel did in fact have the right qualifications to complete a similar task in a Chinese context. He therefore stressed to Copenhagen that "... besides necessary technical qualifications [it is] very important that he is in possession of a nice personality". To make sure this was the case, he suggested that Hardvendel should travel to Canton via Tokyo so that he could size him up and travel on with him and make sure he was well introduced to the Chinese. The head office assured him that Hardvendel possessed "a very good character".[70]

For practical reasons, by the beginning of April, it had still not been possible to organise Hardvendel's journey to Tokyo. Stig-Nielsen began to feel nervous about this as it was important to have a Dane in place in Canton very soon. When he sent a reminder to the head office in April, this was primarily based on his wish to establish a position that could ensure a reliable insider information level regarding other orders from the Chiang kai-Shek regime:

> I am most anxious to get a man from our firm on the job as soon as ever possible, because we can hardly rely on statements from outsiders, and as, of course, it is of very great importance for me to receive regular reports from Canton partly dealing with the plant itself, and partly dealing with developments in the province of Kwangtung.[71]

In addition to this, he was worried about Hardvendel's English proficiency, in particular because, as he said: "It goes without saying that our man in charge of the job in Canton will have to carry out numerous negotiations with the Canton Government, in the same way as he will no doubt have to write them letters from time to time". In spite of Stig-Nielsen's anxiety, it took some time still to get Hardvendel to

Canton, not least because the conditions in China were still turbulent. Both travel planning and organising an insurance policy against kidnapping took all summer, and it was not until the autumn of 1929 that he succeeded in reaching the building site.[72] However, with the amiable Hardvendel in place in Canton, F.L. Smidth & Co. had done what was so far possible to place a candidate in position. For the time being, there was nothing to do but to exercise patience. Expectations were, however, completely fulfilled. In August 1930, Stig-Nielsen reported that Hardvendel carried out first-class work, and in January 1931, when the factory was about to be completed, the Chinese informally leaked the information that they would be willing to continue their close collaboration if Hardvendel remained in charge as a factory manager.[73]

So far, so good in Canton. In the other companies where the Danes had till then been firmly in charge of plant operations, experiences were mixed, however.

At the Green Island Cement Company, F.L. Smidth & Co. had not really regained its foothold since the death of the Danish burner master in 1924. The Danes had certainly succeeded in making good contact with the English factory manager Henry Pooley, even though he was actually closely attached to their German competitors. However, when an extension to the factory in Hong Kong was back on the drawing board in 1929, Pooley began negotiations with Polysius and Vickers.[74] At F.L. Smidth & Co., this was perceived as a U-turn. Stig-Nielsen saw it as a sign that Pooley, who had repeatedly expressed a wish to work for F.L. Smidth & Co., had been disappointed when the position as head of the London office had been refilled in February 1929:

> If he had hoped to get a position in our firm, and then saw when there might have been a chance, he was not considered, then he may, of course, have come to the conclusion that there would be no possibility for him in F.L. Smidth & Company.[75]

Although Stig-Nielsen was well aware that "... it is not the general policy of our Company to take in any foreigners ...", he still recommended to Poul Larsen to offer Pooley the prospect of the responsibility of the China office when the upswing in the Chinese market made it necessary to upgrade.

The FLS people got a chance to discuss this with Pooley when he visited Europe in July 1929 and called in at both the Copenhagen head office and the factories in Aalborg.[76] Officially, technical discussions were on the agenda, but the actual reason for Pooley's visits was to discuss the possibility that F.L. Smidth & Co. might employ him. From a Danish point of view, the outcome of the meetings was mixed. Pooley foreshadowed that F.L. Smidth & Co. had to be prepared to offer particularly favourable credit terms to win the order for the expansion in Hong Kong, and during the meetings he was far from as amiable as might be desired. However, when Pooley mentioned that the order might go to either Polysius or F.L. Smidth & Co., O.V. Mørch, who was responsible for F.L. Smidth & Co.'s operations in Asia, took the chance to ask Pooley directly whether he might see himself as head of FLS activities in China. To this question, Pooley enthusiastically replied that the thought of an FLS position appealed to him, and he privately promised to make sure the order would go to Copenhagen.

In other words, a strong effort was made to regain control of the Green Island Cement Company. F.L. Smidth & Co. had gone quite far – and even beyond their normal national framework – and the risk this implied was accentuated when, in the autumn of 1929, the order went to Vickers after all.[77] Apparently, Vickers had contributed actively with very favourable credit terms to finance the factory extension. It also became clear to F.L. Smidth & Co., however, that during the building phase Pooley had passed on much of the information he had received about the Danish equipment directly to the English competitor. At lightning speed, the prospect of control with the Green Island Cement Company had thus been turned into the recognition of a complete loss of control.

Better luck was had with the situation in Tangshan, where the precondition for continued Danish control was that the agreement regarding the three-year employment so far of factory manager Emil Schmit-Jensen might be extended. This turned out to be no problem, since when the period was about to expire in 1928, the Chee Hsin Cement Company prolonged the agreement to 1933 without further ado.[78] In February 1929, Stig-Nielsen therefore summarised to Poul Larsen that the secured position had been followed up by new orders to F.L. Smidth & Co. for new mill shells for the cement mill. Moreover, extensive FLS reconstruction work at the Hubei factory had been initiated as planned, and work was in progress to install systems for pneumatic transportation and packing of cement in both Hubei and Tangshan.[79] This meant that with Schmit-Jensen as their key figure, F.L. Smidth & Co. continued to be firmly in charge of both the operation and the development of the plant of their main customer in China.

Network Coordinator

By the end of the 1920s, the Danes could safely conclude that on important parameters they had succeeded in maintaining and strengthening their informal grip of the operation and development of the Chinese cement factories. It even appeared that on this basis, new opportunities were about to emerge to take the level of influence and control of the development of the entire cement industry to new heights – and in an even larger area beyond the Chinese borders. The fact was that the influential Danish positions in China and Siam were not exceptions at all. Over time, F.L. Smidth & Co. had come to occupy a position as the natural hub for a major part of key actors in the Asian cement industry. Consequently, the Danes were beginning to see their opportunity to act as a key connecting link between actors who would not otherwise have been connected but would, on the contrary, have been solely competitors. In other words, in Burt's and Kogut's terminology, it became relevant for F.L. Smidth & Co. to more explicitly assume the role of *research centre* in a larger constellation of companies, thus harvesting profit by filling a *structural gap* in a network whose existence in fact depended on an actor that was able and willing to assume such a unifying and coordinating role.[80] Towards 1930, the companies in the Asian cement industry were indeed competitors. However, if confidence in F.L. Smidth & Co. was high, there was a potential to turn the Danish technology supplier into a unifying actor in situations where collaboration was obvious. Basically, the entry of a Danish company in such a coordinating role would constitute the existence of a network of competing cement manufacturers. Such a role would also greatly enhance the Danish possibilities of influence on and control with the overall market development. This was therefore what the FLS people sought to achieve when given the chance as the 1920s came to a close.

The opening came when, in 1929, moves were being made for a cartel-like sales agreement regarding the one million barrels of cement delivered to Shanghai on an annual basis; this paved the way for decisive contacts to be made by Schmit-Jensen in Tangshan, the FLS people at other factories and Stig-Nielsen, who was based in Tokyo. The preliminaries had been settled already in 1928. Both the Japanese Asano Cement Company and the Siam Cement Company had independently approached Stig-Nielsen and asked for his assessment of the possibility of the Chee Hsin Cement Company to be part of this agreement. The Asano Cement Company had just become one of F.L. Smidth & Co.'s major customers (chapter 5), whereas the proposal made by the Siam Cement Company was communicated through the Danish manager Erik Thune and the Danish/Swedish chairman of the board Lennart Grut. Schmit-Jensen held a key position in the Chee Hsin Cement Company, and in January 1929, Stig-Nielsen therefore wrote to him about the matter.[81] The Japanese-Siamese wish to establish a cartel agreement was sparked by the year-long problems caused by Shanghai's corrupt city government. Schmit-Jensen confirmed that this was also the experience of the Chee Hsin Cement Company. In fact, no cement had been sold by the Tangshan factory to the *Shanghai Municipal Council* since 1920, when it had become an established practice that the results of the city government's tests of the strength of the delivered cement were 50% below the results of the tests conducted by the factory itself.[82] With the sales contracts made, the Chee Hsin Cement Company had therefore been obliged to pay for the purchase of cement from other suppliers. As re-marked by Schmit-Jensen, this had been *"an excellent basis for squeezing"*.[83] Their experiences had not improved since then. Attempts at new agreements in 1928 had led to similar hoaxes. Schmit-Jensen's assessment was still that "... everyone agrees that this is the most rotten foreign institution in China, and that absolutely nothing can be done about it". In his view, teaming up against the corrupt city government was therefore an excellent idea. At the same time, however, he said that establishing such teamwork might well prove difficult, mainly because similar collaboration between a number of the Chinese cement manu-facturers, including the Chee Hsin Cement Company, was already in the pipeline.

In February, both the Japanese and the Siamese asked Stig-Nielsen to initiate actual negotiations. Once more, Lennart Grut asked for an as-sessment of the possibility for collaboration between the Siam Cement Company and the Japanese association of cement manufacturers, and to avoid misunderstandings, he asked Stig-Nielsen to pass on his offer to travel to Japan to discuss the topic in more detail. The Japanese took this in good spirit and suggested that the FLS people might act as a "medium for start of negotiations".[84] The matter seemed promising. If an agree-ment was successfully made, F.L. Smidth & Co. would be in an ex-tremely favourable position. This was not just a matter of the prospects of future orders from all the parties included in the agreement, but also of F.L. Smidth & Co.'s role as an unbiased watchdog regarding com-pliance with the agreement – i.e. the risk of cheating. Stig-Nielsen therefore turned to Poul Larsen for advice, and he did not hesitate to accept Stig-Nielsen's role as chief negotiator. At the same time, however, Larsen advised against attempts to reach a contract-bound agreement regarding F.L. Smidth & Co.'s role. In his view, the parties involved were already so closely linked to the Danish side that they might resent a request for a written proof of their positive response, and at the same time, such an agreement might stand in the way of future orders from manufacturers outside of the narrow circle.[85]

On this basis, Stig-Nielsen continued the negotiations, which required a great deal of his political savvy. A key issue was the Chee Hsin Cement Company's negotiations with the other Chinese cement factories. Stig-Nielsen might well convey the informal confirmation from the Chinese side of the complications apparently caused by the Shanghai city gov-ernment, but of course passing on Schmit-Jensen's confidential in-formation about the preparations for a Chinese agreement would cause him to lose credibility. However, the Japanese learnt of the Chinese negotiations from other sources, i.e. through the Asano Cement Company's representative in Shanghai. When they declared that in their view, this did not stand in the way of a Chinese-Japanese agreement, Stig-Nielsen could approach Schmit-Jensen again in April 1929. With the statements from Siam and Japan, Stig-Nielsen concluded to his FLS colleague in Tangshan that a basis had been created for collaboration, and that "... if now the Shanghai Municipal Council can be frozen out also by other cement companies, the whole thing may prove to be of interest and also of business value to you".[86] The intervention of the FLS people had helped prepare the ground for Siamese-Chinese-Japanese negotiations.

From then on, fast progress was made in the case. In mid-April, Erik Thune presented the collaboration proposal to the Siam Cement Company's board of directors, who authorised Lennart Grut to travel to Japan. Simultaneously, Schmit-Jensen asked Stig-Nielsen to come to Tangshan afterwards to present his view of the case to the Chinese management.[87] So far, prospects seemed positive from a Danish point of view. The parties were successfully convened around the negotiation table – and even with Danish/Swedish participation in the shape of Lennart Grut. However, it was beyond the power of the FLS people to determine the results of the negotiations. So far, they had reached the limit of Danish control.

Lennart Grut arrived in Tokyo around the middle of May. When he left to travel home at the end of the month, internal disagreements among the Japanese companies and what he experienced as negligent Japanese treatment of himself had caused the negotiations to break down.[88] After the meeting, Lennart Grut emphasised that he appreciated Stig-Nielsen's efforts. However, implying the threat of an impending price war, Erik Thune subsequently pointed out to Stig-Nielsen – in a message intended for the Japanese – that the purpose of his journey to Japan had been "... a square proposal aiming at avoiding to cut one another's throats".[89] He added that he was convinced that in time, the Japanese would realise that an agreement would have been the wisest outcome. This tirade indicated that the thought of cartel collaboration which would have covered the main part of the East Asian cement production had so far been dismissed. In spite of this unfortunate outcome, the FLS people had demonstrated, however, that they were willing to act as a connecting link between the cement manufacturers and co-ordinate joint action in the Asian cement market.

At the beginning of 1929, Stig-Nielsen reported to Poul Larsen how the FLS organisation in China should no doubt

> ... for next few years be very strong: namely, our man at Canton paid for by the clients; Leth Moller & Nyholm in Peking, and, possibly, Nanking, ... and Schmitt-Jensen paid for by Chee Hsin right up north; in other words, a complete chain, covering the whole China coast, with Consul Jacobsen in Harbin to give us a hint from that corner.[90]

Regarding his own role, there was also reason to be optimistic in view of the initial Chinese reconstruction activities following the civil war:

> If, however, things move on in the right direction, it will be necessary to have a permanent man there, as it is quite impossible for me to do everything in China with the Japanese business to attend to at the same time. If, however, a man were in China permanently, it would be possible for me to go over and help him at times a job was about to be finally settled.

Expansion and Loss of Control (1931–1936)

Following his journey to Shanghai in February 1931, Stig-Nielsen concluded that F.L. Smidth & Co. needed to expand their presence in China. He therefore recommended to the headquarters in Copenhagen that a new permanent office should be established in Shanghai, where – as in southern China in general – the market potential was booming. China's new political and financial centre of gravity was beginning to emerge around the axis between the fast expanding city of Shanghai and Chiang kai-Shek's government city Nanjing a little less than 300 km to the west.[91] The new stability around the power base of the Generalissimo revived the more promising prospects of the building sector, and there was reason to believe that new cement factories would be needed. Shanghai in particular was anticipating a speedy development. Both American and British interests had already begun to invest massively in the city's companies and infrastructure, and plans to turn Shanghai into a freeport under international protection were in the pipeline. Moreover, it seemed likely that the old and fairly dilapidated government city of Nanjing would be expanded considerably as regards infrastructure, industry and housing stock.

There were thus strong arguments in favour of a new permanent FLS office in Shanghai, and in Stig-Nielsen's view, opportunities were emerging for innovation of FLS' collaboration with the Chinese customers. One argument was that Nanjing's housing stock was so run-down that Chinese politicians and government officials did not want to live there permanently. Instead, they would spend a large part of their time in Shanghai, and if F.L. Smidth & Co. were to hope for a share of orders from the new regime, they would have to establish contact with them there. Orders for large-scale plants such as cement factories required a green light from the government apparatus, and Stig-Nielsen also stated – without directly describing the administration as corrupt – that in order to make things run smoothly, it was usually necessary to acquire "... special help from the Government in one form or another". Seen in an FLS perspective, it was decisive that this was something the Chinese were not sufficiently well-organised to provide themselves. As expressed by Stig-Nielsen: " ... unless we back them up and help them with their general arrangements, they get nowhere". In other words, it was necessary to get so close to official China that it became possible to take on the role as a driving force in the customers' projects – "... so that at the right moment we can use our influence, and help our clients to pull the right strings". In other words – and roughly speaking – Stig-Nielsen's opinion was that F.L. Smidth & Co. had to start from scratch and organise the customer base that was necessary to sell the Danish machines.

However, in Stig-Nielsen's view, it was not only vis-à-vis the politicians and government officials that the FLS people needed to be prepared to carry out the work on behalf of their Chinese customers. Something similar would become necessary regarding their customers' sources of financing, which would expectedly also be concentrated around Shanghai. Actors abroad were holding on tightly to their lucrative positions in China, and as the Chinese were unable to organise their own reconstruction work, foreign capital from both governmental and private sources had begun to flow into the country. As described by Stig-Nielsen, this money would flow through Shanghai because on a Chinese scale, the city's financial world was well-developed, but the ongoing planning process regarding a freeport status and international protection also played an important role. FLS' presence in Shanghai would therefore make it possible to include contact with the financial backers in their role as a driving force regarding their customers' factory plans in order "... to keep in touch not only with our Chinese clients who want to build factories, but also with the most important financiers".

All of this went beyond the strategy so far followed by F.L. Smidth & Co. in China. Up to this point, the Danes had indeed delivered technology and informally taken control of the running of cement factories. But their contribution to the establishment of new factories had been limited to the technical project planning. Now Stig-Nielsen formulated a strategy according to which the Danes would specifically target the control of more basic tasks and move across to the customers' side of the negotiation table; this might well make it even more difficult to distinguish between the Chinese cement manufacturer and the Danish technology supplier. Their aim was not vertical integration; they were aiming to exploit their Chinese customers' insufficient organisation level and, informally and without risk, drift into a role that implied taking contact to the political and financial networks. If FLS succeeded, the cement manufacturers would be even more dependent on the Danes. F.L. Smidth & Co. would avoid investing money in the projects and at the same time – particularly with the support of the financial backers – end up with very strong tools to control the activities of their customers. It seemed obvious to imagine scenarios in which extensive Danish control could be exercised without any direct financial risks, i.e. informally speaking, direct investments in multinational enterprise – but with other people's money.

In the spring of 1931, Poul Larsen replied that he generally shared the understanding of the situation in China, and Stig-Nielsen could therefore establish an office in vacant rooms at the Danish consulate-general at The Bund.[92] It now remained to be seen if Stig-Nielsen's plans would become a reality.

Chinese Cement Manufacturers Association

Stig-Nielsen's thoughts regarding increased control with the Chinese cement industry did not appear out of the blue. They emanated from various other indications emerging that F.L. Smidth & Co. might be able to expand their influence on the Chinese cement industry. Since the end of 1930, one potential in particular had emerged, i.e. for FLS to act as a connecting link between the Chinese cement factories and their customers.

In concrete terms, one of the causes was that Japanese cement manufacturers had acquired a large part of the market share in China through a price dumping policy financed by income from the cement market in Japan. The Japanese downward pressure on prices was about to draw the home market-dependent Chinese cement factories into a destructive negative spiral. Under the heading *Chinese Cement Manufacturers Association* (CCMA), the Chee Hsin Cement Company, Shanghai PCW and the China Portland Cement Company therefore entered into negotiations concerning a cartel agreement which involved a joint effort regarding a political request for a customs barrier and the coordination of production, sales and prices in order to avoid a back-breaking price war.[93] In total, this involved more than half of China's production capacity, and as the Chee Hsin Cement Company accounted for 60% of this, their voice carried substantial weight in the negotiations, which on 1 July 1931 resulted in an initial one-year agreement. Thanks to Schmit-Jensen's influence in Tangshan and his – and his Shanghai-based FLS colleagues' – close collaboration with managing director Li Shi Ming, this agreement heralded great prospects for F.L. Smidth & Co.[94]

Under the agreement, the sale of cement was to be distributed according to the proportions between the cartel members' production capacities. This was not an easy volume to determine, unless you possessed thorough knowledge of the machinery and the technological development. The production plants had been established successively over a large timespan, and their capacity depended not only on size, but also on factors such as the extent to which they were worn down and the stages of their technological development. The precondition for a well-functioning cartel agreement was therefore that the parties agreed on the appointment of an impartial body that could step in in the long term and assess the production capacity of the factories when the need for expansion arose again. To begin with, a joint committee with representatives from each factory was appointed for this task. But it was part of the agreement that collaboration be entered into with one of the technology suppliers of the cement factories; the former would thus profit from their favourable role as a type of technical consulting department in a sales cartel that supplied cement to half of the Chinese cement market.

A golden chance was about to present itself. But although Li Shi Ming argued in favour of F.L. Smidth & Co.'s appointment as consulting engineers to CCMA, there was the obstacle that both Shanghai PCW and the China Portland Cement Company had up till then made use of Polysius.[95] Shanghai PCW even chose to appoint a man from Polysius as their representative in the interim committee. Thus, the German competitor stepped directly into the committee even before an external technical consultant had been appointed. This caused E. Schmit-Jensen – who, as we know, now participated as an informal FLS representative – to take immediate action. When the committee announced their arrival in Tangshan in August 1931, he urged Li Shi Ming to deny the German Polysius engineer called Schmidt access.[96] In Schmit-Jensen's view, Schmidth's intention was espionage, but the German envoy would also have an opportunity to criticise the FLS machinery and raise questions about the trustworthiness of the Danes: "Consequently I personally, resp. F.L. Smidth & Co., and perhaps also Chee Hsin shall get a reputation in Shanghai for trying to give out false statements as to the capacity of F.L.S. machinery, which might be detrimental to future relations and dealings in Shanghai". It might also be that Schmit-Jensen had things to hide that Schmidt would be able to point out. Nonetheless, following consultation with Stig-Nielsen, Li Shi Ming ordered the German to be welcomed into Tangshan.[97]

However, this accommodating gesture was a cover-up for a trap, as Stig-Nielsen explained to the baffled Schmit-Jensen. Li Shi Ming's secret thought had been that

> ... by letting Polysius' man into the negotiations, he will later on be able to state to his co-directors that, as far as he himself is concerned, he considers F.L.S. the best firm, but that, on the other hand, he has certainly given their competitor every chance.[98]

Li Shi Ming had thus asserted himself as a strong business partner and guaranteed Danish control of the situation in Tangshan, and it appears that, as expected, the German did make a poor showing. Being prepared for combat, Schmit-Jensen had got Schmidth – who had only been in China a short while – to sign a draft report about the factory's capacity, which the Dane subsequently criticised so harshly that it had to be rewritten in the presence of the entire committee.[99] This was a serious loss of face for the Germans – Schmidt as well as Polysius. When it also appeared that Schmidth had in mind a position as chief engineer for

CCMA, the Chee Hsin people had made it clear, according to Schmit-Jensen, that "... we do not need a chief engineer from Polysius here".

Things were under control in the Danish quarters, and in September 1931, Stig-Nielsen concluded that so far, F.L. Smidth & Co. was in a favourable position: "Altogether I am under the Impression that things have gone very nicely for us".[100]

A Very Great Victory in China

A position as consulting engineer for the CCMA would expand and formalise F.L. Smidth & Co.'s influence on the Chinese cement factories, but still no direct Danish investments would be involved. This option was introduced, however, when the Danish contractor Aage Corrit, who had resided in Shanghai since the early 1920s, contacted Stig-Nielsen in 1930 regarding the possibilities to enter into partnership on a "Ready Mixed Concrete Plant". Aage Corrit needed a financially strong partner, and as F.L. Smidth & Co. had taken out a patent in Denmark for concrete production machinery and specialised lorries for delivery, Stig-Nielsen took to the idea of partnership. In early 1931, he therefore asked the head office for a survey of the operating costs of the Danish Concrete Factories' (De Danske Betonfabrikker) plants in Copenhagen.[101] The scale was completely different, of course. Whereas in Copenhagen 100,000 barrels of cement were used in 1930, the annual consumption in Shanghai was, as mentioned, around one million barrels. However, this only improved the potential, and the FLS headquarters green-lighted the further planning activities.

Corrit therefore continued the preparation work in collaboration with Leth-Møller & Company, who, in April 1931, submitted a report to the FLS headquarters.[102] However, the latter requested more information about the financial risks and were therefore reluctant to promise financial support. In order to calm down the impatient Corrit, Stig-Nielsen had to reassure him in May that the headquarters' interest in the project was genuine, and that he himself would "... use my influence to try to induce them to come in".[103] In reality, the optimistic tone used by the Shanghai office manager probably reflected his own wish to keep the project alive. To a colleague, he expressed that he was well aware that an investment in it would probably exceed the FLS senior management's general strategy. As phrased by Stig-Nielsen, "... it may be their general policy at present not to support anything but actual cement factories".[104]

In late summer 1931, Stig-Nielsen repeated his request for Danish investment to the Copenhagen staff responsible for FLS business in China and Japan, O.V. Mørch. And at this time he supported his arguments by referring to the opportunities that seemed to be emerging from the collaboration with CCMA. If F.L. Smidth & Co. was to contribute actively to the establishment of the cement factory, both Schmit-

Jensen and Li Shi Ming had assured Stig-Nielsen that the Chee Hsin Cement Company would follow suit with similar investments. In this case, it would only be a matter of time before Shanghai PCW and China Cement Company followed the heavyweight of the cartel with further investments.[105] The dream result would then be a business circle in which F.L. Smidth & Co., in addition to their role as technology supplier, would also be in control of a considerable part of the cement production and the sale of cement to the growing Shanghai market. Stig-Nielsen was therefore not afraid to paint a very optimistic picture when approaching his superiors in Copenhagen:

> If we can succeed in getting into close business relations with the Shanghai Portland Cement Works, ... and if on top of that we have a certain participation in the ready-mixed concrete plant, our position will be very strong indeed in and around Shanghai, which is the part of China where we have not been able to secure our position to the same degree as elsewhere in China. If we succeed in establishing a strong position in Shanghai, in which region German influence has been considerable in the past, then we will win a very great victory in China.[106]

Stig-Nielsen was at the head of it all, but FLS' informal presence in Tangshan, personified by E. Schmit-Jensen, was decisive for the success of the big plans. Unless the Chee Hsin Cement Company was strongly lobbied, there was a risk that they would withdraw their support, and that the Danish advantage position vis-à-vis CCMA – and consequently their possibilities to pull the entire cartel into a Danish-Chinese partnership on the cement factory in Shanghai – would be lost. The Chee Hsin Cement Company was the lever for the Danish strategy of control of the Chinese cement industry.

Retreat in Tangshan

As more than the day-to-day Danish presence in Tangshan was at stake, Li Shi Ming's sudden death in February 1932 was a serious blow for F.L. Smidth & Co.'s position in all of China.[107] Since Schmit-Jensen's arrival in China ten years earlier, Li Shi Ming had to a great extent drawn on him in a close partnership which benefitted both parties. This backfired in the power struggles that broke out following Li Shi Ming's death.

Schmit-Jensen himself was of the opinion that he was the only person who knew the factories properly and that he was therefore indispensable.[108] Moreover, following Li Shi Ming's death, H. W. Yuan – son of Yuan Shikai, the man behind the establishment of the Chee Hsin Cement Company – was chosen for a position as managing director. This meant continuity in the top management, and in August, Schmit-Jensen's contract was extended by five years. However, when he discovered a couple of weeks later that the new 16-member board of directors which had been elected at a general assembly in July had requested that the agreement should also be negotiated by them, it became clear that problems were looming.[109] In Schmit-Jensen's view, the problem was his own skills and success, which had secured him such great control as a factory manager that H.W. Yuan was now forced to eliminate him to secure his own position. Seen from a distance, it seems obvious to interpret this to be an attempt by the Chinese to take the opportunity to break away from a Danish dominance which was of less benefit to the Chee Hsin Cement Company than to F.L. Smidth & Co. However, Schmit-Jensen maintained that his own outstanding qualities were the reasons why several of his and Li Shi Ming's closest staff members were laid off and replaced by Yuan's friends during the summer of 1932.[110]

The situation did not improve when the senior management and the shareholders formed four groups. In addition to the family and friends supporting Yuan, two other clan-like groups led by deputy directors Chow Chi Chi and Wang had emerged, as well as a group consisting of a number of banks. Following the July general assembly, they were all represented in the management and systematically obstructed the Yuan Shikai group, for instance through an attempt to eliminate the old Danish business partner. When the new senior management announced that they had appointed an American educated Chinese for a position in the factory management – a family member of one of the board members – and that they, as a compromise with the Yuan fraction, offered to extend Schmit-Jensen's contract by three years, it was clear to the Danes that "... the intention was to break off the existing relationship with F.L.S. as soon as possible".[111]

Schmit-Jensen insisted on his standpoint and stated how "... keen both Yuan and Liu were for me to stay and accept the three years because they realise they cannot do without me for the time being". But in November 1932, he had to ask Stig-Nielsen for assistance.[112] In reality the game was up. Stig-Nielsen referred to the fact that the technical management were dependent on assistance from F.L. Smidth & Co. He succeeded in organising talks with the Chinese management group who emphasised to Schmit-Jensen that "... he would have to realize now that he was working with Chinese and not with foreigners".[113] But in March 1933, managing director Yuan informed Schmit-Jensens that his contract would not be extended at all. Even though he emphasised that the Chee Hsin Cement Company wished to continue to do business with F.L. Smidth & Co., it was evident that the conditions had been radically changed.[114]

Any thought of using the Chee Hsin Cement Company as a lever for greater overall control of the Chinese cement industry had in reality been eliminated following the death of Li Shi Ming. Accordingly, in the negotiations in 1932, 1933 and 1935, the question regarding F.L. Smidth &

Co.'s role did not reappear.[115] And for the establishment of the concrete mixing plant in Shanghai, they could not hope to gain control via the Chee Hsin Cement Co. and consequently via CCMA. The project was dead. The glorious victory of F.L. Smidth & Co. in China now suddenly faded away.

Focusing on the Key Role (1933–1936)

From the autumn of 1932, the FLS management insisted on results in China; otherwise, the offices in both Shanghai and Beijing would be eliminated, which was the message from Copenhagen.[116] In November, Stig-Nielsen was even transferred to New York, and his colleague Tyge Møller took over his job in Shanghai. Focus now became directed towards F.L. Smidth & Co.'s key role as a supplier of machinery and plants for cement production, whereas Stig-Nielsen had envisaged that the customers needed assistance with political and financial contacts. In the course of the following three years, the scope of F.L. Smidth & Co.'s possibilities of influence and control became particularly tested in connection with extensions of the Sai Chuen factory in 1933 and 1936, the planning of new government factories in the Guangxi and Sichuan provinces and the establishment of a new factory in Nanjing in 1935–1936.

Extension in Sai Chuen (1933)

The Sai Chuen factory at Canton was a basic pillar in the nationalist government's reconstruction activities in southern China and seemed to become a strong Danish benchmark. In the summer of 1932, Harald Hardvendel was still the candidate for the position as factory manager, and a number of the other Danes who had participated in building the factory were intended for leading positions.[117] However, when Harald Hardvendel lost courage regarding his future prospects in China, the result was that in 1933, engineer Svend Bonde and leading machine fitter Ejnar Larsen assumed positions as what managing director C.G. Liu described as "engineers of the plant under the control of the director of the Sai Chuen Cement Works".[118]

Svend Bonde subsequently coordinated everything carefully with F.L. Smidth & Co. He made sure in particular to safeguard the asymmetrical knowledge base to an extent that caused the Chinese to request, in 1933, that the technical data and drawings they had ordered and bought from Copenhagen should be forwarded directly to managing director C.G. Liu and not to Bonde privately as had happened previously. In return, the Danes expressed their clear expectation that the Chinese share with them any confidential information they might have of their line of business. At the same time, the FLS people secretly agreed that drawings sent to Sai

Chuen should only include a minimum of information, whereas they would send material with more details to Svend Bonde and Ejnar Larsen.[119] Admittedly, the two Danes were employed by the Chinese government firm, but they blindly obeyed orders from the FLS office in Shanghai.

From 1932, plans were being made to install another rotary kiln line, and at this point it soon became clear to the Danes that they would need to take action on behalf of the Chinese if they were to hope for this expansion to proceed and make sure the order was placed with F.L. Smidth & Co.[120] The reason was that during the autumn everything came to a standstill for the simple reason that the nationalists did not possess the required capital themselves and did not manage to raise it either. From the Danish quarters, an initiative was therefore taken to begin negotiations chaired by Tyge Møller. The vulnerability of the project became clear when he accepted to carry on working on a contract proposal which entailed that two-thirds of the payment must be guaranteed by the Standard Chartered Bank in Hong Kong by opening a credit for the nationalist government. According to Tyge Møller, the bank had namely "... as a matter of fact flatly refused to have anything to do with Government orders".[121] The only response from the government was an attempt to push F.L. Smidth & Co. to accept extraordinarily long credits, or pure and simple "... the creation of a machinery loan", which would essentially mean Danish co-financing of the project.[122] However, at the same time, the Danes were given authority to make further attempts at negotiating on their own with the Standard Chartered Bank, i.e. without intervention by the Chinese government officials.[123] In April 1933, Tyge Møller therefore made contact with James Walker, who was now in the bank management in Hong Kong but had been the manager of its branch in Canton in 1929, when the Sai Chuen factory was established. This time the response was that the bank would like to help the Danes and would welcome a credit request from the government. Tyge Møller and the top bank manager A. Brearley then visited Sai Chuen, accompanied by Kai Neckelmann, the Danish consul in Hong Kong. According to Tyge Møller, this visit was characterised by pleasant confidentiality.

Afterwards, the Danes made new contact with the Chinese, but as it seemed the government apparatus did not sufficiently support the project, it was only when Tyge Møller succeeded in bringing about negotiations with Y. Y. Chang, the top manager of the provincial government's reconstruction commission, that the process was restarted. But from then on things moved fast. Already after one week of negotiations, a contract could be signed. In the process, it had been necessary for the Danes to promise a number of government officials a considerable "secret commission", but in return, Lum Wan Kai, the chair of the commission, expressed his official satisfaction with their effort.[124]

Apparently, it was now acceptable to the nationalist regime that the main initiative to such a large project had been taken over by the Danes. The situation looked promising – also in other places such as Guangxi, where work was in progress from 1932 to establish a government factory.

Guangxi (1933–1935)

In the autumn of 1932, Tyge Møller initiated collaboration with the provincial government in Nanning to establish Guangxi's own cement factory. However, from the very outset, it became clear that F.L. Smidth & Co. could not simply take full control of the project.[125]

In the summer of 1932, Tyge Møller had spent seven weeks travelling in Guangxi, paid by Marshal Li Zongren, the ruler of the province, to collect raw material samples and explore any possible factory locations and prepare profitability calculations. His main conclusion was that the expected return on invested capital would be approx. 30% per year. But then the project came to a complete standstill, mainly because the marshal was busily engaged in politics and acts of war.

When Li Zongren's chief of staff, General Chang, visited Canton in December, Tyge Møller therefore made contact with him. Tyge Møller realised, however, that the general was not in favour of such entrepreneurial behaviour, and the primary objective therefore turned out to be to try to calm him down:

> We told him that we had not at all come around to try to force the matter in any way, but just to learn a little about how things were progressing, in order that we might be able to arrange our own plans for the immediate future.[126]

After consulting with Li Zongren in Nanning, Chang announced, however, that the project would be initiated, but that talks with the Danes would not be undertaken until the financial aspects had been settled.

The Danes were now forced to take a back seat, and they therefore chose to draw on an unofficial government contact established when, in 1931, Stig-Nielsen had helped a key government official, lawyer Li Fong, get out of a financial fix.[127] This turned out to be a good investment. In 1933, Li Fong had advanced to a position described by Tyge Møller as "… a kind of secretary to the Chairman of the Kwangung Provincial Governement". From this position, he informed the Danes that the provincial government actually had the resources to build the factory, but that they wished to involve private capital and had therefore made contact to one of Shanghai's richest people, gangster and mafia boss Du Yuesheng, who had previously provided financial and military support to Chiang kai-Shek.[128] This made the Danes nervous, but although it was implied that some of the money was to come from Shanghai's opium trade, prostitution and gambling activities, they considered the financial aspects settled.

Secretly, Tyge Møller therefore proceeded with the work involved in obtaining bank guarantees. This time, this took place through the Shanghai Commercial & Savings Bank, which was extremely non-committal. Tyge Møller therefore invited bank representative David Au on an inspection trip to Sai Chuen, and he went so far as to offer a Danish buy-back guarantee of the machinery if it turned out that the Guangxi backers were unable to pay. However, it was not until it became clear to David Au that the main backer of the factory project was Li Zongren – who was a close friend of the bank manager K.P. Chen – that he allowed the Danes to leak the information that the Shanghai Commercial & Savings Bank would respond favourably to a credit application from the government.

At the turn of the year 1932–1933, Li Zongren then announced that he would travel to Canton to complete discussions.[129] When the marshal finally turned up in July, he only accepted to attend a meeting when hard pushed, and even announced that the money was not available in the provincial government's 1933 budget. When pushed by Tyge Møller, the marshal turned out to be "... disinclined, and I considered it unwise to put more pressure on him, so I stopped".[130] When Li Fong succeeded in arranging new negotiations in 1934, it was suddenly imperative that F.L. Smidth & Co. would invest directly in the factory. However, this marked the limit of the Danish contribution to the project, and the process came to a standstill.[131] The Danes had to realise that even though they had organised the necessary bank contacts, the control of the Guangxi project had not been achieved at all.[132]

Sai Chuen (1936)

From the mid-1930s, the failed Guangxi project was followed by several problems for F.L. Smidth & Co. concerning the control they had hoped to obtain over the factories. Altogether a pattern was beginning to emerge, and the size of the problems only seemed to increase.

The fact that the situation was about to fundamentally change became clear when the Sai Chuen factory was about to be expanded by another rotary kiln line. When the idea of another expansion was launched in 1935, the FLS people were carefully consulted. However, when the planning work began in 1936, the political winds were blowing in a completely different direction.[133] At the beginning of the year, Svend Bonde took stock of his possibilities to extend his contract as a manager.[134] In his own opinion, he was doing a good job and had managed to obtain strong support from the managing director G.C. Liu. But he also had to add that hostile sentiments towards the west in the government apparatus had meant that several of his acquaintances who had served the Chinese faithfully for many years in other companies had been removed from their positions. It was not at all unlikely, he said, that he was also approaching a similar exit.

The negotiations in 1936 regarding the order for the rotary kiln line became uncompromising. Now the Chinese claimed that they had invited offers from the Danes' German competitors, which was soon discovered by the FLS people to be untrue as they received information from their paid personal connections inside the nationalist government's civil service system.[135] And no further mention was made that the Danes were to handle the bank connection.[136] F.L. Smidth & Co. won the order in March 1936, which coincided with the extension of Bonde's and Larsen's contracts.[137] However, this involved Danish acceptance of an extraordinarily long credit, meaning that the last 20% of the payment was not to be made until 1942. This meant that in reality, F.L. Smidth & Co. had had to take on a long-term co-ownership of the factory without any prospect of direct control of the investment or share in the returns from the cement production there.

Jiang Nan (1935–1936)

The pattern of the pressure suddenly felt by the Danes in China became clear when the contract was finally settled in May 1936 for the delivery of a new cement factory at the village of Jiang Nan on the Yangtze river approx. 30 km east of Nanjing. The Jiang Nan plant, which would be China's largest cement factory with two rotary kilns of 131 m each, would be able to provide the booming construction activities along the Nanjing-Shanghai axis with cement at unprecedented low prices. In other words, this was an attractive order, but it was only landed after a tough negotiation process during which any thought of strong influence on the customers' political and financial foundations was irrelevant.[138] This was not least due to the fact that the Kiang Nan Cement Company was in reality established at the initiative of the Chee Hsin Cement Company, which two years earlier had managed to eliminate the strong Danish control of the factory in Tangshan. When Niels Jensen, who at this time had replaced Tyge Møller as manager of FLS' work in China, and Erik Nyholm from Leth Møller & Co. turned up for the negotiations in Tianjin in March 1935, they were met by a strong counterpart.

From a Chinese point of view, these negotiations were their first opportunity to seriously reap the benefits from the Danish elimination from the core of the Chee Hsin Cement Company, marked by Schmit-Jensen's exit. Thus liberated, the Chinese were able throughout the negotiation process to play off the Danes against their German competitors Polysius, Krupp and Miag. Considering the Danish prices, which were far above those of their competitors, Erik Nyholm concluded that the Danish starting point was poor. In other words, the Danish-German competition enabled the Chinese to reduce the unnecessarily high costs of their previous collaboration with almost exclusively F.L. Smidth & Co.

The Chinese exercised their control of the negotiations by deliberately leaking the German prices to the Danes so that the latter were forced to make competitive counter offers. In Erik Nyholm's view, it was only when, following "... endless whiskeys and sodas at Chinese dancing halls and at less respectable Chinese houses with virgins", they had succeeded in establishing trust with a high-ranking member of the Yuan-Shikai family who through managing director Yuan in Tangshan still held considerable power in the group, that the Danes had learnt about the German prices and had thus been able to make a lower offer.[139] But in reality, the Chinese pressure was becoming increasingly heavy.

A month passed before the negotiations were completed, following a final phase during which it had occurred to Erik Nyholm – again according to himself – to suggest doubling the factory's capacity. If the Chee Hsin Cement Company agreed to such a large-scale purchase, they could be offered such low prices by F.L. Smidth & Co. that they could sell their cement at prices so low that it would be possible for them to win the cement market in the entire Yangtze valley. For the Danes, this resulted in large financial concessions. First of all, the Chinese were allowed to wait five years before paying the last 20% of the purchase sum. This meant that Nyholm and Jensen accepted that not only the extension in Sai Chuen, but also the new and very large cement factory at Jiang Nan would be partly owned by the Danes – including the risk this implied – into the 1940s. At the same time, they were forced to reduce their prices to a level which was so low that internally among the FLS people, this was seen as a downright investment in the future Chinese business. Stig-Nielsen's reaction to the order was that no profits would probably be earned, but that spare part orders would result in some business: "I am inclined to think that with our present plants in China... spare part orders will so to speak almost be able to run the Shanghai Office".[140]

Although the Jiang Nan order might be seen as an investment, it did not in any way commit the Chinese. Formally, F.L. Smidth & Co. had no influence at all on the way in which the Chinese chose to manage the Danish investment. Direct co-ownership – possibly achieved by payments in shares for machine deliveries – might have been a more attractive solution. But this was hardly a real alternative – in the eyes of neither the Chinese nor the Danes. To the Chinese on their part, Danish management control was hardly imaginable. They had only just succeeded in eliminating this type of control in Tangshan – after 25 years. Accepting an offer of prices so low that the Danes in fact paid some part of the technology transfer was a much smoother path to take towards a more trusting relationship. As Stig-Nielsen summed this up to Niels Jensen:

Personally, I believe that we are now facing a radical change in our relationship to Chee Hsin. As you know, when a man in China who has been in power for many years dies, all his advisers are always outed or in some other way rendered impossible. We also saw this when Li Hsi Ming died; at that time, not only his Chinese helpers but also Schmit-Jensen – and to a certain extent F.L. Smidth & Co. – had to be thrown overboard according to Chinese custom ... . All of this has probably been strongly instrumental in prices becoming so low, and my present view of the Kiang Nan affair is that in the ongoing construction of this factory and in your day-to-day contact with the new people you must make sure to build a trusting relationship with the new generation similar to that which had for many years been developed with the Li Shi Ming generation. It is evident that you have a large task ahead of you, and I believe we cannot overestimate the importance of your active and abundant involvement with the people at Kiang Nan.[141]

With a trusting relationship reestablished, an effort had to be made to convince the Chinese that their money would stretch further when buying from the Danes than from the German competitors. This was because the experience from the Niang Nan order was that competing exclusively on prices was not a Danish possibility. As expressed by Stig-Nielsen: "This is of course a completely insane approach, and if our firm were to win orders on this basis we would soon be out of business". Instead, it was necessary to convince the Chinese that the key issue

> ... was not solely the question of manufacturing and selling machines, but that the issue regarding the service we can deliver is at least as important, and that a staff of trained people as is available in our company should not be overlooked, which means that at the end of the day, our prices must be higher than those of our competitors, but that this is again a bigger advantage for our customers than the disadvantage the price difference might be.

In a Danish perspective, direct investment in the Chinese cement factories was not a desirable alternative either. If the Danes stepped into the circle of Chinese cement producers, the other cement producers would immediately be transformed into direct competitors who would seek to obtain machinery from other suppliers. Unless they joined a cartel or monopoly-like setup, as had been in the pipeline with CCMA, or they were in an extraordinarily strong position as in Siam in the 1920s, their direct investment in a cement manufacturer would, in other words, exclude them from the technological field which constituted a key area and their basis for existence.

With the loss of control emerging in China around 1935, the strategy had to be based in a new way on F.L. Smidth & Co.'s role as research centre and directed towards the customers' wishes to have access to the globally compiled knowledge bank administered – in China – by the staff at the company's offices in Shanghai. The competences at the Shanghai office therefore needed to be adjusted to match the strategy. This was why Niels Jensen had been appointed office manager. His profile was namely primarily within engineering, and thus of a completely different nature than that represented by Stig-Nielsen, whose diplomatic skills had, in the previous period, been supplemented by more technologically strong profiles at the factories. This became apparent in particular on a number of occasions when Erik Nyholm complained about what he saw as Niels Jensen's lack of understanding of the role the Danes should seek to play in China. He exemplified this in 1934, referring to Niels Jensen's contribution to the FLS activities regarding the factory plans about to materialise in Chongqing in the Sichuan province:

> One thing about Niels Jensen – if only he would stop being too clever and believe that everything is as in Europe, because out here you often need to be a promoter and guide the Chinese, he doesn't understand this – particularly not a scheme such as that in Szechuan in the interior – there you need to tell the Chinese to do so and so. I have tried to inform him of this without putting pressure on him.[142]

Whereas in previous times both diplomatic and technical skills had been represented by one person – Stig-Nielsen – an effort was now being made to specialise and thus upgrade within both fields. As was formulated by the FLS senior management in 1934, the reason for acquiring Erik Nyholm from Leth-Møller & Co. was indeed that F.L. Smidth & Co. were in need of a China expert with a large network. A person who knew the codes regarding "... squeeze questions arising from time to time", and who would be able to handle different "... delicate matters which under no circumstances can be arranged by any newcomer to China".[143] In contrast to this, Niels Jensen clearly represented the engineering skills which caused Erik Nyholm to characterise him as "clever", and which also manifested themselves on several occasions when Niels Jensen requested that the Shanghai office be expanded by another engineer rather than the "... non-technical" Erik Nyholm.[144]

Chongqing (1935–1936)

Erik Nyholm's reference to the Chungking project as an illustration of Niels Jensen's incompetence was not accidental. When this project began to stir in 1934, it was on the cards that there would be a need for a Danish contribution of the type he himself would be able to deliver.

At the end of 1934, Erik Nyholm reported that he had made contact with "... some big strong French and English finance groups which intend to invest money here in China", and that these capitalists would not only finance a railway line from Chongqing to Chengdu, but were also contemplating building a cement factory in Sichuan.[145] The groups in question consisted of "... the French Fathers (Catholic Millian, who is extremely rich) and the French finance group as well as a bit of Chinese capital", and although this was evidently a French undertaking, it was Nyholm's opinion that F.L. Smidth & Co. could expect to become involved in the project as he personally was "... a member of the French syndicate". Based on this description, the organisational and financial contexts might well seem rather vague. F.L. Smidth & Co. therefore felt a need to mobilise their political/organisational resources so as to make their partners and investors come together and set the project in motion. Following Niels Jensen's visit to Chongqing in November 1934 to make sure suitable sites were actually available for the establishment of cement factories, this meant that the project was now in the hands of Erik Nyholm. Thus, in November 1935, he was staying in Chongqing to pull the right strings: "But, by being constantly with the Chinese, I got into the 'Marrow of the bone', learning about the intrigues between the promoters and also their weaknesses".[146] His attention was not only directed towards identifying the group that appeared to be the most promising business partner, but also towards the financial basis necessary to ensure that the project was in fact brought into being. Independently of the business partners involved in the project, Nyholm therefore held a number of meetings with "... the Commissioner of Finance and the Government people here who are going to put up a substantial part of the money". However, in December, offers of long credits and low prices made by German competitors once more placed the FLS people in an unfavourable negotiating position.[147] The offer of privileged access to the Danish technological know-how was not sufficient for the Chinese backers – led by the local financier K.P. Hu – to be willing to accept the higher Danish prices. Nyholm therefore saw only two possible solutions. One was "... to apply to Nanking and Generalissimo Chiang Kai-shek who is very interested in Szechuan", because, as he mentioned to Stig-Nielsen and the FLS management, "*you yourself know from experience that something can always be done through the upper ten of China*". In other words, Erik Nyholm wanted to make use of Denmark's good connections in the political and financial support base. The other possible solution was to indirectly provide the capital necessary to accommodate the higher Danish prices. In Nyholm's own words, "... we must arm ourselves against the Germans' long credits by cooperating with local financiers in China".

In mid-January 1936, Erik Nyholm was back in Shanghai, where he and Niels Jensen spent some time talking to guarantors from Bank of China and meeting with Chiang Kai-shek's vice-minister of industries,

Dr. Hsü. Following a decision by the Generalissimo himself, the result seemed to be that the factory would receive an investment of USD 400,000 from the nationalist regime as well as contributions from Erik Nyholm's financially strong network in Shanghai.[148] When the contract with the Szechuen Cement Company was signed in March, both Nyholm and Jensen stated that they had been successful in utilising their contacts in their political and financial support base to place pressure on the promoters of the factory. Erik Nyholm summed up how

> In the last days just when we were negotiating here about the contract, Mr. Ou the Salt Bank manager, the Commissioner of Finance, Mr. Ning and my old friend from Tientsin Mr. Yen were all here and that, combined with the good influence of Dr. Hsü, made them decide to buy our machinery, even if they did cut us down.[149]

In Erik Nyholm's view, his old friendship with Mr. Yen had been particularly valuable: "... he even got Mr. Ou the Salt Bank manager come down to Shanghai to be there to see that I did not lose the order ...", whereas Niels Jensen considered the pressure from the nationalist regime through direct contact between Dr. Hsü and Chiang Kai-shek to be decisive. Erik Nyholm once more displayed his self-confident evaluation of his own role and, in spite of his status as newly married, added a sleazy comment suggesting that his intimate acquaintance with K.P. Hu's wife had played a decisive role: "In spite of the rotten life in Shanghai, you get compensations now and then". The order was won, helped along by various assistance and pressure from a Chinese and Western network of politicians, government officials and financiers – and not as a result of competition based exclusively on price and quality.

War Precautions (1937–1938)

Since the Japanese invasion of Manchuria in 1931 and the establishment of the puppet state of Manzhouguo in 1932, the political situation in China had been marked by Chinese guerrilla warfare and Japanese attempts to provoke an excuse to expand the invasion southward. From 1937, southern China did indeed become the target of a Japanese invasion, and F.L. Smidth & Co. had to adapt to the situation that the long credits they had provided when selling equipment to Sai Chuen and Jiang Nan now involved major political risks. Cement was an important strategic resource for the building of fortifications and infrastructure. In other words, the Danes were now suddenly in possession of major shares of an industry that would become interesting to both of the warring parties – but of course without control possibilities of the sort that would have been implied in case of direct investments.

During the summer of 1937, the political conflict developed into full-scale warfare.[150] The Battle of Beijing was commenced in July, and in August, Chiang Kai-shek let his troops retreat to the Yangtse valley around Shanghai and Nanjing. Mid-August saw the beginning of the Battle of Shanghai, and at the beginning of November, Chiang Kai-shek had to order withdrawal to Nanjing. The Japanese campaign was now directed towards the government city, and in mid-November, evacuation of Nanjing's western population groups had to be initiated. Following the Japanese decision on 7 December to capture the city, only 13 days passed before the last fortifications fell. The Chinese army was routed, while Nanjing suffered a seven-week long genocide by the Japanese army of the civilian population during December-January 1937–1938.[151] At the same time, Japanese troops continued to move towards Jiangsu and Wuhan, which were captured in October 1938, while the Chinese nationalist government fled to Chungking. Concurrently, enclaves along the Chinese coast fell, including Canton. For F.L. Smidth & Co. the situation had changed drastically. Was complete or partial withdrawal from the ownerships in Sai Chuen and Jiang Nan possible as in 1926 in order to escape the political risks? Or was it necessary for the Danes to stay in the area in an attempt to control the situation and make sure F.L. Smidth & Co. received the money owing to them?

If the official FLS representatives left China, their possibilities to control the investments would, in a very short time, be reduced to an absolute minimum. However, the question soon emerged whether the same resources as previously were needed. As it became clear that no further factory projects would be initiated for a long time, sales and engineering competences had to take a step back in favour of actors who were able to navigate Danish interests through a situation of war. Towards the turn of the year 1937–1938, Erik Nyholm returned to Copenhagen at his own initiative, and Niels Jensen asked for permission to also travel home to Denmark.[152] However, Copenhagen asked him to travel to the Philippines to explore the possibilities of a contract for an asbestos-cement factory.[153] Moreover, the head office was somewhat puzzled that Erik Nyholm had travelled to Copenhagen without first asking for permission since their plan was that he, who was their politically trained resource, together with the FLS office's secretary, American born Margaret Stang-Lund, was to stay, whereas Niels Jensen could be transferred to other tasks.[154] It was their clear assessment that their primary need was now to have a person well versed in Chinese political conditions at the Shanghai office. However, with Erik Nyholm no longer there, Niels Jensen had to take his place. Following his trip to the Philippines in the winter of 1938, Niels Jensen therefore conducted F.L. Smidth & Co.'s business in China, primarily from Hong Kong and Canton.

At the Shanghai office, day-to-day operations were in the hands of a secretary. However, Stang-Lund was an independently operating personality who enjoyed great trust among the other FLS staff. Moreover, as regards the handling of interests at the Chinese factories, it soon turned out to be an advantage that the day-to-day operations of the office were taken care of by a person in a formally inferior position who was unable to initiate negotiations with the Japanese who now began to arrive – often armed to the teeth.

Exit from Sai Chuen (1937–1938)

The Danish de facto co-ownership of the Chinese cement industry was the result of the strong pressure F.L. Smidth & Co. had been subjected to during the negotiations regarding the orders for the building of the factories. This left F.L. Smidth & Co. with poor possibilities to control their investments. In Sai Chuen, the debts owing to the Danes from the building of the factory in 1937 were instalments for the delivery of the latest extension in 1936, which were supposed to have been paid in full but had only been paid in part. In addition to this was the 20% credit, which, according to the agreement, was not to be paid until 1942. In other words, large sums were at stake when Niels Jensen travelled to Canton in 1937 to negotiate, assisted by Svend Bonde, with the factory's senior management under the leadership of managing director Sun Fo and the government apparatus represented by Chui King Tong.[155]

The Chinese relied on the terms of payment in the contract and referred to the conditions caused by the war. At the negotiations in January 1938, the response from the Chinese was thus indeed very brief; they would like to help the Danes, but they were out of funds. This did not mean that all options were exhausted, however. Niels Jensen leaked via his Chinese interpreter that F.L. Smidth & Co. would be satisfied if they received 85% of the outstanding amount. This caused Chui King Tong and Sun Fo to suggest that F.L. Smidth & Co. would get the 85%, provided it could be arranged that the provincial government first paid the full amount and the Danes then refunded approx. 15% in cash. Niels Jensen accepted this, only to receive a new Chinese message that due to the war situation, they were only able to raise half of the outstanding amount. Managing director Sun therefore suggested that the Chinese paid the 50%, and that the Danes then refunded 15% of this in cash. On the face of it, this was a very poor solution for F.L. Smidth & Co. However, at this time, the factory had been targeted several times by Japanese air raids, and as the risk of a Japanese invasion seemed imminent – which would cause the Chinese to blow up the factory – the conclusion was, as formulated by Niels Jensen, that "... we considered it advisable to try to take whatever we could get as soon as possible ...".[156]

F.L. Smidth & Co. had now reduced their investments in Sai Chuen by 50%, and the options for control that followed from the asymmetrical relationship between the technology supplier and the technology buyers were still in play. At the turn of the year 1937–1938, the lack of spare parts in Sai Chuen was so great that a complete shutdown was looming. When the factory was expanded in 1936 and the Chinese had committed to buy new parts from F.L. Smidth & Co., this had provided the FLS people with a means of exerting pressure. As soon as the Danes had received the first instalment in February 1938, they therefore placed renewed pressure on the Chinese.[157] In a written request to the provincial government for another instalment to be paid, Niels Jensen hinted that this might be decisive for the shipment from Copenhagen of a major consignment of spare parts ordered in April 1937. This was a clear Danish threat to bring the factory to a standstill.

In June 1938, the spare parts were still in Copenhagen, and the Chinese were now requested to not only pay 50% of the spare parts order for this to be shipped but also to pay their remaining debts connected to the expansion in 1936.[158] Bringing factory operations to a standstill was not an alternative for the Chinese at this time. Cement was badly needed, and as stated by Niels Jensen "... as the spare parts are now urgently needed, we are convinced that they will do everything in their power to release the documents ...". The provincial government did indeed agree to fulfil the Danish requests. Hard pushed by the need to keep the factory running, at the end of June 1938, the Chinese government officials had therefore – helped along by further secret commission – produced the money, which settled the Danish account with the Canton government.[159]

Chaos in Jiang Nan (1937–1938)

The rapid Japanese advance towards Nanjing in the autumn of 1937 prevented a fast phasing-out of the Danish involvement in the Kiang Nan Cement Company. Focus was primarily on completing the building of the factory. In September, the project was so far advanced that burner master Oscar Mortensen was on his way from Denmark to Jiang Nan to oversee the start-up. It was a race against time. When the railway lines south of Shanghai were bombed, Oscar Mortensen's journey was disrupted in Hankou, whereas, following Japanese warnings of air raids on Nanjing, the leader of the factory building project, engineer Harald Badstue, fled to Shanghai on a British gunboat on the Yangtze river on 21 September.[160]

From then on, the factory building activities were at a standstill – much to the regret of both the Kiang Nan Cement Company and the main investor, the Chee Hsin Cement Company, which was the real decision-maker from Tianjin. In October, Niels Jensen travelled to Tianjin to discuss the problem with the Chee Hsin Cement Company. His point of departure was the Danish belief that it was only a matter of a short time before Shanghai would fall, and that a brand new and fully operational cement factory near Nanjing would be in imminent danger of Japanese seizure. And if the factory was seized, both the Chinese and the Danish investments would be out of control and very likely lost. In contrast, a plant that was not yet operational would hardly attract the same attention from the Japanese. The Danes had to accept, however, that the Chee Hsin Cement Company held a different opinion:

> Right from the beginning we tried to get them away from their ideas of starting the factory, but unfortunately it was impossible to convince them that this would be the right thing to do. They maintained that big quantities of cement were required by the Central Government; and partly because they wanted to keep their good relations with the Government and partly because they did not want China Portland Cement Works to skim all the cream, they were set upon getting the factory running.[161]

When the Chinese then provided guarantees of large compensation sums in case of murder of or injuries to Danes, Harald Badstue returned to Jiang Nan on 5 November. However, only a few days passed before Chiang Kai-shek ordered the Chinese troops to retreat from Shanghai, and when this turned into headlong flight, the Japanese army could advance on Nanjing. On 15 November, Harald Badstue telegraphed to Shanghai that an empty test-run of the machinery had now been completed, and that test production was being prepared. At this time, the Japanese army was very close to the factory, and on 17 November, Kiang Nan Cement Company told Harald Badstue to take flight.

The cement factory was located close to the railway line Shanghai-Nanjing, which was monitored by the Japanese 16th division. When the main attack on Nanjing was launched on 7 December, the Japanese had been present in the Jiang Nan area for some time. At the same time, the focus of the collaboration between F.L. Smidth & Co. and the Kiang Nan Cement Company/the Chee Hsin Cement Company became directed towards securing the interests of the parties in the cement factory.[162] From both sides it was made clear that F.L. Smidth & Co. had to claim a direct interest in the factory plant. If they failed to do so, the factory would appear to be Chinese property, in which case it was likely to be destroyed or seized by the Japanese. Niels Jensen consulted the Danish representative in China, Oscar Oxholm. In November, this resulted in a suggestion from Niels Jensen that an official joint message be sent from the Danish legation and F.L. Smidth & Co. to inform the Japanese navy and army as well as Japan's representative in Shanghai that the factory had not been completed, and that F.L. Smidth & Co. had not yet fulfilled their guarantees. Considering that the last 20% of the purchase sum was not due until 1942, it was Oxholm's assessment that this would enable them to assert to the Japanese that the machinery was still to be considered Danish property. This would seem even more likely if an FLS employee made an appearance in Jiang Nan – "... as a kind of supervisor, and so that the Danish flag might be hoisted near to his house at the works".[163] At the beginning of December 1937, the Danish consul general in Shanghai, Poul Scheel, wrote to his Japanese colleague about the matter, asking the army, navy and air force to avoid destruction and seizure of the factory plant. Scheel also organised a private dinner party, making sure that Niels Jensen was seated next to the Japanese consul general in Shanghai, Okazaki, who through his father was connected to one of F.L. Smidth & Co.'s largest customers in Japan, the family-owned Asano Cement Company.

At the same time, F.L. Smidth & Co. had succeeded in finding a Danish person, Bernard Sindberg, who was based in Shanghai and, according to Margaret Stang-Lund, would be able to handle the dangerous task it was to travel to Jiang Nan. Sindberg had come to Shanghai as a sailor in 1937 but had no employment when Stang-Lund contacted him about the watchman job, which would be quite well paid. He was therefore keen to get the job, and as Niels Jensen described the situation, Sindberg represented completely new competences at F.L. Smidth & Co.:

> Mr. Sindberg has previously been in the Foreign Legion, and he had been working as chauffeur for Mr. Pembroke Stephens, the English journalist who was recently killed in the French concession during the siege of Nantao. He is a young chap at about 30, and is somewhat of a rough-neck and a die-hard.[164]

On 2 December 1937, Sindberg travelled to Jiang Nan accompanied by a representative from the German company Siemssen & Co., which had delivered the factory's electrical equipment. They arrived in Jiang Nan on 5 December and found the machinery unharmed, but the Chinese fortifications were so extensive that the factory appeared to be an obvious target of attack for the Japanese. In order to emphasise the foreign interests, they planted two flagpoles, one flying the Danish Dannebrog, and one flying the flag of Nazi Germany.[165]

The factory got through December unharmed, and after the turn of the year, the Japanese consul general in Nanjing, Okamoto, stated that the atmosphere between Sindberg and the Japanese troops was positive.[166] At the same time, however, representatives from the Japanese industry began to arrive at the factory, which was housing approx. 100 employees with their families, while 3–4,000 Chinese refugees had sought protection under the Danish flag in a refugee camp outside of the factory fence.[167] At the beginning of January, an employee from the Tokyo Chamber of Commerce and Industry in Japan inspected the factory and took a series of photos of the plant. It was now clear that the Japanese interest in the plant would not cease.

In February, the machinery was scrutinised by a representative from the Onoda Cement Company, Japan's second-largest cement group, who stated openly that the Japanese would like the factory to begin production so as to manufacture cement for the army.[168] The Danes were successful in putting off the Japanese wish during the winter and spring, but as time passed, the pressure increased, and it became clear that the situation was unsustainable. In March 1938, Sindberg was replaced by another Dane, Einar Nielsen, following a number of clashes with the Japanese soldiers over his efforts to save the Chinese refugees at the factory.[169] In May, the FLS office in Shanghai was ransacked by the Japanese, searching for information about the factory.[170] While this was happening, the line of action regarding the critical situation with the Japanese was being managed by the secretary Margaret Stang-Lund.[171] The outcome was that F.L. Smidth & Co. acknowledged their ownership of the machinery. At the same time, an intermediary position had to be sought by reference to the fact that the decision-making authority regarding the factory rested with the Chinese. This might result in one of two possible scenarios. Either, the Japanese army would seize the factory, or the Japanese would try to initiate negotiations for a take-over, which might place the Danes in a difficult situation. Stang-Lund therefore suggested that FLS should try to evade the overall responsibility in their talks with the Japanese:

> ... if they wish to make concessions to the fact that we still have money owing us by Chee Hsin on the plant, and guarantees to fulfil under our contract with Chee Hsin, then the obvious thing is for them to negotiate with Chee Hsin ... In any case it seems to me advisable for us to keep out of it as much as we possibly can ... .

Their wish to receive their last money owing to them, combined with their wish to be on good terms with the Japanese cement groups, might make it difficult to resist the pressure from the Japanese. But if F.L. Smidth & Co. entered into such negotiations on their own, they would in reality have fallen out with the Chee Hsin Cement Company and thus outplayed their role in China.

In March 1938, both the Onoda Cement Company and the Asano Cement Company contacted the FLS office in Tokyo to obtain information about the factory and the Danish interests in it. The reaction from Copenhagen was to try to avoid further involvement:

> As you will realize, this question may develop into a very complicated affair, if the Japanese – as your telegram seems to indicate – should offer to pay us the last instalment, release us from the guarantees, and take over the factory – with or without the consent of the Chinese. It would, of course, be very tempting for us to get our money for the machinery supplied from one of the said Japanese firms, but we may run the risk of spoiling our good relationship with the Chee Hsin Cement Co. On the other hand, we fully realize that care must be taken not to jeopardize the good relation to the Onoda

Cement Company or the Asano Cement Company, but we hope that these firms will understand that we also have to pay regard to our Chinese clients.[172]

So far, the order was therefore to evade the enquiries from the Japanese cement manufacturers to the extent possible.

However, in April–May 1938, the view of the senior management in Copenhagen began to change, not least because the Chinese owners were forced to change theirs. The prospects of a prolonged Japanese occupation of eastern China and a continued war with the Chiang Kai-shek regime led from remote western China turned the Jiang Nan factory into a millstone around the necks of its owners. As long as the risk of Japanese seizure persisted – which would be the case for the duration of the Japanese occupation – starting the plant or announcing it to be functional would seem to be acts of treachery. Moreover, they would need to maintain that the plant could not be started, since they had insisted for a long time that it was not functional. And for as long as the factory was not running, neither the Danish nor the Chinese investors were profiting from it. An actual sale to the Japanese would be tantamount to treachery.

In June, the Chee Hsin managers H.W. Yuan and J.L. Chen and the Kiang Nan manager Wang Dao arrived at the office in Shanghai to inform the FLS people that they had been approached by Mitsui Bussan Kaisha – the Onoda Cement Company's representative in China.[173] This direct contact between the Chinese and the Japanese opened a possibility for the Danes to keep out of the scrape. While negotiations still appeared to be taking place at the end of a Japanese gun barrel, the Chinese had had no other options but to try to win time by maintaining that the factory had not been completed. Several attempts had certainly been made to secretly initiate negotiations with the Onoda people, but as Niels Jensen reported this to Copenhagen, the risk of internal Chinese conflicts was far too high while it was still almost certain that the cement would end up in the hands of the Japanese army:

> The Chee Hsin and Kiang Nan people have always been on very good terms with the Chinese Government and have a lot of connections among the highest officials, and Chee Hsin and Kiang Nan would therefore spoil their future in China entirely if they agreed to come to some understanding with the Japanese.[174]

The Japanese request for the transfer of 51% of the share capital had been unacceptable to the Chinese. In Shanghai, J.L. Chen and Wang Dao discussed the matter with Niels Jensen. Chen then travelled to Europe in July to negotiate with Siemssen & Co. and F.L. Smidth & Co. about whether a change in ownership of the factory might be a way out of the deadlock.[175] The result was that Germany and Copenhagen gave their consent, and

Chen instructed his people in Tianjin and Shanghai to investigate the possibilities of a new German-Danish ownership construction. J.L. Chen remained in Europe to proceed with the negotiations.

In November 1938, the tactics had been settled by mutual understanding between J.L. Chen and the F.L. Smidth & Co. management. The German-Danish take-over of the factory was to take place by:

> ... arranging an ostensible foreign ownership of the Kiang Nan Cement Co., in the way that a large proportion of the company's shares are turned over to a German firm in Tientsin as "payment" for the motors, etc. installed by them, the idea being to approach our firm upon Mr. Jensen's return to Shanghai and for us to take over further shares in the same way.[176]

This model would enable the Chinese to legitimately insist that the shares had been turned over to the German and Danish companies in return for the machinery they had delivered. With co-ownership transferred to western European actors, the factory could then be started at less risk of Japanese seizure, and the various actors could expect to begin receiving return on their investments. F.L. Smidth & Co. would then be free to phase out their involvement, even by selling shares to the Japanese. This outcome of the chain of events might not be desirable from a Chinese point of view, but in a formal sense this was an issue to be sorted out by F.L. Smidth & Co., who could, in this way, accommodate both the Chinese wish to get the factory started and the Japanese wish to take possession of it.

Notes

1 For the changed relations between the continents after 1700, see Kenneth Pomeranz: *The Great Divergence: China, Europe and the making of the Modern World Economy* (Princeton, 2000). The overall description in the following of the Chinese conditions is based Lloyd E. Eastman: *Family, Fields, and Ancestors. Constancy and Change in China's Social and Economic History, 1550–1949* (Oxford, 1988). Philip Richardson: *Economic Change in China, c. 1800-1950* (Cambridge, 1999). Erik Baark: *Lightning Wires. The Telegraph and China's Technological Modernization, 1860–1890. Contributions in Asian Studies, Number 6* (Greenwood Press, 1997). Jonathan Fenby: *The Penguin History of Modern China. The Fall and Rise of a Great Power 1850–2009* (London: Penguin Books, 2008). For western companies in China, see G. C. Allen and Audrey G. Donnithorne: *Western Enterprise in Far Eastern Economic Development. China and Japan* (London, 1954).
2 Richardson, *Economic Change*, 13.
3 Baark, *Lightning Wires*, 2.
4 Fenby, *The Penguin History of Modern China*, 38.
5 Allen and Donnithorne, *Western Enterprise*, 25.
6 Allen and Donnithorne, *Western Enterprise*, 25, 69–75 and 133ff.

7 Richardson, *Economic Change*, 92.
8 Ole Lange: *Finansmænd, stråmænd og mandariner: C.F. Tietgen, Privatbanken og Store Nordiske: etablering 1868-76* (København, 1978), passim.
9 *Betænkning afgiven af den af Udenrigsministeriet i Henhold til kgl. Resolution af 24. Juli 1906 nedsatte Kommission til Forberedelse af en Omordning af Udenrigsministeriet og Danmarks Repræsentation i Udlandet* (København, 1908), 84. Mads Kirkebæk: "The Establishment of a Danish Legation in China in 1912," in *China and Denmark: Relations since 1674*, ed. Keld Erik Brødsgaard and Mads Kirkebæk, Nordic Institute of Asian Studies (København, 2001), 48–72.
10 Lange, *Finansmænd*, 171–173.
11 Steen Andersen and Kurt Jacobsen: *Foss* (København, 2008), 74–75. Lange, *Finansmænd*, 171–172.
12 Knudåge Riisager: *F.L. Smidth & Co. 1882-1922* (København, 1921), 194, Morten Pedersen: *De danske cementfabrikkers bebyggelsesmiljø: en undersøgelse af forandringer i en branches industrielle miljø ved den anden industrielle revolution* (Odense: University Press of Southern Denmark, 2008), 36–37.
13 *The Chronicle & Directory for China, Japan, Corea, Indo-China, Straits Settlements, Malay States, Siam, Netherlands India, Borneo, The Philipines etc. for the Year 1899* (Hong Kong, 1899), 238. *20th Century Impressions of Hongkong, Shanghai and Other Treaty Ports of China. Their History, People, Commerce, Industries, and Ressources* (London, 1908), 828.
14 Riisager, *F.L. Smidth & Co.*, 194. *Cement Plants and Schemes in the Far East. Compiled by F.L. Smidth & Co., A/S, Shanghai August 1932* (FLSA). Nigel Cameron: *Power* (Oxford: Oxford University Press, 1982).
15 Det Danske Udvandrerarkiv, Aalborg Municipal Archives. Green Island Cement Co. Hongkong, Museum of Northern Jutland (sagsnr. 6272).
16 Riisager, *F.L. Smidth & Co.*, 194. *Kominorer 1901-1937* (FLSA). *Rotary Kilns supplied by F.L. Smidth & Co., 1938* (FLSA). *Cement Plants and Schemes in the Far East. Compiled by F.L. Smidth & Co., 1932* (FLSA).
17 Det Danske Udvandrerarkiv, Aalborg Aalborg Municipal Archives. Green Island Cement Co. Hongkong, Museum of Northern Jutland (sagsnr. 6272).
18 Unless otherwise stated, the following account of the Chee Hsin Cement Company's role in Chinese industrialisation is based on Albert Feuerwerker: "Industrial Enterprise in 20th-Century China: The Chee Hsin Cement Co.," in *Studies in the Economic History of Late Imperial China. Handicraft, Modern Industry, and the State*, ed. Albert Feuerwerker, Michigan Monographs in Chinese Studies, Vol. 70 (Michigan, 1995), 273–308.
19 Feuerwerker, "Industrial Enterprise." Elisabeth Köll: *From Cotton Mill to Business Empire. The Emergence of Regional Entreprises in Modern China*. Harvard East Asian Monographs No. 229 (Harvard, 2003), 41.
20 Feuerwerker, "Industrial Enterprise," 276–280.
21 *Rotary Kilns Supplied by F.L. Smidth & Co. 1938* (FLSA). *Cement Plants and Schemes in the Far East* (FLSA).
22 Jonathan Fenby: *Generalissimo. Chiang Kai-Shek and the China he lost* (London, 2003), 30.
23 *Kraks Blaa Bog 1949* (København, 1950), Harry Schrøder.
24 According to F.L. Smidth & Co.'s anniversary publications, Harry Schrøder assumed the role as company manager, whereas internal notes more carefully placed him in positions as chemical engineer and company manager for long periods when H. Günther was displaced and only held the company

manager position as a matter of form. Risager, *F.L. Smidth & Co.*, 211. *Cement Plants and Schemes in the Far East. Compiled by F.L. Smidth & Co. 1932* (FLSA).

25 *Rotary Kilns Supplied by F.L. Smidth & Co.* 1938 (FLSA). "The New Plant of The Chee Hsin Cement Co., Ltd.," in *The Far Eastern Review*, December 1921.

26 Povl Drachmann: *F.L. Smidth & Co. 1922–1932* (København, 1932), 91–93.

27 *T. Stig-Nielsen to Poul Larsen*, 18 November 1924; *O.V. Mørch to T. Stig-Nielsen*, 16 August 1924, T. Stig-Nielsen, Oriental 1922–1926; *Cement Plants and Schemes in the Far East. Compiled by F.L. Smidth & Co.* (FLSA).

28 *O.V. Mørch to T. Stig-Nielsen*, 16 August 1924; *F.L. Smidth & Co. to T. Stig-Nielsen*, 21 August 1932; *T. Stig-Nielsen to F.L. Smidth & Co., Copenhagen*, 11 September 1924, Japan-Kina 1923–1932 (FLSA).

29 *T. Stig-Nielsen to Poul Larsen*, 18 November 1924, Japan-Kina 1923–1932 (FLSA).

30 *O.V. Mørch to T. Stig-Nielsen*, 16 August 1924, Japan-Kina 1923–1932 (FLSA).

31 *T. Stig-Nielsen to Poul Larsen*, 18 November 1924, Japan-Kina 1923–1932 (FLSA).

32 *Axel V. Jensen to T. Stig-Nielsen*, 27 February 1924, T. Stig-Nielsen, Oriental 1922–1926 (FLSA).

33 *Axel V. Jensen to T. Stig-Nielsen*, 27 February 1924, T. Stig-Nielsen, Oriental 1922–1926 (FLSA).

34 *T. Stig-Nielsen to Mssrs. F.L. Smidth & Co., Copenhagen*, 11 July 1924, T. Stig-Nielsen, Oriental 1922–1926 (FLSA).

35 *O.V. Mørch to T. Stig-Nielsen*, 8 August 1924, T. Stig-Nielsen, Oriental 1922–1926 (FLSA).

36 *T. Stig-Nielsen to Mssrs. F.L. Smidth & Co., Copenhagen*, 11 July 1924, T. Stig-Nielsen, Oriental 1922-1926 (FLSA).

37 *T. Stig-Nielsen to Mssrs. F.L. Smidth & Co., Copenhagen*, 20 March 1925; *Axel V. Jensen to T. Stig-Nielsen*, 24 October 1924, T. Stig-Nielsen, Oriental 1922–1926 (FLSA).

38 *Axel V. Jensen to T. Stig-Nielsen*, 24 October 1924, T. Stig-Nielsen, Oriental 1922–1926 (FLSA).

39 *T. Stig-Nielsen to Poul Larsen*, 18 November 1924, T. Stig-Nielsen, Oriental 1922–1926 (FLSA).

40 *T. Stig-Nielsen to Mssrs. F.L. Smidth & Co., Copenhagen*, 20 March 1925, T. Stig-Nielsen, Oriental 1922–1926 (FLSA).

41 Feuerwerker, "Industrial Enterprise," 275, 283–284. *Cement Plants and Schemes in the Far East. Compiled by F.L. Smidth & Co.* (FLSA).

42 *T. Stig-Nielsen to Poul Larsen*, 6 December 1923, T. Stig-Nielsen, Oriental 1922–26 (FLSA).

43 *T. Stig-Nielsen to Poul Larsen*, 6 December 1923, T. Stig-Nielsen, Oriental 1922–26 (FLSA).

44 The following overview on the partners and networks are based on *T. Stig-Nielsen to Poul Larsen*, 19 May 1924; *F.L. Smidth & Co. Copenhagen to T. Stig-Nielsen*, 20 May 1924, T. Stig-Nielsen, Oriental 1922–26 (FLSA). *Cement Plants and Schemes in the Far East. Compiled by F.L. Smidth & Co.* (FLSA).

45 *T. Stig-Nielsen to N. Max Jensen*, 10 November 1924, T. Stig-Nielsen, Oriental 1922–26 (FLSA).

46 T. *Stig Nielsen to Poul Larsen*, 20 November 1924, T. Stig-Nielsen, Oriental 1922–26 (FLSA).

47 Rajeswary Ampalavanar Brown: *Chinese Business Enterprise in Asia* (Cengage Learning EMEA, 1995), 137. W.G. Huff: *The Economic Growth of Singapore. Trade and Development in the 20th Century* (Cambridge, 1995), 147, 225, 459.

48 T. *Stig Nielsen to Poul Larsen*, 20 November 1924, T. Stig-Nielsen, Oriental 1922–26 (FLSA).

49 Howard Boorman, ed.: *Biographical Dictionary of Republican China*, Vol. III (New York, 1970), 362–365.

50 Fenby, *The Penguin History of Modern China*, 145.

51 T. *Stig-Nielsen to Axel V. Jensen*, 29 September 1924, T. Stig-Nielsen, Oriental 1922–26 (FLSA).

52 T. *Stig-Nielsen to Poul Larsen*, 20 November 1924, T. Stig-Nielsen, Oriental 1922–26 (FLSA).

53 T. *Stig-Nielsen to C.A. Møller*, 22 December 1923; T. *Stig-Nielsen to C.A. Møller*, 15 January 1924; *Axel V. Jensen to T. Stig-Nielsen*, 29 February 1924, Japan-Kina 1923–1932 (FLSA).

54 T. *Stig-Nielsen to Axel V. Jensen*, 29 September 1924, T. Stig-Nielsen, Oriental 1922–26 (FLSA).

55 T. *Stig-Nielsen to Poul Larsen*, 6 December 1923, T. Stig-Nielsen, Oriental 1922–26 (FLSA).

56 T. *Stig-Nielsen to Poul Larsen*, 20 November 1924, T. Stig-Nielsen, Oriental 1922–26 (FLSA).

57 T. *Stig-Nielsen to Poul Larsen*, 25 July 1926, T. Stig-Nielsen, Oriental 1922–26 (FLSA).

58 T. *Stig-Nielsen to O.V. Mørch*, 17 September 1924, T. Stig-Nielsen, Oriental 1922–26 (FLSA).

59 T. *Stig-Nielsen to Poul Larsen*, 17 December 1926, Japan-Kina 1923–37 (FLSA).

60 T. *Stig-Nielsen to Poul Larsen*, 5 February 1929, T. Stig-Nielsen, Oriental 1929 (FLSA).

61 T. *Stig-Nielsen to Poul Larsen*, 5 September 1929, T. Stig-Nielsen, Oriental 1929 (FLSA).

62 T. *Stig-Nielsen to Poul Larsen*, 5 February 1929; *Cement Plants and Schemes in the Far East. Compiled by F.L. Smidth & Co.* (FLSA).

63 T. *Stig-Nielsen to O.V. Mørch*, 17 December 1927, Japan-Kina 1923–1932; T. *Stig-Nielsen to C.A. Møller*, 10 July 1929, T. Stig-Nielsen, Oriental 1930 (FLSA).

64 Feuerwerker, "Industrial Enterprise," 285–286.

65 *Henrik Kauffmann to Minister of Foreign Affairs, L. Moltesen, 10 August 1928*, Japan-Kina 1923–1932; *Henrik Kauffmann to T. Stig-Nielsen*, 28 September 1929, T. Stig-Nielsen, Oriental 1929 (FLSA).

66 The order was signed by the government representative of the Canton province on 25 February 1929. T. *Stig-Nielsen to Poul Larsen*, 5 February 1929; T. *Stig-Nielsen to F.L. Smidth & Co.*, 25 February 1925, T. Stig-Nielsen, Oriental 1929 (FLSA).

67 T. *Stig-Nielsen to C.A. Møller*, 26 November 1929; T. *Stig-Nielsen to O.V. Mørch*, 30 December 1929, T. Stig-Nielsen, Oriental 1930 (FLSA).

68 C.A. *Møller to T. Stig-Nielsen*, 30 March 1930, T. Stig-Nielsen, Oriental 1930 (FLSA).

69 T. *Stig-Nielsen to F.L. Smidth & Co.*, 13 February 1930; *Carl Sørensen to T. Stig-Nielsen*, 25 June 1930; *T. Stig-Nielsen to Carl Sørensen*, 3 October 1930, T. Stig-Nielsen, Oriental 1930 (FLSA).

70 O.V. *Mørch to T. Stig-Nielsen*, 14 March 1929, T. Stig-Nielsen, Oriental 1929 (FLSA).

71 T. *Stig-Nielsen to F.L. Smidth & Co.*, 4 April 1929, T. Stig-Nielsen, Oriental 1929 (FLSA).

72 F. *Nissen to T. Stig-Nielsen*, 7 May 1929, T Stig-Nielsen, Oriental 1929; *Harry Schrøder to T. Stig-Nielsen*, 29 July 1929, Japan-Kina 1923–1932; *T. Stig-Nielsen to F.L. Smidth & Co.*, 8 August 1929, Japan-Kina 1923–1932; *Harry Schrøder to T. Stig-Nielsen*, 23 September 1929, Japan-Kina 1923–1932 (FLSA).

73 T. *Stig-Nielsen to F.L. Smidth & Co.*, 6 August 1930, Japan-Kina 1923–1932; *T. Stig-Nielsen to F.L. Smidth & Co.*, 15 February 1931, T. Stig-Nielsen, Oriental 1931 (FLSA).

74 T. *Stig-Nielsen to Poul Larsen*, 5 February 1929, Japan-China 1923–1932; *T. Stig-Nielsen to Poul Larsen*, 8 July 1929, T. Stig-Nielsen, Oriental 1929 (FLSA).

75 T. *Stig-Nielsen to Poul Larsen*, 8 July 1929, T. Stig-Nielsen, Oriental 1929 (FLSA).

76 O.V. *Mørch to T. Stig-Nielsen*, 1 August 1929, Japan-China 1923–1932 (FLSA).

77 Cement Plants and Schemes in the Far East. Compiled by F.L. Smidth & Co. O.V. *Mørch to T. Stig-Nielsen*, 5 February 1932, Japan-China 1923–1932 (FLSA).

78 T. *Stig-Nielsen to F.L. Smidth & Co.*, 19 April 1928, Japan-China 1923–1932 (FLSA).

79 T. *Stig-Nielsen to Poul Larsen*, 5 February 1929, Japan-China 1923–1932 (FLSA).

80 Bruce Kogut: "The Network as Knowledge: Generative Rules and the Emergence of Structure," in *Strategic Management Journal*, Vol. 21 (2000), 414. R. Burt: *Structural Holes: The Social Structure of Competition* (Cambridge, MA: Harvard University Press, 1992).

81 T. *Stig-Nielsen to Poul Larsen*, 5 February 1929, Japan-China 1923–1932 (FLSA).

82 E. *Schmit-Jensen to T. Stig-Nielsen*, 20 January 1929, Japan-Kina 1923–1932; *Aage Smith to T. Stig-Nielsen*, 4 March 1931, Japan-Kina 1923–1932 (FLSA).

83 E. *Schmit-Jensen to T. Stig-Nielsen*, 20 January 1929, Japan-Kina 1923–1932 (FLSA).

84 T. *Stig-Nielsen to F.L. Smidth & Co.*, 25 February 1929, T. Stig-Nielsen, Oriental 1929 (FLSA).

85 Poul *Larsen to T. Stig-Nielsen*, 27 February 1929, T. Stig-Nielsen, Oriental 1929; Valby.O.V. *Mørch to T. Stig-Nielsen*, 15 March 1929, T. Stig-Nielsen, Oriental 1929 (FLSA).

86 T. *Stig-Nielsen to E. Schmit-Jensen*, 5 April 1929, T. Stig-Nielsen, Oriental 1929 (FLSA).

87 Erik *Thune to T. Stig-Nielsen*, 15 April 1929, T. Stig-Nielsen, Oriental 1929; *E. Schmit-Jensen to T. Stig-Nielsen*, 19 April 1929, T. Stig-Nielsen, Oriental 1929 (FLSA).

88 T. *Stig-Nielsen to Erik Thune*, 29 May 1929, Japan-Kina 1923-1932; *T. Stig-Nielsen to F.L. Smidth & Co.*, 29 May 1929, Japan-Kina 1923–1932 (FLSA).

89 W. L. *Grut to T. Stig-Nielsen*, 30 June 1929, T. Stig-Nielsen, Oriental 1929; *Erik Thune to T. Stig-Nielsen*, 22 June 1929, Japan-Kina 1923–1932 (FLSA).

90 T. *Stig-Nielsen to Poul Larsen*, 5 February 1929, Japan-China 1923–1932 (FLSA).

91 O.V. *Mørch to T. Stig-Nielsen*, 6 November 1930, Japan-Kina 1923–1932; *T. Stig-Nielsen to F.L. Smidth & Co.*, 6 February 1931, T. Stig-Nielsen, Oriental 1931 (FLSA).

92 T. *Stig-Nielsen to F.L. Smidth & Co.*, 1 March 1931; *O. V. Mørch to T. Stig-Nielsen*, 12 March 1931; *O. V. Mørch to T. Stig-Nielsen*, 28 April 1931, T. Stig-Nielsen, Oriental 1931 (FLSA).

93 Feuerwerker, "Industrial Enterprise," 294.

94 A translated version of the agreement is available in T. Stig-Nielsen, Oriental 1931 (FLSA).

95 T. *Stig-Nielsen to O.V. Mørch*, 29 July 1931, T. Stig-Nielsen, Oriental 1931 (FLSA).

96 E. *Schmit-Jensen to Li Shi Ming*, 18 August 1931, T. Stig-Nielsen, Oriental 1931 (FLSA).

97 *Li Shi Ming to E. Schmit-Jensen*, 20 August 1931, T. Stig-Nielsen, Oriental 1931 (FLSA).

98 T. *Stig-Nielsen to E. Schmit-Jensen*, 14 September 1931, T. Stig-Nielsen, Oriental 1931 (FLSA).

99 E. *Schmit-Jensen to T. Stig-Nielsen*, 4 September 1931, T. Stig-Nielsen, Oriental 1931 (FLSA).

100 T. *Stig-Nielsen to E. Schmit-Jensen*, 14 September 1931, T. Stig-Nielsen, Oriental 1931 (FLSA).

101 *Aage Smith to T. Stig-Nielsen*, 4 March 1931, Japan-Kina 1923–1932; *T. Stig-Nielsen to Aage Corrit*, 2 May 1931, T. Stig-Nielsen, Oriental 1931 (FLSA).

102 *Aage Corrit to T. Stig-Nielsen*, 18 April 1931; *T. Stig-Nielsen to Aage Corrit*, 24 April 1931, T. Stig-Nielsen, Oriental 1931 (FLSA).

103 T. *Stig-Nielsen to Aage Corrit*, 2 May 1931, T. Stig-Nielsen, Oriental 1931 (FLSA).

104 T. *Stig-Nielsen to P. Mogensen*, 18 August 1931, T. Stig-Nielsen, Oriental 1931 (FLSA).

105 T. *Stig-Nielsen to Aage Corrit*, 26 August 1931, T. Stig-Nielsen, Oriental 1931 (FLSA).

106 T. *Stig-Nielsen to O.V. Mørch*, 25 August 1931, T. Stig-Nielsen, Oriental 1931 (FLSA).

107 P. *Antonsen to T. Stig-Nielsen*, 19 February 1932, T. Stig-Nielsen, Oriental 1932 (FLSA).

108 E. *Schmit-Jensen to T. Stig-Nielsen*, 30 June 1932, T. Stig-Nielsen, Oriental 1932 (FLSA).

109 E. *Schmit-Jensen to T. Stig-Nielsen*, 5 August 1932; *T. Stig-Nielsen to E. Schmit-Jensen*, 30 August 1932; *E. Schmit-Jensen to T. Stig-Nielsen*, 15 September 1932; *E. Schmit-Jensen to T. Stig-Nielsen*, 22 October 1932, T. Stig-Nielsen, Oriental 1932 (FLSA).

110 E. *Schmit-Jensen to T. Stig-Nielsen*, 22 October 1932, T. Stig-Nielsen, Oriental 1932 (FLSA).

111 E. *Schmit-Jensen to T. Stig-Nielsen*, 22 October 1932, T. Stig-Nielsen, Oriental 1932 (FLSA).

112 E. *Schmit-Jensen to T. Stig-Nielsen*, 23 November 1932; *E. Schmit-Jensen to T. Stig-Nielsen*, 1 December 1932; *E. Schmit-Jensen to T. Stig-Nielsen*, 16 December 1932, T. Stig-Nielsen, Oriental 1932 (FLSA).

113 *T. Stig-Nielsen to F.L. Smidth & Co.*, 27 January 1933, T. Stig-Nielsen, Oriental 1933 (FLSA).

114 *H.W. Yuan to E. Schmit-Jensen*, 6 March 1933; *H.W. Yuan to F.L. Smidth & Co.*, 7 March 1933; *E. Schmit-Jensen to T. Stig-Nielsen*, 7 March 1933; *T. Stig-Nielsen to F.L. Smidth & Co.*, 8 March 1933, T. Stig-Nielsen, Oriental 1933 (FLSA).

115 Feuerwerker, "Industrial Enterprise," 295.

116 *O.V. Mørch to T. Stig-Nielsen*, 31 October 1932, T. Stig-Nielsen, Oriental 1932 (FLSA).

117 *T. Stig-Nielsen to O.V. Mørch*, 27 July 1932, T. Stig-Nielsen, Oriental 1932 (FLSA).

118 *G.C. Liu to T. Stig-Nielsen*, 9 January 1933, T. Stig-Nielsen, Oriental 1933 (FLSA).

119 *G.C. Liu to T. Stig-Nielsen*, 16 November 1933, T. Stig-Nielsen, Oriental 1933; *O.V. Mørch to G.C. Liu*, 22 January 1934; *T. Stig-Nielsen to G.C. Liu*, 19 February 1934;, 14 June 1934, T. Stig-Nielsen, Oriental and American 1934 (FLSA).

120 *Tyge Møller to T. Stig-Nielsen*, 22 July 1933, Japan-Kina 1933–1936 (FLSA).

121 *Tyge Møller to T. Stig-Nielsen*, 22 July 1934, T. Stig-Nielsen, Oriental and American 1934; *Tyge Møller to T. Stig-Nielsen*, 8 November 1932, T. Stig-Nielsen, Oriental 1932 (FLSA).

122 *C.G. Liu to F.L. Smidth & Co.*, 22 December 1932, T. Stig-Nielsen, Oriental 1932 (FLSA).

123 *Tyge Møller to T. Stig-Nielsen*, 22 December 1932, T. Stig-Nielsen, Oriental 1932; *Tyge Møller to T. Stig-Nielsen*, 22 July 1933, Japan-Kina 1933–1936 (FLSA).

124 *T. Stig-Nielsen to F.L. Smidth & Co.*, 14 November 1933, T. Stig-Nielsen, Oriental 1933 (FLSA).

125 Where nothing else is stated, the following description of the course of events is based on *T. Stig-Nielsen to O.V. Mørch*, 21 November 1932; *Tyge Møller to T. Stig-Nielsen*, 6 December 1932; *Tyge Møller to T. Stig-Nielsen*, 22 December 1932; *Tyge Møller to T. Stig-Nielsen*, 26 December 1932, T. Stig-Nielsen, Oriental 1932 (FLSA).

126 *Tyge Møller to T. Stig-Nielsen*, 26 December 1932, T. Stig-Nielsen, Oriental 1932 (FLSA).

127 *T. Stig-Nielsen to P. Antonsen*, 26 November 1931, T. Stig-Nielsen, Oriental 1931; *T. Stig-Nielsen to O.V. Mørch*, 27 January 1932, T. Stig-Nielsen, Oriental 1932 (FLSA).

128 *Tyge Møller to T. Stig-Nielsen*, 22 July 1933, T. Stig-Nielsen, Oriental 1933 (FLSA). Fenby, *The Penguin History of Modern China*, 176–177.

129 *Tyge Møller to T. Stig-Nielsen*, 30 December 1932, T. Stig-Nielsen, Oriental 1932 (FLSA).

130 *Tyge Møller to T. Stig-Nielsen*, 7 July 1933, T. Stig-Nielsen, Oriental 1933; *T. Stig-Nielsen to F.L. Smidth & Co.*, 7 June 1935;, 18 June 1935, T. Stig-Nielsen, Oriental 1935 (FLSA).

131 *Lee Fong to T. Stig-Nielsen*, 8 December 1933, T. Stig-Nielsen, Oriental 1933; *T. Stig-Nielsen to Lee Fong*, 2 April 1934, T. Stig-Nielsen, Oriental and American 1934 (FLSA).

132 *Lee Fong to T. Stig-Nielsen*, 26 September 1935; *T. Stig-Nielsen to Lee Fong*, 7 October 1935, T. Stig-Nielsen, Oriental 1935; *T. Stig-Nielsen to Niels Jensen*, 19 December 1935; *Niels Jensen to T. Stig-Nielsen*, 15 June 1935; *Niels Jensen to T. Stig-Nielsen*, 14 September 1935, T. Stig-Nielsen, Oriental 1935 (FLSA).

133 *Svend Bonde to T. Stig-Nielsen,* 5 June 1935; *T. Stig-Nielsen to G.C. Liu,* 9 September 1935; *T. Stig-Nielsen to Niels Jensen,* 12 September 1935; *G.C. Liu to T. Stig-Nielsen,* 12 October 1935, T. Stig-Nielsen, Oriental 1935 (FLSA).

134 *Svend Bonde to T. Stig-Nielsen,* 18 January 1936, T. Stig-Nielsen, Oriental 1936 (FLSA).

135 *Tyge Møller to T. Stig-Nielsen,* 17 February 1936, T. Stig-Nielsen, Oriental 1936 (FLSA).

136 *T. Stig-Nielsen to Niels Jensen,* 10 March 1936; *Erik Nyholm to T. Stig-Nielsen,* 18 March 1936, T. Stig-Nielsen, Oriental 1936 (FLSA).

137 *T. Stig-Nielsen to Svend Bonde,* 19 March 1936, T. Stig-Nielsen, Oriental 1936 (FLSA).

138 *Erik Nyholm to T. Stig-Nielsen,* 20 February 1935; *Niels Jensen to T. Stig-Nielsen,* 12 April 1935; *Niels Jensen to T. Stig-Nielsen,* 24 May 1935; *T. Stig-Nielsen to Erik Nyholm,* 5 June 1935; *T. Stig-Nielsen to Niels Jensen,* 5 June 1935; *Erik Nyholm to T. Stig-Nielsen,* 7 June 1935, T. Stig-Nielsen, Oriental 1935 (FLSA).

139 *Erik Nyholm to T. Stig-Nielsen,* 7 June 1935, T. Stig-Nielsen, Oriental 1935 (FLSA).

140 *T. Stig-Nielsen to Niels Jensen,* 5 June 1935; *Erik Nyholm to T. Stig-Nielsen,* 7 June 1935; *T. Stig-Nielsen to Sigurd Pedersen,* 18 June 1935, T. Stig-Nielsen, Oriental 1935 (FLSA).

141 *T. Stig-Nielsen to Niels Jensen,* 19 December 1935, T. Stig-Nielsen, Oriental 1935 (FLSA).

142 *Erik Nyholm to T. Stig-Nielsen,* 26 July 1934, T. Stig-Nielsen, American & Oriental 1934 (FLSA).

143 *T. Stig-Nielsen to Niels Jensen,* 30 July 1934, T. Stig-Nielsen, American & Oriental 1934 (FLSA).

144 *Niels Jensen to T. Stig-Nielsen,* 25 August 1934, T. Stig-Nielsen, American & Oriental 1934 (FLSA).

145 *Erik Nyholm to T. Stig-Nielsen,* 12 November 1934, T. Stig-Nielsen, Oriental 1935; *Niels Jensen to T. Stig-Nielsen,* 19 October 1934, T. Stig-Nielsen, American & Oriental 1934 (FLSA).

146 *Erik Nyholm to T. Stig-Nielsen,* 15 November 1935, T. Stig-Nielsen, Oriental 1935 (FLSA).

147 *Erik Nyholm to T. Stig-Nielsen,* 23 December 1935, T. Stig-Nielsen, Oriental 1936 (FLSA).

148 *Erik Nyholm to T. Stig-Nielsen,* 16 January 1936; *Tyge Møller to T. Stig-Nielsen,* 23 January 1936; *Erik Nyholm to T. Stig-Nielsen,* 7 February 1936; *Niels Jensen to T. Stig-Nielsen,* 1 May 1936, T. Stig-Nielsen, Oriental 1936 (FLSA).

149 *Erik Nyholm to T. Stig-Nielsen,* 18 March 1936, T. Stig-Nielsen, Oriental 1936 (FLSA).

150 Fenby, *The Penguin History of Modern China,* 265–303.

151 For an account of the genocide and its role in both Chinese and Japanese historical awareness in the present time, see Iris Chang: *The Rape of Nanking. The Forgotten Holocaust of World War II* (Penguin Books, 1997).

152 *Niels Jensen to F.L. Smidth & Co. Copenhagen,* 28 December 1937, Japan-China 1937–38 (FLSA).

153 *F.L. Smidth & Co. Copenhagen to Niels Jensen,* 28 December 1937; *F.L. Smidth & Co. Copenhagen to Niels Jensen,* 30 December 1937, Japan-China 1937–38 (FLSA).

154 *F.L. Smidth & Co. to Niels Jensen*, 6 January 1938, Japan-China 1937–38 (FLSA).
155 *Niels Jensen to F.L. Smidth & Co. Copenhagen*, 31 January 1938, Japan-Kina 1937–38 (FLSA).
156 *Niels Jensen to F.L. Smidth & Co. Copenhagen*, 31 January 1938, Japan-China 1937–38 (FLSA).
157 *Niels Jensen to F.L. Smidth & Co. Copenhagen*, 26 February 1938, Japan-Kina 1937–38 (FLSA).
158 *Niels Jensen to F.L. Smidth & Co. Copenhagen*, 9 June 1938, Japan-China 1937–38 (FLSA).
159 *F.L. Smidth & Co. Shanghai to F.L. Smidth & Co. Copenhagen*, 15 June 1938; *F.L. Smidth & Co., Copenhagen to F.L. Smidth & Co. Shanghai*, 1 July 1938, Japan-Kina 1937-38 (FLSA).
160 *F.L. Smidth & Co. Shanghai to F.L. Smidth & Co. Copenhagen*, 21 September 1937; *F.L. Smidth & Co., Copenhagen to F.L. Smidth & Co. Shanghai*, 1 October 1937, Japan-Kina 1937–38 (FLSA). The following account of the Danish factory building activities during the time leading up to the Japanese capture of Nanjing is based on various correspondence, primarily telegrams, in the correspondence folder Japan-China 1937–1938, which makes it possible to follow the events in detail, and also on an overall summary in *Niels Jensen to F.L. Smidth & Co. Copenhagen*, 23 November 1937 (FLSA).
161 *Niels Jensen to F.L. Smidth & Co., Copenhagen*, 23 November 1937, Japan-China 1937–38 (FLSA).
162 The following account is based on various correspondence from December 1937 in the correspondence folder Japan-China 1937–1938, and primarily the summary in *Niels Jensen to F.L. Smidth & Co. Copenhagen*, 10 December 1937, Japan-China 1937-38 (FLSA).
163 *Niels Jensen to F.L. Smidth & Co. Copenhagen*, 10 December 1937, Japan-China 1937–38 (FLSA).
164 *Niels Jensen to F.L. Smidth & Co. Copenhagen*, 10 December 1937, Japan-China 1937–38 (FLSA). For a more in-depth description of Bernard Sindberg as a person, see Peter Harmsen: *Sindberg. Den danske Schindler og Nanjing-massakren 1937-38* (København: Lindhardt og Ringhof, 2019).
165 *Bernard Sindberg to F.L. Smidth & Co., Shanghai*, 6 December 1937, Japan-Kina 1937-38 (FLSA).
166 *Poul Scheel to Niels Jensen*, 8 January 1938, Japan-Kina 1937–38 (FLSA).
167 *Bernard Sindberg to Niels Jensen*, 11 January 1938, Japan-China 1937–38 (FLSA).
168 *Bernard Sindberg to Niels Jensen*, 4 February 1938;, 8 February 1938, Japan-China 1937-38 (FLSA).
169 *Niels Jensen to Kiang Nan Cement Co., Tientsin*, 16 May 1938; Niels Jensen to F.L. Smidth & Co., Copenhagen, 16 June 1938, Japan-China 1937–38 (FLSA). Harmsen, *Sindberg*.
170 *Margaret Stang-Lund to Niels Jensen*, 7 March 1938, Japan-China 1937–38 (FLSA).
171 *Margaret Stang-Lund to Niels Jensen*, 8 February 1938; *Niels Jensen to Bernard Sindberg*, 13 February 1938, Japan-China 1937–38 (FLSA).
172 *F.L. Smidth & Co., Copenhagen to F.L. Smidth & Co., Tokyo*, 26 March 1938, Japan-China 1937–38 (FLSA).
173 *Niels Jensen to F.L. Smidth & Co., Copenhagen*, 21 May 1938; *F.L. Smidth & Co., Tokyo to F.L. Smidth & Co., Copenhagen*, 24 May 1938; *F.L. Smidth & Co., Copenhagen to Niels Jensen*, 25 May 1938; *F.L. Smidth & Co.,*

Copenhagen to F.L. Smidth & Co., Tokyo, 9 June 1938; Niels Jensen to F.L. Smidth & Co., Copenhagen, 29 June 1938, Japan-Kina 1937–38 (FLSA).
174   Niels Jensen to F.L. Smidth & Co., Copenhagen, 29 June 1938, Japan-Kina 1937–38 (FLSA).
175   Niels Jensen to F.L. Smidth & Co., Copenhagen, 1 December 1938, Japan-Kina 1937–38 (FLSA).
176   Niels Jensen to F.L. Smidth & Co., Copenhagen, 1 December 1938, Japan-Kina 1937–38 (FLSA). The efforts made to transfer the Jiang Nan factory to German-Danish ownership are also described in Einar Nielsen to Margaret Stang-Lund, 3 November 1938 and Margaret Stang-Lund to F.L. Smidth & Co., Copenhagen, 26 November 1938, Japan-China 1937–38 (FLSA).

References

Albert Feuerwerker: "Industrial Enterprise in Twentieth-Century China: The Chee Hsin Cement Co.," in *Studies in the Economic History of Late Imperial China. Handicraft, Modern Industry, and the State*, ed. Albert Feuerwerker, Michigan Monographs in Chinese Studies, Vol. 70 (Michigan, 1995), 273–308.

Betænkning afgiven af den af Udenrigsministeriet i Henhold til kgl. Resolution af 24. Juli 1906 nedsatte Kommission til Forberedelse af en Omordning af Udenrigsministeriet og Danmarks Repræsentation i Udlandet (København, 1908).

Bruce Kogut: "The network as knowledge: Generative rules and the emergence of structure," in *Strategic Management Journal*, Vol. 21 (2000), 405–425.

Elisabeth Köll: *From Cotton Mill to Business Empire. The Emergence of Regional Entreprises in Modern China*. Harvard East Asian Monographs No. 229 (Harvard, 2003).

Erik Baark: *Lightning Wires. The Telegraph and China's Technological Modernization, 1860-1890. Contributions in Asian Studies, Number 6* (Westport: Greenwood Press, 1997).

G. C. Allen & Audrey G. Donnithorne: *Western Enterprise in Far Eastern Economic Development. China and Japan* (London, 1954).

Harry Schrøder: *Kraks Blaa Bog 1949* (København, 1950).

Howard Boorman, ed.: *Biographical Dictionary of Republican China*. Vol. III (New York, 1970).

Iris Chang: *The Rape of Nanking. The Forgotten Holocaust of World War II* (Penguin Books, 1997).

Jonathan Fenby: *The Penguin History of Modern China. The Fall and Rise of a Great Power 1850-2009* (London: Penguin Books, 2008).

Jonathan Fenby: *Generalissimo. Chiang Kai-Shek and the China He Lost* (London, 2003).

Kenneth Pomeranz: *The Great Divergence: China, Europe and the Making of the Modern World Economy* (Princeton, 2000).

Knudåge Riisager: *F.L. Smidth & Co. 1882-1922* (København, 1921).

Lloyd E. Eastman: *Family, Fields, and Ancestors. Constancy and Change in Chinas Social and Economic History, 1550-1949* (Oxford, 1988).

Mads Kirkebæk: "The Establishment of a Danish Legation in China in 1912," in *China and Denmark: Relations since 1674*, ed. Keld Erik Brødsgaard and Mads Kirkebæk (København: Nordic Institute of Asian Studies, 2001).

Morten Pedersen: *De danske cementfabrikkers bebyggelsesmiljø: en undersøgelse af forandringer i en branches industrielle miljø ved den anden industrielle revolution* (Odense: University Press of Southern Denmark, 2008).

Nigel Cameron: *Power* (Oxford: Oxford University Press, 1982).

Ole Lange: *Finansmænd, stråmænd og mandariner: C.F. Tietgen, Privatbanken og Store Nordiske: etablering 1868-76* (København, 1978).

Peter Harmsen: *Sindberg. Den danske Schindler og Nanjing-massakren 1937-38* (København: Lindhardt og Ringhof, 2019).

Philip Richardson: *Economic Change in China, c. 1800-1950* (Cambridge, 1999).

Rajeswary Ampalavanar Brown: *Chinese Business Enterprise in Asia* (London: Cengage Learning EMEA, 1995).

Ronald Stuart Burt: *Structural Holes: The Social Structure of Competition* (Cambridge, MA: Harvard University Press, 1992).

Steen Andersen & Kurt Jacobsen: *Foss* (København, 2008).

The Chronicle & Directory for China, Japan, Corea, Indo-China, Straits Settlements, Malay States, Siam, Netherlands India, Borneo, The Philipines etc. for the year 1899 (Hong Kong, 1899).

Twentieth Century Impressions of Hongkong, Shanghai and Other Treaty Ports of China. Their History, People, Commerce, Industries, and Ressources (London, 1908).

W.G. Huff: *The Economic Growth of Singapore. Trade and Development in the Twentieth Century* (Cambridge, 1995).

5 Samurai and Cement Factories. Japan 1922–1938

The Japanese Context at the Turn of the 20th Century

In Japan, F.L. Smidth & Co. had to adapt to the idea of collaborating with the cement industry on conditions that in many ways resembled those encountered by the company in the industrialised West.[1] The Japanese tradition of scepticism regarding impulses from the outside world did in fact set the scene for political small-state advantages as in Siam and China. However, from the beginning of the 20th century, Japan appeared as a modernised nation which, as the only state in Asia, was able to compete independently and on equal terms with the western world. This created completely different preconditions for the Danish opportunities to capture a market position.

The background was a fast industrialisation and modernisation process from the 1860–1870s onwards, which had eliminated the possibilities of western companies to profit by an asymmetrical knowledge basis as in other parts of Asia. The abolition of the shogunate in 1868 and the establishment of a new government with Emperor Meiji as the unifying figure had been the starting signal of an extensive political, economic and social revolution, which was to safeguard the existence of a strong and independent Japan. The counter-image was the West, but only as regards politics, as the endeavours were directed towards drawing on western inspiration to such a pervasive extent that traditional Japanese conventions were more or less abandoned in the course of one generation. One example was that a group of Japanese managers visited Denmark in 1873 which subsequently became a source of inspiration for the early reforms of the Meiji regime. However, Prussia was the main inspiration source for the extensive industrialisation and militarisation under Itô Hirobumi and Ôkubo Toshimichi's government from the 1880s.[2] The previous traditional feudal division of the population was replaced by a general citizen status, which turned the Japanese into payers of tax to the state and made them subject to general compulsory education and military service. Farmers, craftspeople and grocers became free to change trade, and social mobility became a real option for many. The Samurai

DOI: 10.4324/9780429446184-5

class, which for a large part had sunk into poverty towards the end of the Tokugawa period, lost their privileges and most of their income. However, they were free to apply for positions in the new civil service and to participate in the work to reform Japan's business life and the creation of an industrial sector. In the 1920s, the development also reached a certain level of democratisation, before Japan, which was by then strongly militarised, in the 1930s moved in a still more imperialist direction with increasing colonisation of other Asian countries and preparations for a major war under Emperor Hirohito's leadership. Already before the year 1900, Japan had been transformed into an industrial nation with heavy industry (iron and steel works, engineering companies and shipbuilding industry) and mining industry (coal, iron and copper in particular). This development had been prompted by government initiatives in the early 1870s and particularly by the building of an extensive railway network. On this basis, changes in business structures had already from the 1880s resulted in privately initiated industrialisation, which involved a comprehensive introduction of the new labour-saving technologies and new commodity groups, which also came to impact the western world of the day. Japan stepped directly into the second *Industrial Revolution*.[3]

As in other parts of Asia, the extensive transfer of technology from the West involved a certain risk of externally imposed dominance. However, in Japan, the technology transfers mainly took place via the marketplace in business transactions controlled by the Japanese themselves. The Japanese were successful in specifically targeting the purchase of the best possible technologies and the full control of these.[4] They often based this on reconnaissance trips to European and American industrial districts. Already from the 1870s, the Japanese were able to draw on experience from a large number of students sent out to study at educational institutions in the western world. From 1868 to 1895, the government sent 2,500 students to Europe and North America to complete technical and natural science studies. Between 1868 and 1910, the Japanese participated in at least 38 major industrial exhibitions across the world. The Japanese competently screened the world for usable technical solutions. In the 1890s, an English machinery supplier gave an illustrative insight into Japanese thoroughness when describing their handling of machines delivered from England. According to him, the urge of the Japanese to be in control combined with their distinct mistrust of western business partners was not only seen in tough price negotiations but also in their meticulous examination of the quality of the machines delivered to them: "It is no unusual thing for them to be pulled apart entirely and for the whole of the paint to be scraped off the surface of the castings and other covered parts".[5]

From the 1880s onwards, external business partners had to relate to a Japanese modernisation process initiated, conducted and controlled with a steady hand by the Japanese themselves. It was not a relevant strategy for western companies to profit from the absence of Japanese skills or will to take responsibility for the technological systems – not in the cement industry either.

Government-Run Transfer of Cement Technology

In 1870, the cement for the building of Japan's first modern harbour had to be shipped out from France. This was an unacceptable situation for the Meiji government, and in 1873, they therefore took the initiative to establish a cement factory in Fukugawa, near Tokyo. The first cement left the Fukugawa factory in 1875, which coincided with the first modern cement factory in the USA launching its product into the market.[6]

In line with the general Japanese utilisation of Prussian models of modernisation, the Fukugawa factory was established with inspiration from Germany. This was a sign that the Japanese had their ear to the ground; however, they were not just content with adopting an import solution but made the state initiative their basis for comprehensive further development in a private setting.[7] This meant that Fukugawa became the centre of the Japanese manufacturers' own experiments to develop new production methods, and both the ordinary operations of the factory and the technological development work thus produced key individuals with competences to build a private Japanese cement industry during the 1880s, with two companies in particular, both based on the experience from Fukugawa, becoming completely dominant.

Overall, this foreshadowed the establishment of a distinct Japanese *business ecosystem* in the cement industry, clearly resembling the constellations which were at the same time being created in Denmark and Germany.

Samurai and Cement Factories

From the 1880s onwards, one of the driving forces in Japan's cement industry was the Asano Cement Company, which was a direct outcome of the government initiative in Fukugawa.[8] The state-owned factory was sold in 1884 to the private individual Asano Sōichirō, who had grown up in the poorest part of the samurai class and, when he was 14 years old, had left his hopeless warrior life to try his luck as a tradesman in Tokyo.[9] Here, he made a living from selling coal, which got him in contact with the cement production in Fukugawa. In 1883, when Asano was 36 years old, he succeeded in renting the Fukugawa factory, which had been closed down since 1879, with financial support from Shibusawa Eiichi, the creator of Japan's first share-based bank. The following year, he managed to buy the plant, and with continued government support, he succeeded in expanding the cement business significantly in just a few years.

The precondition for this was the development and acquisition of technological expertise. During the years leading up to 1890, Asano Sōichirō sent 14 members of staff from the Fukugawa factory to Germany to study the latest German production methods and to buy equipment to take home to Japan. Indirect state subsidies in the shape of large orders for cement for the government's infrastructure projects paved the way for Asano Sōichirō and for the Fukugawa factory, which had increased its production fivefold by 1889. On this basis, Asano Sōichirō was able to expand his business, which meant that from the beginning of the 1890s, it included not only a number of cement factories, jointly called the Asano Cement Company, but also a range of businesses, the largest being shipping, shipbuilding, coal mining, ironworks and electricity power plants. Thus, he came to be at the head of one of the around 20 Japanese *zaibatsus* which were to dominate Japan's economy during the years leading up to World War II.

The second of the two main actors of Japan's cement industry was established at the initiative of another samurai, Junpachi Kasai, when he, in 1880, gathered a group of 37 of his former warrior colleagues for the formation of the Onoda Cement Company.[10] This was also based on subsidies from the Meiji government and on technology transfers from Germany. In terms of finance, the Onoda Cement Company was established with the help from loan programmes earmarked for the support of samurai initiatives within farming and industry. When the first factory was built from 1881 to 1883 at the city of Onoda in the Yamaguchi region at the most southern tip of Honchū, the Fukugawa factory served as a technological model. Five of the Onoda Cement Company's technicians spent ten months at Fukugawa to be introduced to its production principles and make drawings of the plant. The Onoda factory was then established with machinery produced at the shipyard of the Japanese army in Osaka. The collaboration between the Japanese companies and sectors across the divide between private and government actors was in no way inferior to that of their counterparts in Denmark and Germany.

In 1886, the Onoda Cement Company succeeded in signing a contract with one of the largest of the old Japanese commercial houses, the zaibatsu conglomerate Mitsui & Co., for the exclusive supply of cement for the state organisation responsible for the modernisation of Tokyo's building stock. The powerful commercial house committed to selling only Onoda cement in several regions. Therefore, when it turned out in 1886 that upgrading was required, German engineering assistance was once more called on. In 1889, a rotary kiln and other machinery were purchased from Germany for the establishment of a second factory, which, in other words, coincided with the installation of the new kiln type at Aalborg Portland and at the factory Hemmoor near Hamburg, i.e. before the English cement factories introduced rotary kilns. In 1895, the Onoda Cement Company built their third factory to accommodate the increasing military and civil demand. Continuous growth subsequently turned the Onoda Cement Company into a multinational company which sold cement both in Japan and in mainland China and Korea via a sales agreement and continued partnership with Mitsui & Co. and which, as mentioned in chapter 4, later on expanded its activities by cement factories in Korea and Manchuria.

Entry into the Japanese Market (1922–1926)

The establishment of the Japanese cement industry shared many similarities with the situation in Denmark and Germany. Key competences were developed for both technology development and the running of the factories, and this took place in a closely coordinated field with both private and government actors. Attempts were even made to expand beyond the Japanese borders, however at a level far below that of the international activities of their Danish and German competitors. In overall terms, at an early stage of their presence in Japan, F.L. Smidth & Co. might have aimed at exploiting their advantages of being a highly specialised, global technology leading company. But not to the same extent as in other parts of Asia. Nor could the political advantages play the same role as in Siam and China, where the threat of unwelcome external influence on the countries' business structures was more imminent. Finally, F.L. Smidth & Co. could not in the same way pull the strings via their Danish networks when dealing with the competent and self-assured Japanese. As might be expected, no Japanese connection was established to F.L. Smidth & Co. in the 1890s, and it was not on the cards that this might happen any time soon. Three decades later, in 1921, Japan was still not among the markets mentioned in F.L. Smidth & Co.'s 40-year anniversary publication to illustrate how the company was conquering the world. When F.L. Smidth & Co. finally accepted the challenge in their "Campaign in the East" in 1922, two apparent points of departure therefore had to be taken into account.

First of all, F.L. Smidth & Co did not need to spend energy on promoting their own market – cement producing companies – as had been the case in other Asian countries. But on the other hand, they could not count on the benefits of such a situation either. Secondly, they had to expect fierce competition from the technology suppliers, Japanese as well as external, who were already well established in the Japanese cement market. So although the internationalisation processes in Siam and China proceeded as a gradual transition from network-based influence to efficient informal Danish control of the customers' factories, it was evident that this was not a path they could follow in Japan. Investments were required, and to outcompete their competitors, they had to expect these to be of a considerable size.

Table 5.1 Catalogue of Japanese cement manufacturing companies and factories 1924, prepared by Aage Bruun 1924.

Name	Location	Founded In	Capital in JPY – Nominal	Capital in JPY – Paid Up	Kilns Number	Kilns Length (Feet)	Method
Aichi	Nagoya	1890	3,000,000	1,650,000	1	150'	Dry
Amaxa	Kyushu						
Asano	Fukugawa (Tokyo)				4	100'	Dry
	Kawasaki (Tokyo)				2	180'	Dry
					2	200'	
—	Moji		56,310,000	24,920,000	5	80'	Dry
					4	200'	
—	Kisugawa (Osaka)				2	125'	—
—	Kamiiso (Hokkaido)				1	100'	—
					1		
					24 shaft kilns	200'	
—	Takao (Formosa)				1	180'	—
					2	200'	
Chuwo	Kyushu	1895	2,000,000	1,250,000	2	150'	—
Chichibu	Tokyo	1923	5,000,000	1,250,000	2	164	—
Donkwa	Kyushu		500,000	500,000	1	150	Vaad
Echigo			3,000,000	375,000			
Hitachi	Tokyo	1916	750,000	450,000	1	120'	Dry
Hokoku	Moji (Kyushu)				4	125'	Dry
	Nagoya	1918	7,500,000	7,500,000	2	150'	—
—	Morotomi (Kyushu)				1	120'	—
					1	125'	
Hinode	Hondo (North)	1918	3,000,000	1,580,000	1	130'	—
					1	200'	
Iwaki	Tokyo	1907	3,000,000	1,800,000	4	125'	—
Mikawa	Nagoya		500,000	500,000	1	125'	Dry
					8 shaft kilns		

(Continued)

Table 5.1 (Continued)

Name	Location	Founded In	Capital in JPY – Nominal	Capital in JPY – Paid Up	Kilns Number	Kilns Length (Feet)	Method
Miyo	Nagoya	1897	1,125,000	1,125,000	1	125'	–
Nippon	Yatsushiro	1888	5,000,000	3,125,000	4	125'	–
–	Okawa	–	–		10 shaft kilns		–
Nihon Chiso Hiriyo	Minamata (Kuyushu)		22,000,000	16,000,000	1	125'	Vaad
					1	150'	
–	Kagami (Kyushu)				1	125'	–
					1	150'	
Onoda	Shimonoseki	1881	7,800,000	7,800,000	2	200'	Dry
–	Shusuishi (Dairen)				2	100'	–
					1	200'	
	Shokori (Korea)				1	200'	–
Osaka Yogyo	Osaka	1877	1,500,000	1,500,000	2	200'	Vaad
Oita	Yura	1918	7,000,000	4,984,000	2	125'	Dry
–	Tsukumi				1	125'	–
					2	160'	
					1	125'	
–	Ofunato				2	160'	–
Sakura	Kyushu	1907	800,000	800,000	2	125'	–
Suzuki	Tokyo	1918	880,000	386,000	1	125'	–
Toikoku	Kyushu	1917	1,000,000	1,000,000	1	125'	–
Tosa	Shikoku	1908	4,000,000	2,500,000	3	60'	Vaad
					2	200'	
Toa	Kobe	1907	1,500,000	1,500,000	1	164'	Dry
Ube	Shimonoseki	1923	3,500,000	875,000	1	164'	–
Yoshikawa	Okayama	1912	200,000	100,000			

Source: FLSA.

Initially, this would involve the presence in Japan of an FLS representative who was capable of rising to the challenge. Stig-Nielsen tried to formulate this in more detail in a message to the Copenhagen headquarters in December 1923, following his own first assessment of the situation – from his base in Beijing.[11] In concrete terms, he said that the long distances made it impossible for one person to be present on location, which was a precondition for the FLS representation to have the intended effect in both China and Japan. Instead, he suggested an expansion of the platform in Japan so as to include collaboration with a local partner, a local FLS representative and remote control by himself from his base in China:

> If we had some arrangement with a firm in Japan and probably one of our own, even a young and not too expensive, man who could do all the general work and prepare the different matters coming on, I could then when necessary support him the best of my ability, and perhaps a means of solving the question could be arrived at on something like these lines.

Mapping the Market (1924–1926)

Stig-Nielsen's proposal was accepted by Poul Larsen in May 1924 and came to shape the following activities in Japan.[12] While Stig-Nielsen was working on securing an agreement with a Japanese business partner, his colleague, the engineer Aage Bruun, spent some time in 1924 on a more technically oriented mapping of the cement industry in the country. This included the collection of general data, but he also travelled to some of the most important factories in order to form his own impression of the states they were in. The FLS people could therefore begin to compile a technically well-based overview of their opportunities in the Japanese market.

It became clear that if they were to use their persuasive skills on one individual customer, the Asano Cement Company was the most promising initial candidate, measured on a quantitative scale. Of the 38 cement factories in Aage Bruun's catalogue at the end of 1924, 19 had only one single plant at their disposal. The other 19 plants were divided among six owners; the Asano Cement Company was the largest with six factories, whereas the Onoda Cement Company and the Oita Cement Company owned three factories each, and the Nippon Cement Company and the Nihon Chiso Hiriyo owned two factories each.

In his reports, Aage Bruun mentioned obvious issues that ought to be improved at the plants he had visited. At the same time, his information confirmed the impression that the Japanese cement industry was based on a solid pool of experience and possessed a sophisticated production apparatus. Nine of the factories listed in the catalogue had been established

Table 5.2 Survey of information regarding machine suppliers obtained during Aage Bruun's visits to 11 Japanese cement factories in 1924–1926.

Factory	Mill	Rotary Kilns	
Asano- Fukagawa	Pfeiffer (DE) Allis Chalmers (USA) Fuller (DE)	Asano Steelworks (Japan)	
Asano- Kawasaki	Pfeiffer (DE) Allis Chalmers (USA) Asano-Kawasaki	Pfeiffer (DE) Fuller (DE)	 Allis Chalmers (USA)
Asano- Kisugawa	Hirotani Steel Works (Japan, Osaka)	Allis Chalmers (USA)	
Onoda-Nagoya (Aichi)	Japanese manufactured (Tokyo) Allis Chalmers (USA)	Allis Chalmers (USA)	
Onoda- Shimonoseki	Worthington McCully (USA) Nagel & Kemp (DE)	Fellner & Zeigler (DE)	
Chichibu Cement Co.	Allis Chalmers (USA) Kobe Steelworks (Japan)	Allis Chalmers (USA)	
Hokoku- Nagoya	Allis Chalmers (USA) Fuller (DE)	Allis Chalmers (USA)	
Osaka-Yogyo	Japanese product	Japanese product	
Sakura	Aero Pulverizer Co. (USA) Hirotani Steel Works (Japan, Osaka)	Traylor Allentown (USA)	
Toa	Allis Chalmers (USA) Worthington McCully (USA)	Allis Chalmers (USA)	
Ube Cement Co.	Allis Chalmers (USA)	Allis Chalmers (USA)	

Source: FLSA.

before the year 1900, which meant that his documentation reflected at least 25 years of production experience at around a quarter of the Japanese cement companies. Two of the companies – Amaxa and Yoshikawa – were so small that they might in reality be left out of consideration, but a number of the factories had very large production facilities. This applied in particular to the Asano Moji factory, which was equipped with nine rotary kilns, four of which were 60-m long and among the largest in Japan. A few of the factories used shaft kilns, one being the Asano Kamiiso factory, which had a large facility with 24 shaft kilns. However, almost the entire industry had now shifted to rotary kilns.

At the same time, Aage Bruun's explorations reflected how the purchase of German machinery in the 19th century had continued, but also how this had been supplemented by Japanese domestic production and imports from the USA in particular. In addition to mills and kilns from German Pfeiffer, Fuller and Fellner & Ziegler, a large market share derived from Allis Chalmers, whereas a few of the larger machines had been manufactured at Japanese steelworks and shipyards. It was clear, in other words, that there were strong competitors in the field, but also that the Japanese imported a large part of their technology. This emphasised to F.L. Smidth & Co. that advantages might be gained from spotlighting their reputation as a highly specialised technology company with a pool of experience harvested from world-wide activity. In other words, Aage Bruun's reconnaissance activities confirmed the assumptions that there was a market to be aimed at and identified advantages which could be exploited.

Mitsui & Co.

While Aage Bruun was compiling his survey, the preconditions for making contact to the Japanese customers were settled in November 1924, when Stig-Nielsen succeeded in establishing collaboration with Mitsui & Co.[13] This was essential since, if acting on their own, it would in reality be impossible for F.L. Smidth & Co. to influence the actors controlling the development of the cement industry.

Since it was established as a family-owned business in the 17th century, Mitsui & Co. had developed into a large group of companies whose core businesses in the 19th century were finance and trade, but which, following the Meiji modernisation, expanded their activities to include the mining and chemical industries, among others. To this was added the cement industry by virtue of their collaboration with the Onoda Cement Company. After the year 1900, their activities had developed to the extent that Mitsui & Co. assumed the role as Japan's largest zaibatsu. In other words, F.L. Smidth & Co. had obtained a business partner with far-reaching influence on both Japan's business life and the country's political sphere. Their opportunities for influence via Japanese partners were decisive for F.L. Smidth & Co. As expressed by Stig-Nielsen: "... we foreigners are powerless when it comes down to Japanese tricks and financial pressures extended by any of the big houses there".[14] Indeed, it soon became clear that Mitsui had no intention to deliver the services of an actual agency, but that the collaboration should rather be viewed as a type of payment for the access to influence in the right circles.

In some sense, it was therefore convenient when, in 1926, F.L. Smidth & Co.'s activities in China became so futile that Stig-Nielsen could break up and head to Japan. After his arrival there in July, he could then start making an effort to improve the results of the collaboration with Mitsui & Co.[15] On a positive note, he concluded that: "It secures our money, which is an important fact". Through Mitsui & Co, insights were gained into conditions which "no foreigner would be able to get down to the bottom of", and access was obtained to the business actors and the political life which had stakes in the cement industry. The latter was reflected in the strategy towards the warlords in northern China. The plan was now to log on to the Japanese imperialism towards the Chinese, who were seen by Stig-Nielsen to be unpredictable:

> It is ... my firm belief that doing business directly with this group of people will be most inadvisable indeed. They are all more or less adventurers and may be in power the one day and absolutely out of power the next day, for which reason, in case we did not get all our money with the order, we should run a very big risk of losing.

However, with the increased Japanese influence in Manchuria, it was now possible to draw on Mitsui & Co.'s more stable connections:

> The question is of course one of high politics and closely connected with the attitude of the South Manchurian Railway. ... It is therefore my idea that gradually we shall try to make Mitsui's and their friends, the South Manchurian Railway, interested in the matter in the way that they perhaps help Chang Tso Lin building of much needed cement works in Manchuria.

It was also an advantage that Mitsui & Co.'s close collaboration with the Onoda Cement Company did not prevent the building of Danish relations with Japan's largest cement group, the Asano Cement Company. "... it does not seem to handicap our endeavors in getting on with Asano", Stig-Nielsen concluded. However, the Mitsui people did not attend to their part of the collaboration agreement quite as desired. "Mitsui's must, however, all the time be pushed, and this particularly applies to the Tokio office ...", Stig-Nielsen stated. It was particularly disadvantageous that while the Mitsui & Co. staff in Osaka were seen as "harder business people" well acquainted with the cement industry through their collaboration with the Onoda Cement Company, this was not the case at their head office in Tokyo, which was in charge of their collaboration with F.L. Smidth & Co. Therefore, Stig-Nielsen's personal presence was required in Tokyo, since, as he described the situation:

> ... anything going on near Osaka will pretty certain come to the knowledge of Mitsui's Osaka office, who will then immediately send me an imperative wire to come down; whereas, if anything happens in Tokio, Mitsui's Tokio people will most likely be slower in drawing my attention to it. From this reason you will see I think it is more necessary to push Mitsui's Tokio people.

Moreover, Stig-Nielsen began to make a targeted effort to take advantage of the opening following from the collaboration with Mitsu & Co. to create and cultivate his own contacts to the largest Japanese cement groups.

Already, requests had been received from the Asano Cement Company regarding cement mills for the factories in Fukugawa and Kawasaki. Stig-Nielsen handled the dialogue personally by calling in at the Asano office in Tokyo. His rapport with the Asano people was good, but, in his view, F.L. Smidth & Co. probably had to be content with their hopes for what might happen in the future. During his visits, Stig-Nielsen learnt about a large-scale reconstruction of the factories of the business group, which was still only at an ideas stage, but of course extremely interesting to F.L. Smidth & Co.

At the Onoda Cement Company, the desire to use imported technology was very limited; according to Stig-Nielsen, this was not least due to the founder's confidence in his own abilities: "Dr. Kasai is, I am told, the type of man who thinks he can do everything better than anybody else in this world". There had been no immediate opportunity for Stig-Nielsen to pay Dr. Kasai a visit, but he expected the collaboration with Mitsui & Co. to prepare the ground for this:

> Mr. Asada in Mitsui's Tokio office is a personal friend of Dr. Kasai and has promised me to take up the matter personally with Dr. Kasai in connection with giving F.L. Smidth & Co. the preference when it comes to placing orders for machinery.

However, at the Iwaki Cement Company, they were focusing their efforts on making the company's production plant more efficient, and they did not in any way exclude the thought of purchasing machinery from the West. Stig-Nielsen therefore launched the tactics of calling personally at the head office as often as possible and subsequently documenting their oral negotiations in letters:

> My impression is that it is hardly sufficient to send a quotation and discuss this quotation verbally with the Japanese, as they do not understand all the points given. If, however, after a long conversation such conversation is confirmed in writing and a call again made, it is generally found that the Japanese, who can generally read English even if they cannot speak it, have studied such letter and underlined numerous points where on the second call full information can be given them.

These meetings must have been attended by interpreters and some Mitsui & Co. staff, even though no mention is made of this in the source

Table 5.3 The value of F.L. Smidth & Co.'s sale of cement machinery in Japan
from 1926 to July 1929.

1926	GBP 10,000
1927	GBP 180,000
1928	GBP 120,000
1929 (January–July)	GBP 10,000
Total	GBP 320,000

Source: FLSA.

material, but it is evident that Stig-Nielsen did the speaking and provided
a veritable sales pitch.

Consolidation (1927–1930)

Four years after F.L. Smidth & Co.'s first venture in Japan, real results
were seen in 1926. From then on, it seemed as if a boil had been lanced.
The opening appeared with orders for cement mills from the Asano
Cement Company and the Chichibu Cement Company, which were won
in competition with German and American companies. It even seemed as
if orders for complete factory plants would follow from the Asano
Cement Company and from a number of the other cement manufacturers.[16] This turned out to hold water. In May 1927, an order arrived from the Asano Cement Company for the reconstruction of the
factories in Katsubo and Kawasaki, and during the same year, orders for
rotary kiln lines were received from the Onoda Cement Company and
the Iwaki Cement Company.[17] In 1928, seven orders for rotary kiln lines
were received, and in 1929, the capacity of the rotary kilns sold to Japan
reached six million barrels a year, corresponding to just over a quarter
(27%) of the total Japanese cement production in that year.[18] Suddenly,
F.L. Smidth & Co.'s activities were no longer focused on entering the
Japanese market, but rather on consolidating their position and obtaining control of their newly acquired market position.

It soon became clear that the risk of Japanese copying of the Danish
technology was great, and any idea of maintaining and exploiting an
asymmetrical knowledge position was illusory. In 1929, Stig-Nielsen
summarised this in a letter to Poul Larsen:

> One condition for getting business in Japan will, however, be that
> we get proper patents for those machines we particularly want to
> sell. It is so that with as strong a patent as our Unax patent, and with
> Mitsui backing us, there should be only little danger of infringe-
> ments. Our Unidan Mills are, as you know, however, not patented in
> Japan, as that could not be done at the time we started our business

there. These mills will, therefore, without a doubt be copied, and it will therefore be of the utmost importance that we get our new construction of mill very firmly patented in Japan before we mention this mill to anybody.[19]

Although the immediate risk of copying might be counteracted by patent protection, it was evidently implied that this tool was of little value without the support of Mitsui & Co. Consolidation in the Japanese market had to be based on influence and control through the powerful actors behind the Japanese cement industry. At the same time, it was a clear conclusion at F.L. Smidth & Co. that their collaboration with Mitsui & Co. was not sufficient. When, in 1929, Stig-Nielsen sent a status report to Poul Larsen on the past five years, his conclusion was that orders had indeed been received, but also that:

> Mitsui would ... be <u>useless</u> unless we had our own men to push them all the time, and it often takes one's patience not to lose one's temper over Mitsui's apathetic attitude. However, when Mitsui is treated in the right way, they are most obliging, and absolutely quite necessary for us when it comes down to the most important factors in our business, viz: – payments, shipping and custom's clearance.[20]

However, the Danish feeling of uneasiness about Mitsui & Co. was not only caused by apathy, but also by fear of opportunism: "... as not only may times change – the fight between Asano and Onoda may be too pointed to retain Mitsui openly as our agents – but also it is always dangerous to be too dependent upon a large firm like Mitsui, as in such case they might well try to dictate terms to us". It was quite simply too risky to be dependent on one business partner with the power to block activities in the entire Japanese market.

The FLS strategy therefore became focused on establishing a situation in which it was possible to manage without Mitsui & Co. at all, should this become necessary. The precondition for this was the upgrading of the staff at the FLS office in Tokyo which had been taking place since 1926 and had ensured that: "As it is, they [Mitsui] perfectly well know that in a tight corner we can quite well go on with our daily work, even if a break should come, and this makes us strong in our small controversies ..."[21] But the objective of acting independently and freely among the Japanese cement manufacturers was particularly meaningful in light of the character of the customer relations which Stig-Nielsen had been building during the previous years.

Profound Personal Customer Influence

A few months after his arrival from war-torn China in 1926, Stig-Nielsen summarised how close relations had been established to the largest

Japanese cement manufacturers: "Asano have full confidence in us and I believe there will be a lot more to do for that Company in connection with reconstruction of their old works", he said, and added that both the Onoda Cement Company and the Iwaki Cement Company were interested in F.L. Smidth & Co.'s products. The consequence was, he continued, that "... to satisfy all these clients it is necessary to visit their works and to spend quite a lot of time with them in their Tokio offices ..."[22] Time was not only spent on discussing technical topics, but also on establishing ties of personal confidence. This applied primarily to their main customer, the Asano Cement Company.

As regards the Asano Cement Company in particular, the support from Mitsui & Co. soon became irrelevant. When the first order was received in 1927, this was the result of negotiations conducted personally by Stig-Nielsen with Asano Sōichirō's son Asano Ryozo, who, as perceived by the Dane, had used all his power to ensure that the order went to F.L. Smidth & Co.[23] And the importance of the personal relations with the Asano zaibatsu's founder was enhanced considerably when, at the end of 1927, Stig-Nielsen returned from a recreational trip to Denmark and, accompanied by Asano Sōichirō, embarked on a tour of the factories of the business group to inspect the plants together with him and discuss the possibilities of reconstruction.[24] It was crucial to make sure that the knowledge of the Danish technology was provided to the right people and groups internally in the customers' organisations and at the same time to suss out where the barriers and aversions against the Danes might be located. Otherwise, the situation would get out of hand.

During his tour with Asano, this was manifested in concrete terms when it turned out that several of the technical reports prepared by F.L. Smidth & Co. had been kept secret to Asano Sōichirō and Asano Ryozo by the two chief engineers, Fujii and Miyagawa, who were anxious about Danish manipulation and felt that their own positions were being threatened by the Danes. At the time, this was a well-known problem. Already in April 1927, the interim manager of the Japan office, Harry Schrøder, referred to situations in which Fujii "... had been reprimanded by his president, who had used som figures against him, which he had received from Stig-Nielsen. Fujii bluntly said that 'the president believes what Stig-Nielsen has said and not what I say'".[25] In other words, the Danes exerted influence and control deep into the Japanese cement group. But managing where information ended up and in what way was decisive for remaining in control.

On his tour with the Asano owners, it was therefore necessary for Stig-Nielsen to make sure, by means of sporadic and well-directed hints, that the Japanese top management was informed of the Danish analyses. Sensitivity to the situation was crucial as humiliating the Japanese engineers in front of their top managers must also be avoided. At one of the meetings, however, Stig-Nielsen ventured to try directly to eliminate their mistrust by speaking openly about it in the presence of the Asano owners. At least this is how he referred to the situation to the FLS management in Copenhagen:

> ... I hinted that perhaps someone in the Asano Cement Company thought we were trying to press orders through in connection with the reconstruction work, and said that I hoped Mr. Miyagawa would see to it that this misunderstanding was entirely removed, stressing the point by adding that I really thought we had on numerous occasions shown that all we were out for was to do the work we were paid for in a satisfactory way, then naturally leaving the final results to be decided by the Asano Cement Company.

This was an offensive tactic. At the meeting, the Japanese engineers could hardly express open mistrust towards F.L. Smidth & Co. and consequently towards their top managers, who had hired the Danes and were now travelling personally with Stig-Nielsen. And as their silence at the same time deprived them of the chance to utter criticism at a later stage, Stig-Nielsen concluded that "As you will see, we are now in a position where absolutely nobody can blame us, and I think that we shall be getting in any case the very best part of the reconstruction work which will come up from time to time".[26]

The Limit to Danish Control

From the very beginning, F.L. Smidth & Co.'s efforts to consolidate their position in the Japanese market were directed towards influence on the dealings of their customers via close personal relations deep within their organisation. This was the step before actually employing FLS staff as in Siam and China, but it was also exactly as far as the Danes were able to go. This became apparent in the few cases where F.L. Smidth & Co. made attempts to establish an informal presence at the Japanese factories.

When Bernard Olsen was sent out to be in charge of the reconstruction of the Katsubo factory in 1927, this was organised as a loan arrangement corresponding to Schmit-Jensen's stay at the Chee Hsin Cement Company's factory in Tangshan. At the turn of the year 1927–1928, it was Stig-Nielsen's assessment that Bernard Olsen "... is really in the service of the Asano Company ...".[27] And to consolidate Bernard Olsen's position as "resident engineer" in Katsubo, Stig-Nielsen asked the head office in Copenhagen in 1928 to send all correspondence regarding the reconstruction work to Olsen, and not to H.S. Nielsen, the machine fitter, at whom the material was directed.[28] There was not a great deal the Danes could do, however. As the Asano Cement Company's Japanese engineers were not enthusiastic about extensive

Danish influence and expressed their dissatisfaction with the thought of Danish "resident engineers", this construction was in reality unsustainable.[29] Consequently, in September 1928, the Danish assessment was that it was difficult to keep Bernard Olsen in the Asano Cement Company's service in Katsubo. In October, the loan agreement was terminated by the Japanese. However, Bernard Olsen remained in his position at the factory until 1930, but now once again as F.L. Smidth & Co.'s field representative.[30] The formation of an informal Danish organisation as an everyday control tool at the Japanese factories was not a feasible strategy.

Networks and Partnerships at the Top Level

The opportunities for influencing the top-ranking Japanese were not confined to Stig-Nielsen's personal acquaintance with the Japanese business owners. It was possible to draw on other Danish-Japanese relations as well, including the diplomatic service at levels up to the Danish royal family and the Japanese emperor's family.

The first opportunity arose in 1929 when Poul Larsen visited Japan as a member of a Danish delegation attending the annual *Tokyo Engineering Congress*. The congress was an exclusive social event, and the FLS people made every effort to secure a high official profile for the Danish delegation, which included both their own people and Danish scientists and technicians.[31] Their wish to secure a high profile was also reflected in the FLS people's attempts to make sure that the Danish government's official envoy, the charismatic Henrik Kaufmann, participated; he was well-liked among the Japanese, and was also infamous for his extensive and extravagant use of the Danish foreign ministry's travel account. The Danish government soon allocated funding for three professors from Copenhagen to attend the congress, but as Stig-Nielsen learnt from Kaufmann himself, there was a certain opposition to his participation: "His only difficulty, however, is that the Danish Foreign Office has certain difficulties in making certain groups in the Danish Parliament realize the necessity of undertaking such trips ...".[32] Stig-Nielsen therefore approached Poul Larsen to get him to provide the director of the Danish foreign office with the best arguments, because, as he said,

> ... the Danish Foreign Office on their part would much easier be able to overcome their trouble if a firm of the high standing of F.L. Smidth & Company expressed to the Foreign Office the advantage it would be to our interests if Mr. Kauffmann could be present during the Conference.[33]

Kaufmann's attendance would make sure the Japanese got the impression that F.L. Smidth & Co.'s operations were supported by the

Danish government. If arrangements could be made for Poul Larsen to meet with the Japanese cement manufacturers, accompanied by official representatives from both Denmark and Japan, this would be an even better result, however. At best, such an opportunity could embed F.L. Smidth & Co.'s work in an overall context of mutual political goodwill. The fact that this was the strategy was reflected in Poul Larsen's travel schedule, which came to include meetings with dignitaries from the Japanese cement industry, from the professional environment surrounding it, and from the highest levels of Japanese political life. On the day of his arrival, Poul Larsen was introduced to "the President of the Congress, Baron Koi Furuichi", who held a leading position in the Japanese ministry of engineering affairs, and this was followed by meetings with leading political actors.[34] On the opening day of the congress, when Poul Larsen was appointed "Honorary Vice-President of the whole Congress", he proceeded to attend an evening reception thrown by the prime minister of Japan, and here "... Mr. Larsen was placed with the high officials in his capacity as Honorary Vice-President". Poul Larsen spent the following days in the company of Henrik Kaufmann, meeting owners and managers from the Japanese companies. These meetings at top level took place during visits to the Japanese company offices, and at social events such as dinners, garden parties and receptions, which were also attended by other key actors such as the head of the Mitsui & Company, "Baron Mitsui", the mayor and city government of Tokyo and leading individuals from other parts of Japan's industrial community. Leading people from the Japanese government attended, among them "Baron Shidehara", who held the position as foreign minister and was married into the Mitsubishi zaibatsu and who, following an assassination attempt against the head of government, Osachi Hamaguchi, in 1930 came to take over the position as prime minister of Japan. At the closing ceremony in the Japanese parliament building, Poul Larsen spoke to the delegates on behalf of both the Danish and Swedish delegations. His itinerary then included a 10-day tour of Japanese sights and cement factories. Several travel days were spent in the company of Japanese factory owners and their wives. The evening before Poul Larsen's departure from Japan was spent at a farewell dinner thrown by Asano Sōichirō in his home in Tokyo. During the following time, the high-ranking relations were confirmed by the exchange of letters of thanks as well as presents and personal photographs between the Danes and the Japanese.[35]

A further contribution to F.L. Smidth & Co.'s work in Japan was made by the Danish royal family when the Danish Crown Prince Frederik spent six days in the country while visiting Asia in 1930. The Crown Prince followed a travel schedule prepared by Stig-Nielsen, who in return benefitted from this royal assistance at nurturing his high-ranking Japanese connections. Afterwards, Henrik Kauffmann concluded that "... the visit would not have proceeded with such effect and success – at least from our business interest perspective – had it not been for the considerable effort made by Mr. Stig-Nielsen".[36] And at an official Danish-Japanese dinner party attended by both Asano Sōichirō and Junapachi Kasai, the Crown Prince personally made sure they were well entertained.

The Danish Japanese Society

Moreover, the endeavours to embed F.L. Smidth & Co.'s activities in Danish-Japanese connections outside of the business community were expanded by a targeted effort to create relations under the joint umbrella of the *Danish-Japanese Society*. Ideas regarding the creation of a Danish-Japanese society had been brewing in various contexts since 1924, but they did not materialise until F.L. Smidth & Co. began their collaboration with the Mitsui & Company and the Asano Cement Company in 1926–1927.[37] When the preparation process for a Danish-Japanese Society in Tokyo was initiated from 1928, the FLS people were therefore the driving forces. The first preparations were made by an "Inner circle", which convened in Tokyo on 3 December 1928.[38] Stig-Nielsen participated in this, together with the diplomats Henrik Kauffmann and Poul Scheel from the Danish legation and J.J. Bahnson, head of the activities of the Great Northern Telegraph Company (Store Nordiske Telegrafselskab) in the Far East. The Japanese members were Admiral Sano, representatives from the companies Mitsui & Co. and Nippon Yusen Kaisha and officials from the Japanese government ministries of infrastructure and farming. Later on, this "inner circle" was supplemented by F.L. Smidth & Co.'s contact person at Mitsui & Co., Mr. Komatsu, Aage H. Hansen, the Danish consul in Tokyo, and Erik Nyholm. In 1929, the people involved spent some time sounding out the sentiments regarding the official formation of a society, and during the first months of 1930, actual steps were made in that direction.

Thus, in January 1930, Stig-Nielsen and Komatsu prepared the draft bylaws of the society, which were adopted at a banquet on 20 March attended by high-ranking individuals from both sides in the shape of the Danish Crown Prince Frederik, the Japanese Prime Minister Hamaguchi, Foreign Minister Baron Shidehara and Princess and Prince Takamatsu, Emperor Taishōs third son and Emperor Hirohito's younger brother. On this occasion, Takamatsu was appointed patron of the society. A crowd of 150 people were also invited, including the heads of the Danish companies in Japan and high-ranking Japanese individuals. Baron Koi Furuichi was chosen as president of the society.

The costs of the banquet were sky-high, but Stig-Nielsen explained the gains to Poul Larsen:

... I have given this whole matter considerable attention, and also spent considerable time in trying to get it into shape. I have done this because I feel that such a Society may on many occasions be useful in transactions between Denmark and Japan, since a Society is a much easier medium to use for a gathering than any private concern or any private individual. Japanese from various camps are most difficult to invite together, but if they are members of the same Society, this can easily be done. I am further of the opinion that possible future Decorations can much easier be distributed through the Japan-Denmark Society, as if done that way will smell much less of business.[39]

Stig-Nielsen also informed the FLS management in Copenhagen that his own offices had been chosen to house the activities of the society and described the opportunities this might offer: "You will no doubt agree that this will be rather useful for us since nearly all Japanese going to Denmark will no doubt call on the Society here before leaving for Denmark". With the initiative to establish the Danish-Japanese Society, F.L. Smidth & Co. had placed themselves in a key position to influence Danish-Japanese relations in general – and consequently to try to achieve optimal conditions for continued control of their own market position with the Japanese cement companies.

Expansion and Loss of Control

At the end of the 1920s, F.L. Smidth & Co. had consolidated their position in the Japanese Market. Collaboration had been established with the country's industrial heavyweights, and channels for influence on the Japanese customers had been formed through a large grey zone of FLS people and various external actors at many levels in and around the periphery of the company. At times, this influence could be of profound and decisive significance. However, the Danes were not able to control the choices made by their Japanese customers regarding F.L. Smidth & Co.'s line of business. This became particularly evident as it turned out to be impossible to resist the increasing Japanese pressure to move the production of cement machinery from Denmark to Japan. In this way, the Japanese were trying to make inroads into the very foundation of F.L. Smidth & Co.'s activities, but at the end of the day, the Danes could not do much else but try to delay the process and mitigate its harmful effects.

Partly for Sentimental Reasons

The Japanese wishes to establish machine production in Japan were expressed at the very first negotiations conducted with the Asano

Cement Company, and during his holiday in Denmark in 1927, Stig-Nielsen and the FLS executive management therefore had to formulate a "general policy" on the topic.[40] Even though it was cheaper to produce the machinery in Denmark, freight rates and custom expenses might soon cause the balance to tip over. To the Japanese, it was decisive that the purchase sum, the jobs and the technological skills were retained in Japan. "For this reason", Stig-Nielsen said in his summary of the course of events,

> and partly for sentimental reasons, we then first started making in Japan kiln shells, mill shells Unax cooler tubes and several other items of a bulky nature – that is items that were costly in freight – and on this base we were fortunate enough to land some very useful jobs.[41]

In other words, the decision to manufacture machine parts in Japan resulted in orders from the Japanese customers. However, this implied the risk that the Japanese cement industry might further develop its capacity as a parallel to both the Danish and the German constellations with F.L. Smidth & Co. and Polysius, respectively, as the core companies. This might be the start of a slippery slope in which the Japanese might eventually threaten the Danish and German positions not only in Japan but also in the world market. Consequently, it became F.L. Smidth & Co.'s "general policy" to try to keep as many activities as possible in Denmark. The arguments were expressed as two considerations regarding the knowledge embedded in F.L. Smidth & Co.'s activities:

> ... keeping in mind, however, all the time that manufacturing in Europe would be preferable, not only because this would give more work to Valby and our other connections there, but also because the Japanese would be less likely to know anything about our margin.[42]

The strategy had to be directed towards containing the risks implied in the use of the Japanese engineering industry as a sub-supplier. The largest risks were evident in case of their weightiest business partner, Asano Sōichirō, whose wish it was that as many orders for machinery to the Asano cement factories as possible should result in orders placed with the machinery works included in his zaibatsu. The Danish deliveries of kiln and mill shells were therefore produced at the Asano-owned Tsurumi Ship Steel Works in Yokohama. This meant that in reality, the sub-supplier and the customer were the very same company, which reflected that what the Japanese had in mind was to put pressure on F.L. Smidth & Co. in order to transfer considerable parts of the technological advantages to one of their major customers. During Poul Larsen's visit to Japan in 1929, Asano Sōichirō even mentioned the possibility of what

Stig-Nielsen referred to as: "a closer co-operation in connection with the manufacture of machinery at Tsurumi".[43]

The thought of such "closer co-operation" was shelved for the time being. However, the FLS people had to be prepared to spend time and resources on making agreements with sub-suppliers and conduct in-process inspection of the quality of the work they delivered. In 1932, Stig-Nielsen concluded that the cooling shells and other minor parts manufactured by Ashizawa Iron Works in Tokyo were of impeccable quality, and that their people were indeed skillful.[44] In contrast, the rotary kiln shells and mill shells delivered from the Mitsui-connected Tama Shipyard had not been first-class work, in spite of the fact that this had been subject to careful inspection by the Danes. In other words, the quality of the locally produced machinery sometimes varied, and to boost the inspection effort and the quality control, the staff at the FLS office in Tokyo was gradually increased by people who were acquainted with the working procedures at the machinery works in Valby in Denmark.[45] However, the head of the Asia department at the head office in Copenhagen, O.V. Mørch, still concluded in 1929 that the use of sub-suppliers was the reason why they were constantly receiving complaints from their customers:

> As regards your remarks concerning faulty machinery, you will know we are doing our best as to inspection, but the very fact that we are manufacturing at so many different places does make it difficult to get all parts of the machinery to fit together as well as it should. If everything was assembled in one shop we would get over the difficulty, but it is quite out of the question to do that, as we should then never be able to compete in prices.[46]

The wording regarding price level suggested that the Japanese customs expenses rendered it unnecessary to consider how the machine production might return home to the factory in Copenhagen. This was not a realistic option.

Up through the 1930s, efforts therefore had to be directed towards attempts at optimising the state of affairs through constant inspection of the quality and price level of the work carried out at the Japanese machinery works.[47] Even though the Danes could still make their influence felt through powerful connections and networks, they were not in any way able to withstand the pressure to place increasingly large parts of the manufacture of machinery for the Japanese customers in Japan – causing the Danish technological advantage to be watered down.

Sales Office or Manufacturing Office?

The pressure on F.L. Smidth & Co. to move their machine production to Japan increased considerably from 1932, following a fall in the Yen

Table 5.4 Production capacities in the Japanese cement industry 1931 according to a survey from F.L. Smidth & Co. 1931.

	Total Capacity of Japanese Cement Works	
	Barrels per Day	Barrels (Million) per Year of 300 Days
Asano Portland Cement Co.	34,000	10.2
Onoda Cement Co.	18,000	5.4
Oita Cement Co.	6,800	2.0
Chichibu Cement Co.	8,500	2.5
Ube Cement Co.	6,500	2.0
Iwaki Cement Co.	6,800	2.0
Nippon Cement Co.	5,700	1.7
Hokoku Cement Co.	5,500	1.6
Osaka Yogyo Cement Co.	4,800	1.3
Tosa Cement Co.	4,000	1.2
Nanao Cement Co.	3,000	0.9
Toa Cement Co.	1,500	0.5
Mikawa Cement Co.	600	0.2
Asahi Cement Co.	500	0.1
Denki Cement Co.	400	0.1

Source: FLSA.

exchange rate and the introduction of new customs rates. In the competition for a larger order from the Ube Cement Company, F.L. Smidth & Co. lost in May 1932 to German Krupp, which offered Japanese manufactured machinery at low prices. In the autumn of 1932, a large number of orders were lost for similar reasons.[48]

In August 1932, Stig-Nielsen therefore opened a new proposal for F.L. Smidth & Co.'s strategy regarding the Japanese market by making it clear that

> ... although it would be better to continue making the largest part of our machinery at home and just the bulky parts in Japan, we will be forced – unless we want to risk losing our business – to reorganize our manufacturing so that as much as ever possible is made here, leaving only certain parts of the most difficult nature to be made at your end.[49]

In Stig-Nielsen's view, the business prospects were so promising that they should be pursued, "... even if we in order to do so have to go a little out of our way". And when, following inspection of a number of machinery works, he was able to document that the necessary competences and facilities were present in the Japanese engineering industry, it was clear to him that the production in Japan should be expanded from kiln and mill shells to almost everything required to build a production line.

The crucial question was therefore how to contain the risk that the Danish technological competitive advantages might be undermined. It was generally expected that the Japanese would make attempts at copying: "... what we risk in the way of, perhaps, giving information away that may make it easier for the Japanese machine works to copy our machinery". At this level, however, the risk would not noticeably increase. As stated by Stig-Nielsen: "The minute we sold our first piece of machinery in Japan we had to be prepared that it might at any time be copied ...". Several of F.L. Smidth & Co.'s small machines had already been copied, he continued, and so had mills and kilns from both Allis Chalmers and Krupp. The danger of copying could be avoided in two ways. One was to make constant improvements of the technology, which the Japanese workshops were unable to make themselves, another was to increase the Danish machine production in Japan on the ground that

> If we ourselves can make the best part of our machinery in Japan – in that way becoming more competitive than we are to-day – we think that the larger companies, who, after all, want to present a bit of face to the outside world, would prefer us to make their machinery ....

At the same time, it was Stig-Nielsen's assessment that even though it was hardly possible to prevent the Japanese from producing machinery on the basis of the knowledge acquired from the Danes, it would probably be possible to prevent them from manufacturing complete plants behind the backs of the Danes. To accomplish this, F.L. Smidth & Co would need to focus on the production of more specialised items such as the Symetro gears. In this case, it would be necessary "... to teach the suppliers and make them acquainted with special tricks in a certain particular manufacture ...". The riskiest move would be to reveal particularly specialised key competences: "The extra danger, therefore, seems to be more n teaching them certain tricks in the manufacture than actually letting them get hold of our drawings". An obvious tool to use to try to remain in control of the technological advantage was therefore to spread production across several sub-suppliers, preferably as many as possible, so that none of them would be able to produce all components for an entire factory on their own.

In Copenhagen, Stig-Nielsen's strategy proposal was taken into account, even though basically this went against the company's overall objectives:

> You will know that we have always held here that the best way of running our business is to concentrate as much as possible in Copenhagen, and when customers send us their inquiry, then they

should be tackled from here as directly as possible, and sales engineers should go and see the customers by journeys straight from Copenhagen.[50]

However, if that was the way, it was also necessary for the corporate management in Copenhagen to emphasise to Stig-Nielsen that the FLS department in Japan should not develop into a competitor of the competence cluster at home in Denmark:

> When you went out there originally it was certainly the intention that proper sales offices should be opened, and so they were. When, however, we have a proper organization in Japan, it seems quite necessary that some sales engineer is there all the time. We do not think it will ever be satisfactory that we keep a manufacturing office there … .

On this basis, F.L. Smidth & Co. embarked on an expansion of their collaboration with Japanese sub-suppliers. In October 1932, work was in progress concerning offers for a number of factories, and F.L. Smidth & Co. were optimistic about the possibility to be included in an expansion programme which was on the drawing board of the Asano Cement Company. The optimism turned out to be well-founded as the order was won a year later, one of the reasons being that competitive prices could be offered on machinery manufactured at the Tsurumi Ship Works.[51]

At the same time, problems soon emerged. The FLS people now had to spend a considerable part of their time negotiating with sub-suppliers.[52] Much energy also had to be used to oversee that good quality products were delivered and at the agreed time, even from large factories such as the Tsurumi Ship Works.[53] In 1938, a Japanese sub-supplier was successful in producing the gear wheels for the Symetro gears for the cement mills in a satisfactory quality.[54] It was an even larger problem, however, that it was almost impossible to avoid that the knowledge transferred to the sub-suppliers was passed on – to F.L. Smidth & Co.'s competitors, among others. This risk was explicitly present in particular when the Asano Cement Company, in 1936, chose to let the order for a new kiln line go to Krupp, while at the same time requesting that the kiln shells were to be produced at the Tsurumi Ship Works, where the necessary competences and facilities were already available by virtue of their collaboration with F.L. Smidth & Co.[55] Evidently, this implied the risk that Krupp would get direct access to information which F.L. Smidth & Co. wished to keep to themselves, and at the same time it was unsatisfactory that the knowledge resources provided to the Japanese machinery works would now be made directly available to the Germans. The FLS people had to accept the outcome of the case, however, even though the contract they had signed in reality made it possible to refuse the Tsurumi Ship Works permission to manufacture machinery for their competitors.[56] However, this was not the first time the Danes encountered these types of problems regarding the Tsurumi Ship Works. One example was that in March 1934, the Japanese made an effort to have the largest iron cast parts for the FLS machinery manufactured at yet another sub-supplier – with the intention to spread the Danish knowledge across a veritable chain of sub-suppliers.[57] Another example followed later in 1934, when the Tsurumi Ship Works themselves had tracked down a cement factory project in Harbin which they wanted to equip with a kiln shell independently of F.L. Smidth & Co., who were, however, requested to consent.[58] F.L. Smidth & Co. obviously protested against the project, but the Danes still had to face the fact that it was impossible to fight fire with fire in the case of the Tsurumi people's initiative – and consequently their Japanese main customer, the Asano Cement Company. The consequence was that the Japanese sold the Danish technology to others at their own initiative.[59]

Towards the end of the 1930s, the Japanese pressure to have the machine production facilities – and consequently F.L. Smidth & Co.'s technological competences – fully located in Japan increased. In August 1937, the war situation made it impossible to have the payment for an order for a factory in Sanchoku paid in British pounds into F.L. Smidth & Co.'s account in London. Mitsui & Co. therefore put pressure on them to have the entire plant manufactured in Japan and paid for in Yen.[60] F.L. Smidth & Co. strongly opposed this and, referring to the question of quality, argued in favour of having the Symetro gears for the cement mill delivered from Copenhagen. This made no difference, however, and in order to obtain a share of the future orders from Japan, the Danes had to accept, in the autumn of 1937, that also the gear parts could be manufactured by a Japanese sub-supplier. With this outcome, the control of the last element in the machine production, which F.L. Smidth & Co. had struggled to maintain around their base in Denmark, had been transferred to their Japanese business partners.[61]

Notes

1 The following description of Japan's modernisation process is based on Elise K. Tipton: *Modern Japan. A Social and Political History*, 2nd ed. (London and New York, 2008). Ian Inkster: *Japanese Industrialisation. Historical and Cultural Perspectives* (London and New York, 2001).
2 Yoichi Nagashima: *De dansk-japansk kulturelle forbindelser 1873-1903* (København, 2012), 31–32.
3 Inkster, *Japanese Industrialisation*, 34–37.
4 Inkster, *Japanese Industrialisation*, 33, 51–58.
5 Inkster, *Japanese Industrialisation*, 52.
6 Taiheiyo Cement Corporation: *International Directory of Company*

Histories, Vol. 60 (Detroit: St. James Press, 2004), 298–299. Soon-Won Park: *Colonial Industrialization and Labor in Korea. The Onoda Cement Factory* (Harvard, 1999), 53.

7 Seiichiro Yonekura: *The Samurai Company: Double Creative Response in Meiji * Japan. The Case of Onoda Cement* (Institute of Innovation Research, Hitotsubashi University, 2012), http://econpapers.repec.org/paper/hitiirwps/12-08.htm

8 In 1998, the Asano Cement Company entered into a merger called the Taiheiyo Cement Corporation.

9 Johannes Hirschmeier: *The Origins of Entrepreneurship in Meiji Japan* (Harvard, 1964), 238–240.

10 For the establishment and initial development of the Onoda Cement Company, see Seiichiro Yonekura, *The Samurai Company.* Like the Asano Cement Company, the Onoda Cement Company joined the merger in 1998 under the Taiheiyo Cement Corporation.

11 *T. Stig-Nielsen to Poul Larsen. 6 December 1923*, T. Stig-Nielsen, Oriental 1922–1926 (FLSA).

12 *T. Stig-Nielsen to Poul Larsen. 18 November 1922–1926*, T. Stig-Nielsen, Oriental 1924 (FLSA).

13 *T. Stig-Nielsen to Poul Larsen. 18 November 1922–1926*, T. Stig-Nielsen, Oriental 1924 (FLSA).

14 *T. Stig-Nielsen to Poul Larsen. 18 November 1922-26*, T. Stig-Nielsen, Oriental 1924 (FLSA).

15 As regards the information on Stig-Nielsen's activities immediately after his arrival in Japan, see *T. Stig-Nielsen to Poul Larsen. 25 July 1926*, T. Stig-Nielsen, Oriental 1922–1926 (FLSA).

16 *T. Stig-Nielsen to Poul Larsen. 29 October 1926*, Japan-China 1923–1932 (FLSA).

17 *O.V. Mørch to T. Stig-Nielsen. 25 May 1927; Harry Schrøder to F.L. Smidth & Co., Japan. 27 November 1927*, Japan-China 1923–1932; *Rotary Kilns supplied by F.L. Smidth & Co., 1938* (FLSA).

18 *T. Stig-Nielsen to The Danish legation Tokyo. 30 July 1929*, T. Stig-Nielsen, Oriental 1929 (FLSA).

19 *T. Stig-Nielsen to Poul Larsen. 5 February 1929*, Japan-China 1923–1932 (FLSA).

20 *T. Stig-Nielsen to Poul Larsen. 5 February 1929*, Japan-China 1923–1932 (FLSA).

21 *T. Stig-Nielsen to Poul Larsen. 5 February 1929*, Japan-China 1923–1932 (FLSA).

22 *T. Stig-Nielsen to Poul Larsen. 29 October 1926*, Japan-China 1923–1932 (FLSA).

23 *O.V. Mørch to T. Stig-Nielsen. 25 May 1929*, Japan-Kina 1923–1932 (FLSA).

24 *T. Stig-Nielsen to Poul Larsen. 19 January 1928*, Japan-China 1923–1932 (FLSA).

25 *Harry Schrøder to O.V. Mørch. 24 March 1927*, Japan-China 1923–1932 (FLSA).

26 *T. Stig-Nielsen to Poul Larsen. 19 January 1928*, Japan-China 1923–1932 (FLSA).

27 *T. Stig-Nielsen to O.V. Mørch. 17 December 1927*, Japan-China 1923–1932 (FLSA).

28 *T. Stig-Nielsen to O.V. Mørch. 10 July 1928*, Japan-China 1923–1932 (FLSA).

29 The resistance against the Danish *"resident engineers"* among some of the Japanese engineers and Bernard Olsen's presence at Katsubo appear from *T. Stig-Nielsen to Poul Larsen* and other sources. *14 February 1930*, T. Stig-Nielsen, Oriental 1930 (FLSA).

30 *T. Stig-Nielsen to F.L. Smidth & Co., Copenhagen. 15 September 1928*; *O.V. Mørch to T. Stig-Nielsen. 4 October 1928*, Japan-China 1923–1932 (FLSA).

31 *T. Stig-Nielsen to Poul Larsen. 22 July 1929*, T. Stig-Nielsen, Oriental 1929 (FLSA).

32 *T. Stig-Nielsen to Poul Larsen. 22 July 1929*, T. Stig-Nielsen, Oriental 1929 (FLSA).

33 *T. Stig-Nielsen to Poul Larsen. 22 July 1929*, T. Stig-Nielsen, Oriental 1929 (FLSA).

34 Information regarding the travel schedule was retrieved from *T. Stig-Nielsen to Poul Larsen. 27 November 1929*, T. Stig-Nielsen, Oriental 1929 (FLSA).

35 The large number of letters of thanks are found in T. Stig-Nielsen, Oriental 1930 (FLSA).

36 *Henrik Kauffmann to Poul Larsen. 9 April 1930*, T. Stig-Nielsen, Oriental 1930 (FLSA).

37 *T. Stig-Nielsen to Poul Larsen. 11 April 1930*, T. Stig-Nielsen, Oriental 1930 (FLSA).

38 *T. Stig-Nielsen to Poul Larsen. 11 April 1930*, T. Stig-Nielsen, Oriental 1930 (FLSA). See also *T. Stig-Nielsen to J.J. Bahnson. 24 February 1930. Soichiro Asano to Henrik Kauffmann. 10 April 1930. T. Stig-Nielsen to J.J. Bahnson. 14 April 1930*, Japan-China 1923–1932 (FLSA).

39 *T. Stig-Nielsen to Poul Larsen. 11 March 1930*, Japan-China 1923–1932 (FLSA).

40 *T. Stig-Nielsen to F.L. Smidth & Co. A/S, Copenhagen. 8 August 1932*, Asano & Onoda, Personal Notes (FLSA).

41 *T. Stig-Nielsen to F.L. Smidth & Co. A/S, Copenhagen. 8 August 1932*, Asano & Onoda, Personal Notes (FLSA).

42 *T. Stig-Nielsen to F.L. Smidth & Co. A/S, Copenhagen. 8 August 1932*, Asano & Onoda, Personal Notes (FLSA).

43 *T. Stig-Nielsen to F.L. Smidth & Co. A/S, Copenhagen. 8 August 1932*, Asano & Onoda, Personal Notes (FLSA).

44 *T. Stig-Nielsen to F.L. Smidth & Co. A/S, Copenhagen. 8 August 1932*, Asano & Onoda, Personal Notes (FLSA).

45 *T. Stig-Nielsen to O.V. Mørch. 22 October 1930*, T. Stig-Nielsen, Oriental 1930 (FLSA).

46 *O.V. Mørch to T. Stig-Nielsen. 30 July 1929*, Japan-China 1923–1932 (FLSA).

47 *Sigurd Pedersen to T. Stig-Nielsen. 22 October 1930*, Japan-China 1923–1932 (FLSA).

48 *O.V. Mørch to T. Stig-Nielsen. 12 May 1932*; *P. Antonsen to T. Stig-Nielsen. 4 October 1932*; *P. Antonsen to T. Stig-Nielsen. 15 October 1932*, T. Stig-Nielsen, Oriental 1932 (FLSA).

49 Here and in the following reference is made to the report "Manufacture of Machinery in Japan," in *T. Stig-Nielsen to F.L. Smidth & Co., Copenhagen. 8 August 1932*, Asano-Onoda, Personal Notes (FLSA).

50 *O.V. Mørch to T. Stig-Nielsen. 31 October 1932*, T. Stig-Nielsen, Oriental 1932 (FLSA).

51 *Sigurd Pedersen to T. Stig-Nielsen. 20 October 1932*, Japan-Kina 1923–1932; *T. Stig-Nielsen to F.L. Smidth & Co., Copenhagen. 27*

October 1932, T. Stig-Nielsen, Oriental 1932; *Sigurd Pedersen to T. Stig-Nielsen. 24 October 1933*, T. Stig-Nielsen, Oriental 1933 (FLSA).

52 *Sigurd Pedersen to T. Stig-Nielsen. 9 December 1933*, T. Stig-Nielsen, Oriental 1933 (FLSA).

53 *Sigurd Pedersen to T. Stig-Nielsen. 24 October 1933*, T. Stig-Nielsen, Oriental 1933; *O.V. Mørch to Sigurd Pedersen. 10 February 1934*, T. Stig-Nielsen, American & Oriental 1934; *Sigurd Pedersen to T. Stig-Nielsen. 7 March 1934; Sigurd Pedersen to T. Stig-Nielsen. 26 July 1934*, T. Stig-Nielsen, American & Oriental 1934 (FLSA).

54 *F.L. Smidth & Co., Tokyo to F.L. Smidth & Co., Copenhagen. 30 August 1937*, Japan-China 1937–1938 (FLSA).

55 *F.L. Smidth & Co., Copenhagen to T. Stig-Nielsen. 6 October 1936*, T. Stig-Nielsen, Oriental 1936 (FLSA).

56 *Tyge Møller to T. Stig-Nielsen. 9 October 1936*, T. Stig-Nielsen, Oriental 1936 (FLSA).

57 *Sigurd Pedersen to T. Stig-Nielsen. 24 March 1934*, T. Stig-Nielsen, American & Oriental 1934 (FLSA).

58 *F.L. Smidth & Co. Copenhagen to F.L. Smidth & Co., Tokyo. 29 August 1934*, T. Stig-Nielsen, American & Oriental 1934 (FLSA).

59 *T. Stig-Nielsen to F.L. Smidth & Co., Copenhagen. 9 October 1934*, T. Stig-Nielsen, American & Oriental 1934 (FLSA).

60 *F.L. Smidth & Co., Tokyo to F.L. Smidth & Co., Copenhagen. 30 August 1937*, Japan-China 1937–1938 (FLSA).

61 *F.L. Smidth & Co., Copenhagen to F.L. Smidth & Co., Tokyo. 7 September 1937*, Japan-Kina 1937–1938 (FLSA).

References

Elise K. Tipton: *Modern Japan. A Social and Political History*, 2nd ed. (London & New York, 2008).

Johannes Hirschmeier: *The Origins of Entrepreneurship in Meiji Japan* (Harvard, 1964).

Ian Inkster: *Japanese Industrialisation. Historical and Cultural Perspectives* (London and New York, 2001).

Seiichiro Yonekura: *The Samurai Company: Double Creative Response in Meiji Japan. The Case of Onoda Cement* (Institute of Innovation Research, Hitotsubashi University, 2012), http://econpapers.repec.org/paper/hitiirwps/12-08.htm

Soon-Won Park: *Colonial Industrialization and Labor in Korea. The Onoda Cement Factory* (Harvard, 1999).

Taiheiyo Cement Corporation: *International Directory of Company Histories*, Vol. 60 (Detroit: St. James Press, 2004).

Yoichi Nagashima: *De dansk-japansk kulturelle forbindelser 1873-1903* (København, 2012).

6 A Strategic Goal of Independence. India 1904–1938

The Indian Context at the Turn of the 20th Century

The Indian cement industry emerged during the first decades of the 20th century and was strongly marked by the contrasts of the colonised world, and of the modernisation process which the country had been undergoing since the 1850s.[1] India's position was that of a regular colony – from 1858 directly under the British crown, and from 1876 onwards as the jewel in the crown of empress Victoria. In other words, the highest Indian authority was British, not Indian, and for this reason India's commercial life was dominated for decades by British interests, which as a matter of course provided for the interests of the companies in the British Isles. From the beginning of the 19th century, the export of commodities such as indigo, silk, rice and timber had led to increasing economic growth. This had the strongest impact on the main city of Bombay, to which enormous riches had been imported by virtue of the British East India Company's trade in opium on China. However, in the major part of the Indian subcontinent, a miserable infrastructure prevented both efficient administration of the country and the exploitation of its resources. Poor road communication and a multitude of monetary and administrative boundaries between federal states raised a multitude of barriers to a very large growth potential. It was therefore a key issue for the colonial power to make amends for this in order to ensure their possibilities to both rule India and ensure earnings for themselves from the country's resources. From the 1850s onwards, the British initiated a modernisation programme led by the East India Company which forestalled several of the western-inspired reforms which followed more than 20 years later in Japan and China. This prepared the ground for the emergence of a number of British-owned companies. Thus, under the management of governor-general Lord Dalhousie, an initiative was taken in 1850 to create a general body of laws, a common administrative language (English, of course) and an educational sector with three universities and other institutions. Moreover, an order was issued to initiate comprehensive road construction work, and from 1854 the construction

DOI: 10.4324/9780429446184-6

of a railway network which was to develop into one of the largest in the world. And when the administrative control of the crown colony was transferred from the East India Company to the British empire, this development was boosted even further.

When F.L. Smidth & Co. first tried to capture market shares in India around the year 1900, it was therefore in a context which had been undergoing Western-dominated modernisation for half a century. While the railway network already spanned 2,550 km in 1851, it had been extended to 15,650 km by 1881, and by 1901 to as much as 38,900 km.[2]

The modernisation initiatives of the colonial power were accompanied by the establishment of a number of Western companies, which were owned and operated in clusters by British so-called *agency houses*. At the same time, from the 1860s, a considerable Indian-owned business life developed, which in line with the British *agency houses* was strongly characterised by conglomerates. Of the company groups established around Bombay's textile industry, several grew to a considerable size. However, the conglomerate established in 1868 by the Tata family, led by Jamsetji Nusserwanji Tata, was completely unequalled.[3] In the beginning, its activity was concentrated around trade, but with the establishment of its flagship, The Central India Spinning, Weaving and Manufacturing Company, the Tata family's business empire was expanded during the decades leading up to 1900 by an extensive textile industry, and also by food exports and other business lines. The diversification process picked up more speed following the turn of the century when the Tata group underwent a dramatic development with the establishment of a number of large heavy industry companies.

In spite of the massive clashes of interest that followed from British colonialism, and which already in 1857 resulted in extensive rebellions in the northern part of India and the East India Company's fall as an Indian holder of power, the emergence of the modern industries occurred in an atmosphere of reasonable harmony between Indian and British interests.[4] The reason was not least that the efforts were distributed across different lines of business and sectors. The Indians focused mainly on the cotton textile industry, whereas the British actors operated in other fields such as jute production, coal mining, steam transport and tea and coffee. Below the surface, however, the Indian actors became increasingly aware of their own identity, and particularly the British abolishment in 1882 of the duty on imports of textile products from Great Britain, which placed the Indian manufacturers in an extremely difficult situation, was seen as a hostile action and led to extensive protests. The creation of the Indian National Congress in 1885 took place with close ties to the Indian industrialists, and a mindset known as *Swadeshi* regarding Indian economic autonomy based on a modern industry and an independent banking system gained momentum.

When Lord Curzon decided, in 1905, to divide Bengal on the pretext of making administration easier, this led to further resistance in the western parts of the region, particularly by the Indian Hindus, who would be reduced to a minority compared to the Muslim population groups, and who saw the division as directly aimed at minimising their considerable economic and political influence. In the wake of the division followed renewed demands for *Swadeshi,* accompanied by a boycott of foreign products. The hostile atmosphere against the British thus paved the way for the creation of a number of Indian companies, some of which became very significant, among them the Tata Iron and Steel Company, TISCO, which was founded in 1907 based on capital investments from Indian investors driven by enthusiasm regarding liberation from British dominance. When World War I tied up almost all the capacity of the European industry in the following years, the result was an extremely favourable business climate in India. This became the basis of a strong consolidation of the new Indian companies and, not least, turned steel-producing TISCO into the Swadeshi movement's largest company.

However, the war-years boom also created a basis for the establishment of new companies within other lines of business which had till then been dominated by European actors in India or by companies based in Europe. One of the lines of business that emerged at the initiative of the Indians in the hostile atmosphere against the western world during the years around World War I was the cement industry.

Entry into the Indian Market and Consolidation (1904–1930)

Comprehensive infrastructure projects were initiated by the British during the second half of the 19th century, but in spite of this, neither they nor the introduction of modern building methods caused an Indian cement industry to be established. For more than half a century, the usage of cement for India's houses, bridges, viaducts, harbour facilities, etc. was dependent on the import of Western-produced commodities, of which 85% derived from the British Isles and thus provided the British industry with massive earnings.[5] When the largest actors in Indian business life began to seriously expand the country's industry by the most capital-demanding lines of business during the early years of the 20th century, the cement industry was therefore first on the list. In this context, it is hardly surprising that this happened on the basis of technology transfers from F.L. Smidth & Co. and to a much lesser extent from their competitors, whose home countries were not only the big industrial nations in the West but also the biggest colonial powers. The British machinery works in particular might have had a good basis for working in a well-known Indian colonial sphere, but they were also so closely linked to the very part of the European cement industry which the Indians primarily wished to outcompete. However, this did not prevent the British from taking their own initiatives.

Indian Cement Industry, British Initiatives

Before the Indians themselves began to establish a cement industry, a British actor, i.e. one of the two partners in the British *agency house* Arbuthnot & Co., P. Macfadyen, managed to initiate the establishment of India's first cement factory at Madras in 1904. Although this was a British initiative, it resulted in close contact between F.L. Smidth & Co. and the Indian sphere from the outset. The factory was constructed around machinery from Copenhagen, including the most recent technology in the shape of a 22-m-long rotary kiln. This provided F.L. Smidth & Co. with advantages that might enhance their possibilities to participate in British initiatives in the Indian market. Since 1890, F.L. Smidth & Co. had had an office in London from which their activities in the British colonies had been taken care of from the very beginning.[6] This meant that for more than ten years, work had been in progress to spread information about the Danish technology supplier in the relevant British business circles and other networks. Moreover, shortly before the Madras factory was established in 1904, i.e. in 1901–1902, F.L. Smidth & Co. had completed the job of fitting out a rotary kiln factory, only the second in England, for the Sussex Portland Cement Co. Ltd.[7] In other words, F.L. Smidth & Co.'s reputation as a technology leader was secured with the British actors with an interest in the cement industry and its development.

The Madras factory never became an important player in the Indian cement industry, however. After a number of failed investments in India, the USA and South America, Arbuthnot & Co. collapsed in 1906.[8] Without a capital base, the company's other quite robust activities in both India and England were also terminated, and the leading figure, Sir George Arbuthnot, had to face the legal consequences, whereas P. Macfadyen took his own life and left his cement business in shambles. However, the work of transferring technology to Madras had earned F.L. Smidth & Co. the opportunity to increase their advantages in the Indian market. The Danes had had an opportunity to form their first impression of the conditions for working in India, and at the same time, knowledge of the Danish business partner had increased, both in the Indian context and with the British businesses that might want to invest in the establishment of cement factories in India.

Indian Cement Industry, Indian Initiatives

F.L. Smidth & Co.'s possibilities to gain a firm foothold in the Indian market arose during the years following 1913, when the Indian Cement Co. Ltd., which had been established by the Tata family the previous year, built a cement factory at Porbandar in the federal state of Gujarat. The Porbandar factory was initially established with machinery from

German Krupp, but when another factory, i.e. the Katni Cement and Industrial Company, Ltd., near Bihar in Madhya Pradesh, followed later in the same year, with the Tata family as the driving force, this was based on technology deliveries from F.L. Smidth & Co. This first collaboration with India's leading industrial conglomerate was followed up when F.L. Smidth & Co. were also hired to take care of expansions of the Porbandar factory in the following years.[9] This meant that the Swadeshi movement's trend-setting activities, which at this point in time were led by Dorabji Tata, had now seriously embarked on the task of adding yet another of the most knowledge- and capital-intensive industries to their portfolio and had, in a very short time, moved on to base their initiatives on collaboration with a technology supplier from the politically harmless Denmark.

Thus, from 1913, F.L. Smidth & Co. assumed the role as the preferred technology supplier to the Indian cement factories, both the factories which were established with the Tata family as the driving force and in the Indian market in general.

Already in 1915, F.L. Smidth & Co. delivered another factory to India, this time for the Bundi Hydraulic Lime & Cement Co. Ltd., which was established at Lakheri in Rajasthan. And yet again, Danish political neutrality provided F.L. Smidth & Co. with a decisive advantage of a slightly different variety. The Bundi factory was established by Killick Nixon & Co., which up through the 1890s had developed into the most significant British *agency house* in Bombay. But again – in spite of the direct British connection – the factory was established with machinery from F.L. Smidth & Co., who could continue, relatively unimpededly, to deliver machinery under cover of Danish neutrality during World War I, whereas the British machinery works had to adapt to war production.[10]

The end of World War I was immediately followed by a wave of factory constructions and expansions, with the Tata family as the primary main investor and based on technology deliveries from Denmark. One exception was a factory in Punjab, which like the Bundi factory was established by Killick Nixon & Co., who once more decided, however, to use technology from F.L. Smidth & Co. Finally followed a last wave of Danish machine deliveries to the Indian customers towards the end of the 1920s. Of the nine cement factories in operation in India at the beginning of the 1930s, six thus consisted of facilities delivered fully or partly by F.L. Smidth & Co., primarily in two phases around World War I and at the end of the 1920s.

In overall terms, during their first 15 years in India, the Danes had managed to maintain such a significant grip of the Indian cement machinery market that their position was beginning to resemble that of a monopoly. However, the backers of the Indian cement industry were partly British and partly strongly self-confident Indians with much experience in modern business enterprise. This was also reflected in the

Table 6.1 Indian cement factories based on machinery deliveries from F.L. Smidth & Co. in 1932 and factories based on machine deliveries from other suppliers. Survey compiled by F.L. Smidth & Co., supplemented by information from the company's own survey of rotary kiln sales 1938 and of the Indian factories' technical equipment 1941

Factory	Year of Establishment	Investors	Machine Supplier of First Facility	Machine Deliveries from FLS in
Factories based on machine deliveries fully or partly from F.L. Smidth & Co.				
Porbandar	1913	Indian investors (Tata and others)	Krupp	1922, 1928
Katni	1913	Indian investors (Tata and others)	FLS	1913, 1919, 1929, 1930
Bundi (Lakheri)	1915	Killick Nixon & Co.	FLS	1915, 1919, 1928/29
Gwalior Cement Co. (Banmor)	1920	Indian investors (Tata and others)	FLS	1920, 1928
Punjab (Wah)	1920	Killick Nixon & Co.	FLS	1920, 1926, 1928
Shahabad	1922	Indian investors (Tata, Maharaja Nizam of Hyderabad and others)	FLS	1922, 1927/28
Factories based on machine deliveries from other suppliers				
Dwarka (Okha Cement Co.)	1919 (Allis Chalmers)			
United Cement Co.	Year of establishment? (Allis Chalmers)			
Sone Valley, Japla	Year of establishment? (Newells and Vickers)			

Source: FLSA.

endeavours made by the Danes to gain control of the Indian cement industry. Thus, the FLS people did not get to control the affairs to the same extent as in Siam and China, but because the Danish tools could be currently adapted to the changing conditions and not least potentials in the Indian context, they did not become restricted either, as in Japan.

Aiming at Danish Influence at Two Levels

For the first many years after the preliminary technology transfers, F.L. Smidth & Co. did not build a permanent representation in India outside of the organisations of their Indian customers. Up until the beginning of the 1930s, they made use of travelling engineers and FLS people placed in positions of trust with their Indian customers.[11] In this regard, they had to take into account that not only did they have two types of

Table 6.2 India's cement factories gathered in administrative groups, led by so-called Managing agents, 1931. Survey prepared by F.L. Smidth & Co. 1932

Managing Agent	Factory
Led by Mulraj Khatau: (C. McDonald & Co), Bombay	Katni Cement Co., Katni
Led by Killick Nixon & Co., Bombay	Bundi Cement Co., Bundi
	Punjab Cement Co., Wah
Led by F.E. Dinshaw, Bombay	C.P. Cement Co., Central Provinces
	United Cement Co., Central Provinces
	Gwalior Cement Co., Gwalior
	Okha Cement Co., Dwarka
Led by Tata Sons Ltd., Bombay	The Indian Cement Co., Porbandar
	The Shahabad Cement Co., Shahabad, Deccan
Led by APCM, England	The Sone Valley Cement Co., Japla

Source: FLSA.

customers, i.e. British and Indian; the development of the Indian cement industry also made it relevant to aim at influence at two levels. F.L. Smidth & Co. might well try to manoeuvre the Danes towards positions where they could control the day-to-day management of the cement factories, but a strong trend towards cartel formation in just a few years also paved the way for them to aim at influence at a level above the individual factories. This opened possibilities to step in as a pivotal actor and connecting link for the circles around the cement industry, but in a much less aggressive manner than in East Asia.

The background was that the establishment of the factories towards 1920 caused the production capacity to exceed the demand to an extent that led to price war and bankruptcies. To counteract and regulate this development, a government intervention in 1925 paved the way for increasing the import duty on cement and for the formation of the price regulating body *The Indian Cement Manufacturers' Association.*[12] This meant that the cement factories now entered into a collaboration agreement which, in 1927, was expanded by a marketing collaboration agreement in *The Concrete Association of India.* From 1930, this collaboration was extended by the sales organisation *The Cement Marketing Company of India Ltd.,* where the cement factories were represented in groups of "managing agents", who at the same time – in the wording of the FLS people – took care of the overall management of the factories "... in terms of business and technically".[13]

This meant that in 1931, the FLS people found that the ten Indian cement factories had come together under five *managing agents.* Dominance by the Tata family was considerable. The factories in Porbandar and Shahabad belonged directly under Tata Sons Ltd. In addition, the overall management of as many as four factories belonged under one of the Tata empire's closest business partners, Framroze Edulji Dinshaw, who occupied a strong position in the Indian business sector. Up through the 1920s and 1930s, he was one of Bombay's largest industrial investors, based on a vast personal fortune, and he also profited from considerable commissions from TISCO, since he had facilitated a loan from the fifth Maharaja of Gwalior, Madho Rao Scindia, for the steel manufacturing company.[14] The Katni factory belonged under another of the Tata family's closest business partners, Dharamsey Mulraj Khatau, who had taken over a considerable industrial conglomerate from his father. This had been founded in 1874 and was based on textile production, chemical industries and shipping operations.[15] Outside of the Tata sphere were only two factories, established by the British *agency house* Killick Nixon & Co., Bombay, and a single plant, the Sone Valley Cement Co., which was represented in the Cement Marketing Company of India by a British company directly from England in the shape of the Associated Portland Cement Manufacturers (APCM).

In other words, two options were available to F.L. Smidth & Co. Their aim could be to have Danes occupy managing position in the individual factories. This would seem obvious. However, if they aimed at supplying FLS people who could also contribute to the work carried out by the respective *managing agents,* they would also have a potential for influence on both the technical management of the factories and on a more overall cartel-like structure which handled the affairs of the Indian cement industry.

Danes in the British-Owned Part of the Indian Cement Industry 1914–1931

F.L. Smidth & Co. soon succeeded in manoeuvring the FLS people into the factory management of the British-owned part of the Indian cement industry. At least, in 1922, the Danish perception of management of the two Killick Nixon factories was that "Bundi and Punjab are managed by engineer A.T. Robinson, who has also come from F.L. Smidth & Co".[16] And in a comment on their collaboration with Killick Nixon & Co. in 1933, Aage Smith concluded that

> They have been our friends ever since we first did business with them in 1914. We have given them Tom Robinson, and we have given them Ewald Christensen and Carlsson, all people we first trained here, and all the machinery we have sold them have been satisfactory … .[17]

Of the three people mentioned, Ewald Christensen for one had been in Killick Nixon & Co.'s service since 1914, when he was sent out from Copenhagen to fit out the factory in Bundi.1

Danes in the Indian-Owned Part of the Indian Cement Industry 1914–1931

Initially, it was not quite as easy to get Danes placed in control of the Tata-dominated factories. Danes were indeed hired to contribute to the running of the factories owned by Indians. Among these were burner master Christensen in Shahabad at the beginning of 1932. But it was apparently a slow process to get the Danes manoeuvred into factory management positions or with the superior *managing agents*.[18] This did not in any way mean, however, that the Danes had no possibilities of gaining profound influence inside the Tata-dominated cement sphere. Only that the possibilities were embedded in their potential to navigate in a field dominated by Indian owners and the British they employed to assist them with business management. How this potential could be unfolded may be illustrated by the role one of the Danish key figures, engineer Ejnar Lassen Landorph, came to play in the establishment of the Gwalior Cement Co. and Shahabad Cement Co. at the beginning of the 1920s.[19]

Landorph came from a job as *Division Engineer* in the Canadian Pacific Railway Company, and after meeting personally with Poul Larsen in New York, he left this job to take on a position in the FLS-owned contracting firm Danalith, which specialised in the casting of reinforced concrete and, as a sub-supplier, performed complicated concrete casting tasks in cement factory construction around the World. His first tasks took him to France, but Landorph was soon redirected to India to be in charge of the reinforced concrete work in the building of the Gwalior Cement Company. Around Christmas 1920 he therefore arrived with his wife Sarah at the town of Gwalior in the federal state of the same name. Here, the couple were introduced to the European community of the town and to the upper echelons of the Indian population, including Gwalior's ruler Maharaja Scindia, and later on to the 800 men, women and children who were involved in the building project.

The task of leading the factory building project involved many challenges. However, in Landorph's everyday life, the biggest challenge was that in spite of the Tata dominance, the Gwalior Cement Company was indeed owned by Indians, the management of the company was in the hands of a staff of English technical experts who had been members of the large Tata workforce since the 1880s. From a Danish point of view, the opportunities to benefit from an asymmetrical knowledge base and thus take control of the factory were therefore well and truly messed up. Landorph's descriptions of his working conditions clearly reflect how he had ended up in a situation where the Indians played the expatriate parties – the Danes and the British – off against each other. Slightly paradoxically, the presence of the British at the factory did, in other words, secure a Danish position and influence. Using F.L. Smidth & Co. as a tool, the Indians were able to establish a checks-and-balances-like situation. With their Danish business partner in place, they could avoid too much British dominance; at the same time, they could place the British in the leading positions of the cement factories and thus avoid becoming dependent on the Danish expertise.

The result was a strained relationship between the Danes and the British, and this appears explicitly from Landorph's letters home to his family in Denmark immediately after his arrival in Gwalior. Already in January 1921, he concluded regarding the English *works manager* R.S. Symonds:

> He is far too English-English for me to approve of his type; he does not want to accept good advice, he will not even discuss this. He always knows best beforehand what to do, and this is despite of the fact that it has appeared on several occasions that it would have been well, had he listened. Result: I only speak when asked, and as you know, this is not to my liking.[20]

This was only the first of a large number of complaints about R.S. Symons during the following two years. However, what was expressed was not just personal conflict material, which appears from a generally negative tone towards those of Tata's British staff who appeared to Landorph to be his direct competitors. For illustration purposes, this was clearly expressed in Landorph's description from July 1927, in which he writes how:

> One of Tata's engineers (at home he would be a constructor), a certain Mr. Jones (Welshman, 56 years of age) arrived here in order to build a power station; he managed to get as far as to the middle of the building site from Banmor Station, then he collapsed and had to be carried into a house, be driven back to Gwailior, treated by a doctor and is now critically ill in bed at Gwalior Hotel from malaria and heatstroke.

Personal acquaintances of Landorph or not, the British were presented in a negative light, and he consistently held them at arm's length.

Towards the end of 1922, Landorph was transferred to the building site of the Shahabad Cement Company, which meant that he was now among new British people. As this move meant that he stepped in as *works manager* during the building period, replacing British Jeffries, the trouble now mainly involved his superiors in technical positions of trust in the parent group and Tata Engineering Co. in particular. This became the beginning of a course of events in which both the Danes and the British spent much energy on bringing their counterparts into discredit with their Indian employer, both orally and in writing. Thus, in February 1923, Landorph reported about the British building manager at Tata Engineering Co.:

Limby came here on the 12th, I think I wrote this previously, he has sent an awfully impudent report about the conditions here; they are indeed not rosy, for this to be the case Jeffries has shown much too little vigilance, but according to Limby's Report, conditions are almost worse now than before, and I have written a very harsh letter to Bombay Office today in which I state that if L. does not contain himself, and "tries to speak the truth", I shall promptly hand in my notice.

Even though the power struggle took its toll on Landorph, he held his ground. Announcements from F.L. Smidth & Co. in Copenhagen clearly expressed an overall strategy of gaining influence at the Tata factories. Landorph therefore held on, even though he was under pressure and strongly motivated to pack up and leave for Denmark.

But there are very likely other and weightier considerations to bear in mind, referring to F.L. Smidth & Co.'s wishes, it is very fair that F.L.S. might think it to be quite favourable for them to have me here as Works Manager while the factory is being constructed, and that they will therefore persuade me to remain, although this will undoubtedly bring about many a harsh dispute with Limby etc.[21]

At a meeting by the Shahabad Cement Co.'s board of directors in the town of Hyderabad in July, to which both Landorph and Limby were invited, matters came to a head, and the Brit was fired. Thus, in this context, the strong opposition displayed by Landorph served as a tool for the Indian owners to regulate their British staff. This did not imply, however, that the British were replaced by Danes. Landorph's conflicts continued, only now with British White in Limby's former position in Tata Engineering Co.'s staff. Although it was Landorph's impression that ideas were circulating at Tata to keep him as *works manager* beyond the construction period, i.e. as cement production manager, the outcome was that when the building activities were completed in March 1924, he had to leave his position as factory manager to R.S. Symon's brother, W.F. Symons, who had till then been the manager of the Tata factory in Porbandar. Landorph then had to travel home to Denmark. In other words, an FLS take-over of the factory management in Gwalior and Shahabad so far did not get off the ground. For this to happen, British dominance was too great, and the interest of the Indians to eliminate this and the advantages it implied were too small.

An Office in Bombay (1932–1936)

In 1932, F.L. Smidth & Co. established itself as an official company in India with an office in Bombay led by Danish Aage Smith, who until then had overseen the company's Indian affairs from the head office in Copenhagen.[22] The opening of this new office marked a new initiative to gain influence and control of the Indian cement industry. As had been the case when F.L. Smidth & Co. opened an office in China ten years earlier, there was a need to get a handle on the Danes working in key positions with their customers in India, as well as a need to access new market opportunities. In India of the 1930s, the challenge for the FLS people was not, however, to maintain the control that was about to slip from their grasp, but rather the need to manoeuvre wisely in the context of an increasing pressure to gain closer contact with parts of the cement industry.

Danish Opportunism

On Aage Smith's arrival in India in 1932, Danes had been employed in key positions at Killick Nixon & Co.'s factories for almost 20 years. It was therefore not surprising that the handling of opportunism came to be included in the to-do list of the newly arrived FLS people in Bombay. In one of the Danes in particular, i.e. engineer Ewald Christensen, loyalty seemed to have shifted from the old Danish parent company to his British employers. Having left his job as machine fitter with F.L. Smidth & Co. almost 20 years earlier, Ewald Christensen was, in 1932, employed in a position of such high trust with Killick Nixon & Co. that it was up to him alone to take care of the company's interests when inviting tenders for a new factory they were planning to establish in collaboration with F.E. Dinshaw at the town of Coimbatore in Southern India.[23] In other words, Ewald Christensen's position was particularly influential. However, as the process proceeded, this seemed to be mainly a problem for F.L. Smidth & Co.

In the negotiations, Killick Nixon & Co. attempted to seize power over the choice of suppliers for the upcoming construction project, which, as expressed by Aage Smith, would mean "strongly favouring – British manufacturers". There was nothing odious about this. What was more annoying was, however, that such a development would strengthen Ewald Christensen's role because, as Aage Smith learnt from personal experience, he no longer worked for F.L. Smidth & Co.'s interests, but rather was no longer controllable. In Aage Smith's perception, Ewald Christensen was instead seeking to construct a factory plant himself with machinery from various suppliers and was in this way attempting to make himself indispensable – at the expense of his Danish parent company. At the beginning of 1933, Aage Smith went as far as to conclude in a telegram that "Ewald Christensen – attitude – to us – has been – quite – hostile – and – some of – his – statements – may be – characterized – as – deliberately – wrong – Stop".[24]

Seen from the outside, this might be interpreted as an indication that Ewald Christensen's technological expertise was no longer up-to-date, and that he was trying to hide this from being exposed in the negotiations so as not to cause this to harm his position with Killick Nixon & Co. In any case, this was how the FLS people saw the situation, having seen how he acted in the negotiations with his counterpart at F.E. Dinshaw, the British engineer H.I. Captain: "We are afraid that Mr. Ewald Christensen has had the idea all the time that Captain could do the job at Coimbatore without Christensen's help if we helped Captain, and therefore he was anxious that we should not get the order".[25] Seen from Copenhagen, Ewald Christensen would not have needed to be anxious if he had concentrated on filling his position with Killick Nixon & Co. – and, that is, if he had done as instructed from Copenhagen. But the FLS people could not ignore his demonstration of distinct lack of loyalty. During the negotiations, they therefore chose to support Captain as manager of the Coimbatore project, assisted by such good Danish forces that he would be able to withstand Ewald Christensen's attempts to obtain power by force. As was expressed by the person in charge of the India department in Copenhagen, O.V. Mørch:

> On receipt of your telegram we at once looked about for an assistant for Captain, who could do the work and who could help Captain in case there came any attacks later on what Captain was doing. It was therefore not only a question of a man who knew about concrete constructional work, but it was very important that he should also be able to counter Mr. Ewald Christensen in any discussion about cement technical problems.[26]

In concrete terms, the outcome was that engineer Bernard Olsen, who had a great deal of experience from building projects for the Asano Cement Company, was appointed for the position as technical assistant to Captain. The situation was now that one FLS man was in reality sent out to fight off another FLS man who had become uncontrollable.

New Market Prospects in India

The lesson learnt from the Coimbatore project was that the Tata-dominated part of the Indian cement industry was no longer dismissive of buying machinery from the British suppliers. This was also seen in 1931 when Katni Cement Co., with Mulraj Khatau at the helm, bought a rotary kiln from British Vickers. The Danes had, at least momentarily, lost one of their oldest Indian customers. In other words, in a worst-case scenario, this was an indication of initial erosion of their monopoly-like position, and in any case of Indian pressure on the Danish exploitation of this.[27]

At the same time, increased collaboration between the Indian cement manufacturers was in the pipeline. Whereas their collaboration so far had included prices, marketing and sale, the operation and development of the production machinery were included after 1930. This represented a decisive argument for F.L. Smidth & Co. to bolster their platform by opening the office in Bombay, which could provide reliable information about any activities and make sure Danish services were promoted in the right places. Such cartel formation signified golden opportunities for a technology supplier, not least because it prepared the ground for the use of external impartial support, completely parallel to the situation in China, where the FLS people, in 1930–1931 as well, were making a great effort to capture the privileged role as advisor to *the Chinese Cement Manufacturers Association*. In India, the ambition level must be at the same high level since what would be more natural for the Indian companies than to approach the business partner they had been sharing for decades?

Collaboration between the Indian cement producers concerning technical matters gathered speed from 1931, when F.E. Dinshaw took on a leading role in this, backed by the Tata influence, and in 1933, this was manifested when the companies under the Cement Marketing Company teamed up and established the factory in Coimbatore to meet the increased need for cement in Southern India. It soon became clear to F.L. Smidth & Co. that exactly because the order for the Coimbatore factory was based on strong Indian collaboration, this was a core order they needed to win. As expressed by Aage Smith:

> It was therefore of paramount importance for us to win this order, and we obtained orders for a rather considerable part of the machinery, that is in addition to the actual cement machineries also for the electric equipment and for a travelling crane for the treatment of the materials, limestone, coal etc.[28]

Without delay, F.L. Smidth & Co. made every effort to become the technology supplier of the new collaboration constellation.

In Close Collaboration with F.E. Dinshaw

Aage Smith had only just arrived in Bombay in May 1932 when he directed most of his attention towards the strongest actor in the collaboration between the Indian cement manufacturers, F.E. Dinshaw. Thus, already a week after his arrival, he was able to report to Copenhagen about the results of promising negotiations he had conducted personally with Dinshaw.[29] Dinshaw had confirmed the rumours that a decision had been made to construct the Coimbatore factory, and Aage Smith had prepared the ground for choosing Captain, i.e. Dinshaw's technical advisor, as project manager, rather than F.L. Smidth & Co.'s own man (theoretically) at Killick Nixon & Co., i.e. Ewald Christensen. From then on, the FLS people concentrated on delivering input to Captain, who on several occasions called upon the support of FLS on-site employee Bernard Olsen in connection with confrontations with Ewald Christensen.[30] It was obvious that the Danish contribution was accepted with enthusiasm by both Captain and Dinshaw. When Aage Smith announced in 1933 that the order for the factory was about to be won, the vibrations were so good that he could report about Dinshaw's "very kind attitude" and say that "... he thinks that our last price was very low ...", adding that for this reason, he had therefore, on his own accord, increased the payment of the work which had already been delivered.[31]

Dinshaw's requests for support from the FLS people in Bombay soon developed into assistance with key challenges in the operation of the Indian's activities. It soon turned out that F.L. Smidth & Co.'s concerns regarding a possible loss of their secure market position following their defeat in Katni against Vickers the previous year could be replaced by hopes of even closer collaborations, which opened big new opportunities for control of the areas which were interesting to the Danes. This was not least apparent when Dinshaw asked Aage Smith to travel to Calcutta in 1933 to negotiate on his behalf with The National Cement, Mines & Industries Ltd. about the purchase of land areas with raw material deposits as a countermove against the plans in Bombay's financial circles regarding the establishment of a new factory in collaboration with German technology suppliers.[32] The delegation of such an entrusted task was an indication of broad collaboration close to the core to the Indians' strategic dispositions, and it can be difficult not to perceive Aage Smith as directly involved in Dinshaw's activities – which of course he was not in a formal sense. However, as of May 1932, another two activity fields came to reflect how the Danes were about to be directly involved in Indian cement production. These were the recruitment of personnel for the Indian factory managements and the preparations for Danish investments.

Danish Staff for Indian Customers

Whereas no Danes had found their way into factory management positions in the Tata-dominated part of the Indian cement industry before 1932, the situation in the following years was almost diametrically opposite. The reason was that the FLS office came to act as F.L. Smidth & Co.'s auxiliary arm when new managerial positions were to be filled in the Indian factories. Immediately after Aage Smith's arrival in Bombay, Dinshaw asked him to find a candidate for the position as joint *works engineer* for Central Provinces Cement Co. and Okha Cement Co.[33] This task was solved in consultation with the headquarters in Copenhagen, which suggested a young electrical engineer, Rüdinger, who had been in F.L. Smidth & Co.'s service for some time. Rüdinger's posting in Okha came to be the first of a number of recruitments from the ranks of F.L. Smidth & Co. for leading positions at factories in Dinshaw's domain, and there were good possibilities for the Danes to control who ended up where. This became particularly evident when leading positions were to be occupied in Coimbatore in 1933–1934. At this point in time, one of the British Symons brothers was still active in the Tata sphere, and he was now brought into play as an obvious candidate for the job. However, in order to eliminate the Brit and his supporters, Aage Smith was able to try to draw actively on the influence from Captain, who was a member of the factory's board of directors and was strongly dependent on the Danish technology expertise to secure his own position. The manoeuvre was successful, and Bernard Olsen could therefore step into the desired position and use this to safeguard F.L. Smidth & Co.'s interests.[34]

Moreover, as of the spring of 1934, the Danish influence on individual staff reached a new level when Bernard Olsen as the first of a number of staff was about to take over one of the positions in "Dinshaw's General Staff", i.e. in the coordinating company overseeing the individual cement factories. From then on, the activities of the FLS office in Bombay were largely to find Danish candidates for jobs at the Indian factories, replacements of these when adjustments were needed, and the handling of a variety of practical issues regarding the Danish expatriates in India.[35] In other words, at management level, the FLS office was more or less an HR office for the Tata-dominated companies, both at the factories and with the superior *managing agents*. This resulted in the gradual elimination of the previous British influence in favour of Danish dominance of the companies – in other words, the building of strong informal Danish control deep into the organisation of the Indian customers.

At the same time, this involved the handling of increased competition for the best of F.L. Smidth & Co.'s people. With the same individuals standing as candidates with several customers at the same time, the scene was set for a balancing act to satisfy everyone's wishes. This was the case, for instance, when efforts were being made in 1933 to find a works manager at Killick Nixon & Co.'s factory in Bundi, which expressed a wish to employ 33-year-old engineer Emil Riisager. He was simultaneously being wanted for a position at the new factory in Coimbatore, and it was therefore clear that it would be impossible to satisfy all parties involved.[36] In 1935, O.V. Mørch reported from discussions that had been conducted from Copenhagen with Ewald Christensen at Killick Nixon & Co. about a number of people who had been brought into play:

> The situation is such that a couple of months ago we made the offer to Ewald Christensen that he might get Tveskov to assist him, and

we did so at a point in time when Ewald Christensen had made it clear to us that he was not completely confident that Schønfeldt was big enough, and he gave us to understand that we had evidently let Mr. Dinshaw have some of our better people. We pointed out that we had offered him Riisager, and that it was a matter of sheer misfortune that he did not get this person, who was in every respect as good as any other man we had given to our customers.[37]

Of course, it was an unpleasant situation if a customer experienced time and again that they had been treated unfairly. Indeed, Ewald Christensen did threaten to let the order for an extension of Killick Nixon & Co.'s factory in Punjab go to F.L. Smidth & Co.'s competitors if he did not in future get access to include the best FLS people in his staff.[38] The threat remained only a threat. The Danish control was too strong for it to be acted out.

Danish Investments in the Pipeline

From 1934, the now ageing and ailing Dinshaw made an effort to secure the continuation of his business. His plans to let F.L. Smidth & Co. take over a major part of the shares in the companies behind the cement factories were key elements in this work. Danish ownership would ensure that the factory's technical management and development remained in the hands of experts, and in July, Dinshaw presented a written proposal to the FLS people explaining which shareholdings he intended for Danish takeover. At meetings in London and Copenhagen, he personally presented his plans to O.V. Mørch and Gunnar Larsen, who was now about to take over the position as FLS group managing director after his father Poul Larsen.[39] From the Danish quarters, this was positively received. The Danish attitude towards Dinshaw's proposal was in clear opposition to the efforts being made by F.L. Smidth & Co. during the same years to stay clear of any economic involvement in the Chinese cement industry. However, under Gunnar Larsen's leadership, the possibility to establish themselves as a cement manufacturer in India was seen as a step in a new strategic initiative to turn F.L. Smidth & Co. into a global cement manufacturer on the basis of select markets. India was a relevant market to aim at in such a global change of strategy, whereas China was not.

The initial plan was that during his own trip to India in the spring of 1935, Gunnar Larsen was to conduct negotiations regarding the further share acquisition process. However, as he was unable to find the required time for this, it became necessary to ask for postponement, knowing full well that Dinshaw's ill health made the matter urgent. Aage Smith was therefore informed of the opinion he was to convey from Copenhagen:

Table 6.3 Survey of proposal from F.E. Dinshaw to Gunnar Larsen, July 1934, regarding F.L. Smith & Co.'s takeover of shareholdings in Indian cement factories

	Rupees	Percentage of Share Capital	Annual Production – Tonnes	Production in Relation to Shareholdings
C.P. Shares	133,00,000	100	180,000	180,000
Okha Shares	14,35,000	28	100,000	28,000
United Shares	4,71,000	16	0	0
Coimbatore Shares	8,25,000	33	60,000	20,000
	160,31,000			228,000

Source: FLSA.

> You may tell them that we fully understand that Dinshaw wishes to include us, and we would like to help him, and we are also ourselves interested in taking over a share in his undertakings, but we are so busily involved in undertakings to which we had promised capital even before he approached us that for this reason as well, we would prefer to postpone our final decision to the autumn. You may say that, on the other hand, there is presently no reason to believe that we might be in a weaker position in terms of finance in the autumn, on the contrary, but one must always be cautious, and it is always best to proceed in small steps, making a forward thrust and clearing up and observing one's position before making the next small forward thrust.

In other words, explicit Danish interest was expressed. As stated by O.V. Mørch:

> As regards the actual question of taking part in Mr. Dinshaw's undertakings, the situation is that we (in Copenhagen) are still greatly interested in such participation. Of course, there are many good reasons for us to obtain financial interests in the Indian factories. The same reasons that caused us to promise to step in as shareholders in the Burma factory speak in favour of our entry as shareholders in the other undertakings in which Dinshaw is interested. Our position in Dinshaw's undertakings would in a sense be better as we would have a larger share in "The Management" than in Burma, but on the other hand, the investment is indeed also of a much larger size.

As it appears, the target was to obtain as much control with the management as possible, and the size of the investment did not intimidate the Danes. In 1935, F.L. Smith & Co.'s resources were certainly tied up in investments in cement factories in America and in an expected government-assigned monopoly position as cement manufacturer in Ireland. Afterwards, however, they were willing to move on to India, albeit on a smaller scale than the acquisition suggested by Dinshaw. The reason was that whereas the value of this was assessed to amount to GBP 1,200,000, the FLS management were, in their own opinion, not able to raise more than GBP 150,000, which they would then earmark for the shares in Central Provinces Cement Co. (C.P.). This would even be close to their limits, but still attractive in light of the fact that

> ... the chances are so good that the Indian cement factories will be able to find not only a market for their present products but will also find locations where they can build new factories. With a large holding of shares in C.P. it should be possible for us to obtain influence in one way and the other.

Aage Smith was therefore given the task of presenting the case to Dinshaw in a way that this would remain open. In March, the Copenhagen office was happy to report that

> the most important thing is that for the time being we have succeeded in keeping the issue alive and retaining the chance of entering into further negotiations with Mr. Dinshaw, and we are exceedingly happy to note that your negotiations have gone so well.[40]

The pot was kept boiling. Moreover, during the summer of 1935, Dinshaw invited F.L. Smidth & Co. to subscribe for shares in a factory that was being planned in Ceylon, and efforts were still being made to let Gunnar Larsen travel to India in November.

At the end of 1935, it looked as though F.L. Smidth & Co. were actively going for a role as key co-owner of the Indian cement industry. However, already the year after it became necessary to carefully reconsider this strategy.

Two-Edged Strategy in a Cartelised Marked (1936–1938)

At the beginning of 1935, F.L. Smidth & Co. were about to step into a role as multinational cement manufacturer with units in India. The basis of this was their close collaboration with F.E. Dinshaw. This was why it became decisive that his company, from 1936, entered into even closer collaboration with the other Indian cement factories in the newly established *Associated Cement Companies Ltd.*, usually referred to as ACC or just *The Merger*. *The Merger* transformed the assembly of Indian cement manufacturers into one single actor with complete market dominance. Only one factory, the Sone Valley factory in Japla in

Table 6.4 The companies joining the Associated Cement Companies Limited in 1936, including annual production figures

Company	Estimated Production Capacity – Tonnes
The C.P. Cement Company Limited	180,000
Bundi Portland Cement Limited	160,000
The Shahabad Cement Company Limited	140,000
The Katni Cement & Industrial Co. Ltd.	87,000
Punjab Portland Cement Limited	80,000
The Okha Cement Company Limited	80,000
The Coimbatore Cement Company Limited	60,000
The United Cement Co. of India Ltd.	50,000
The Gwalior Cement Company Limited	45,000
The Indian Cement Company Limited	40,000

Source: FLSA.

northeast India decided not to join.[41] Seen from a Danish perspective, the target was now no longer to become connected to the strongest among a number of collaborating companies. With *The Merger*, they would need to collaborate with a cartel construction that commanded the production apparatus of almost the entire Indian cement industry. In light of this, the question was whether it was still relevant to seek Danish control through direct investments.

The reason for the establishment of *The Merger* was overcapacity. Whereas in 1934, the production capacity of the Indian cement factories amounted to 135% of the total Indian cement consumption, this had already increased to 158% the following year (see the table below). Therefore, the key task for ACC was to ensure the appropriate geographical dispersion of factories across India, and a distribution of the production that would counteract a back-breaking price war. This also made it obvious that there would be specific tasks that might result in disputes among the cartel members, each of which might be interested in getting hold of the largest possible slice of the pie. This meant that a new opportunity had emerged for F.L. Smidth & Co. to become included as a mediating technology-savvy assistant, due to their detailed knowledge of the factories' components and their condition. This was already evident by virtue of the model selected for the inclusion of the individual factories in ACC. The agreement immediately placed F.L. Smidth & Co. at the centre of the cartel construction.[42]

Thus, it was agreed that the individual companies were to be taken over by ACC against the payment of 60 rupees per tonne of what was described as the factories' so-called "rated capacity" – i.e. their assessed annual production capacity. Moreover, ACC's takeover of the companies' cash holdings, shares, amounts due to them, stocks, etc. was to be

Table 6.5 Survey of the development 1914–1936 of the Indian cement industry's production capacity and the Indian cement consumption

Year	Number of Factories	Total Capacity (Tonnes)	
1914–1916	3	85,000	
1924	10	581,000	
1934	11	1,072,000	
1936	12	1,465,000	
Cement sales during the accounting year	Indian cement (tonnes)	Imported cement (tonnes)	Total consumption in India (tonnes)
1931–1932	583,000	59,000	642,000
1933–1934	642,000	49,000	791,000
1935–1936	886,000	43,000	929,000

Source: FLSA.

paid in addition to this, using the capital provided by the payment by each company of 10 rupees per tonne of their assessed annual capacity. Large sums of money were at stake, and determining the factories' *rated capacity* was a key task that could not be solved by the counting of rotary kilns, mills, etc. It was also necessary to assess to what extent the plants were technologically up-to-date and, not least, their standards of maintenance. A committee was appointed to review the factories and assess these conditions, and both Ewald Christensen and Aage Smith became members of this. The touring of the factories and the preparation of the necessary reports took place during the first months of 1936. In January, when Aage Smith fell ill, the Danish contribution to this work was supplemented by the visiting O.V. Mørch, which meant that not only the local FLS people in India but also people from the very top level of management in Copenhagen came to be involved in the preparation of the core basis of the ACC construction. This meant that the ground was prepared for close collaboration between F.L. Smidth & Co. and ACC's management level led by the chairman of the board of directors Sir Nowroji Saklatvala – head of the entire Tata & Sons – and E.C. Reid from Killick Nixon & Co.

From a Danish point of view, the question was how best to seek influence over the Indian cement manufacturers and whether this should necessarily take place through direct investments and integration.

"... Not to Encourage Outsiders"

It was evident that ACC wanted F.L. Smidth & Co. to become so closely attached that more or less sole and exclusive rights of the Danish competences were achieved. This clear Indian wish reflected the fact that the cartel did indeed include almost all of the country's cement manufacturers, but this did not signify that competitors might not appear, and it was important to be on good terms with these in advance. From a Danish viewpoint, a close merger with ACC was of course an obvious path to take. This was also risky, however, for with *The Merger*, the market situation in India had in some sense become critical. The possibility to rely on several actors had disappeared and been replaced by either the chance of a monopoly-like situation or the risk of complete failure. At the same time, the negotiation initiatives from the ACC partners made it clear that F.L. Smidth & Co. might end up in a difficult position in case new cement manufacturers appeared on the Indian scene.

Thus, at Killick Nixon & Co. the opinion was that ACC should give preference to F.L. Smidth & Co. regarding orders from ACC, against their obligation, as expressed in a telegram style "... not to encourage outsiders, and if outsider projects do become reality after all, we must notify Merger no later than the time when the machine order is placed. But we must be allowed to work freely to obtain orders". The objective of the notification duty was to enable ACC to persuade new actors to join the cartel and thus to avoid competition. But although this preferential status of orders from ACC might seem tempting, it potentially implied large negative consequences for the Danes; basically, the aim of new cement manufacturers must of course be to enter into competition with the cartel, and for them, it would be anything but tempting to begin collaboration with a technology supplier who was obliged to keep ACC closely informed. In other words, Killick Nixon & Co.'s proposal would more or less pull F.L. Smidth & Co.'s competitors directly into the Indian market, while the Danes would be forced into strong dependence on ACC.

There were even signs indicating that the Tata-dominated part of ACC would want to restrict F.L. Smidth & Co. even further. At least this is what engineer Niels Holck-Larsen, who worked at the FLS office, reported from talks with Captain in Bombay, stating that

> ... he has said to me several times that he would not mind if Krupp, Miag or Vickers would want to build factories for outsiders out here – as long as <u>we</u> do not help the outsiders. Captain's opinion is that factories built by our competitors who do not have our experience with Indian conditions will operate poorly – and that such a poorly operating factory, which may operate at a loss, will be a useful lesson learnt.[43]

A merger as intimate as indicated would ensure orders from ACC, which implied that F.L. Smidth & Co. would be a type of technical project engineering and operations management unit in the cartel. However, the result would most certainly be that orders from outsiders would pass by the Danes and go to F.L. Smidth & Co.'s competitors.

Ramkrishna Dalmia and Rothas Sugar Ltd.

The reason why *outsiders* were on everybody's lips in the middle of 1936 was that the risk of serious competition to ACC was looming on the horizon. In July 1936, rumours of plans to build a cement factory at Dehri on Sone in western Bihar reached Killick Nixon & Co., and directly asked, the FLS people had to admit that they were already informed of the project and considered it to be serious. Subsequently, the Danes decided to inform Captain of the project and tell him that the person behind this was the Punjabi businessman Ramkrishna Dalmia, who ran the company Rothas Sugar Ltd. with five sugar factories: "After some consideration I decided to tell the name of Dalmias to Mr. Captain also before he got it through Killick Nixon & Co., and accordingly I visited him to-day and gave him the name of the people behind the Dehri scheme".[44] Of course, this implied a risk that word of this would get out to the circle around Dalmia and cause information to be leaked. However, if Holck-Larsen had not made this confession, this might, on the other hand, have harmed the confidence shown to them by their old business partners in ACC. To maintain the confidence of one party, it was necessary to compromise the confidentiality of another.

By chopping a toe and squeezing a heel, the FLS people succeeded in getting through the first round of their endeavours to maintain both their close relationship with ACC and the possibility of collaboration with Dalmia and Rothas Sugar Ltd. F.L. Smidth & Co. had no possibility to influence ACC's objective of an overall cartel covering all of the Indian market, but the question was how tightly attached to the cartel the Danes wished to be.

Technical Office in The Merger or Consulting Engineer?

During the summer of 1936, ACC insisted that F.L. Smidth & Co. should refuse to collaborate with *outsiders* in return for a guarantee of the cartel's orders.[45] The Danes, on their part, continued to express their scepticism. In September 1936, Dalmia travelled to Copenhagen, and in the consultations held there regarding his factory plans, the FLS people insisted that their position had been released.[46] There was every good reason to try to win yet another order, and if F.L. Smidth & Co. refused to meet with a customer based on their exclusive collaboration with another customer, or if this was suspected to be the case, the possibility to claim to be acting neutrally would of course be very difficult to uphold. This gave rise to fundamental considerations concerning the Danish strategy. Their considerations regarding the neutrality-conditioned competitive advantages were the preconditions for taking on and benefitting from the role as *research centre* for the constellations surrounding the cement industry. Ultimately, a reputation as a biased business partner might spread and cause reservations regarding business collaboration with Danish partners in other countries and continents.

In their relationship with ACC, F.L. Smidth & Co. were at the same time in possession of good possibilities to dictate the conditions for collaboration. Not only had their close collaboration so far placed the Danes in an insider-like relationship in the cartel with thorough knowledge of the factories they had for the most part delivered themselves and which they had also by now come to manage; an asymmetrical knowledge base to the advantage of the Danes had also been established which the Indians could not expect to easily break free from. First of all, a competing technology supplier would lack the knowledge of the factories and the Indian market which the Danes had accumulated; they would also be forced to collaborate with the large number of FLS people who had ended up in leading positions at the factories. If ACC decided to collaborate with competitors, this would at the same time most certainly cause F.L. Smidth & Co. to link up with Dalmia and other competitors.

In other words, F.L. Smidth & Co. was in quite a strong position, and as it turned out, it became difficult for the ACC people to get the Danes to accept a role that was as intricately connected as they wanted. At meetings in London at the end of August 1936, the FLS top management made their standpoint completely clear to Killick Nixon & Co.'s chief executives, English E.C. Reid and the Tata manager Nowroji Saklatvala. Thus, O.V. Mørch summarised, in short, that the Danish point of departure must be that: "... of course, with all the new inquiries in hand we are more and more disinclined to tie ourselves too much to the Merger".[47] The possibility of a more independent role as consulting engineers was to be preferred, and developments were beginning to move in this direction.

In September, Captain revealed to Holck-Larsen that Killick Nixon & Co. wanted "... a technical central management of all the Merger factories – and that Killick's idea was for Ewald Christensen to become head of such an office". Captain said that the suggestion had met with resistance from himself and from the Tata sphere, who did not wish to hand over the power to the British-dominated side in ACC. This was to the advantage of the FLS people. Combined with the fact that they considered Ewald Christensen to be disloyal, the Danes had no ambition to take over such a central technical management position. As expressed by Holck-Larsen: "... such a close connection to the Merger would make it <u>very difficult</u> to receive orders from other customers".[48] In Holck-Larsen's view, the problem would solve itself as a result of the ACC management's internal differences of opinion regarding the issue. If the ACC people could not agree on establishing such an office, this would strengthen the possibilities of the Danes of being hired as "consulting Engineers for the Merger". When Captain's resistance subsequently developed into an open veto against any power of control to be given to Ewald Christensen, this did in fact cause the matter to be settled.[49]

Following negotiations in the autumn of 1936, an agreement was signed at the beginning of 1937 which committed F.L. Smidth & Co. to contribute with "the operation, reconstruction and expansion of existing or acquired factories and the construction of new factories".[50] In return, the Indians were committed to

> order all machine deliveries for cement machinery from F.L.S. at fair prices, calculated on the same basis as deliveries from F.L.S. to A.C.C. in the most recent years prior to the signing of the contract. The fee payable by A.C.C. will be 5% of all new acquisitions and new buildings ... .

> The contract did not imply, however, that F.L. Smidth & Co. were free to collaborate with anyone they wanted. Within a five-year agreement period, the Danes had to accept to refrain from "... delivering to or providing consultative services to other companies in India" – except relating to the negotiations and orders which had already been commenced with Dalmia and with the federal state of Mysore regarding a factory. This meant that the relationship had now become more regulated. The Danes were certain to receive orders from ACC, and knowledge and control of the running of the cement production of the Indians were secured by contract. In return, the Danes were tied to ACC for five years, but the movement towards integration of the companies had been stopped, which meant that F.L. Smidth & Co. were free to continue their collaboration with the competitors to which they had made contact. As regards other outsiders, however, the FLS people were instructed to show reluctance: If you get inquiries from people you do not know, we think that in most cases it will be best to reply that we regret we are not able to help them, as we have made agreements with other people making it impossible for us to quote them for machinery to be erected in the district they mention, and, of course before you give this reply you may write them and ask them in which district they are going to build their factory, and you may learn something to the advantage of the A.C.C.[51]

Danish Investment Plans Shelved

In consequence of the objective of a freer Danish position, the thought of Danish ownership interests in the cement factories needed to be revised. To attach the Danes more closely to the Indian factories, Nowroji Saklatval did in fact, in 1936, offer F.L. Smidth & Co. to buy, at a "... particularly favourable price ..." a considerable part of his own shares in ACC. The FLS people in India considered this idea to be "... rather interesting ...". However, an announcement to the contrary was soon received from Copenhagen:

As regards the actual question of acquiring shares or not, the situation is, as we know, that to the Merger it makes no difference whether we own shares or not, and we will hardly be able to acquire much more influence of the company if we own shares than if we do not. We might well be able to raise the money to acquire more shares, but GBP 50,000, for instance, would not, of course, ensure any great influence on the company. We would therefore prefer to wait and see how our further negotiations regarding the question of acting as consulting engineers proceed before making any decisions.

This settled the matter. With the prospects of doing business with one customer only and not achieve more control, any thought of Danish-owned cement shares in India was ready to be scrapped. F.L. Smidth & Co.'s influence on their Indian customers would be much greater if this continued to be based on the delivery of staff, knowledge and technology for the operation and development of the production plants.

This meant that at the beginning of 1937, the FLS people could look back on a U-turn in India during the past six months. The movement towards integration with the Tata-dominated companies which had been in progress since 1932 had been replaced by a collaboration type with ACC that appeared to merely include products and services regulated by contract, and any thoughts of becoming co-owners of the Indian cement factories had been abandoned. Now the question was whether this change of policy was sufficient, i.e. whether it was now possible to establish parallel and free collaboration with competing Indian customers.

"… So That We Cannot Afterwards Be Blamed for Being Indiscreet in Any Way"

In addition to the ongoing technical consultancy services, F.L. Smidth & Co. also made their own engineers available for the management of ACC's factories, and at the end of 1937, a contract was signed for the delivery of three new factories in Sind, Bezwada and Patiala. To this was added the expansion of the Coimbatore factory.[52] In other words, the Danes were in strong control of the development of the Indian cement industry. They currently became involved in tasks which reflected fundamental and profound influence on the decisions of their Indian business partner. For instance, during O.V. Mørch's visit to India in the winter of 1937–1938, the chairman of AAC's board of directors, E.C. Reid, asked him to conduct an overall analysis of ACC's administration and bureaucracy in order to prepare a proposal for the establishment of a new management structure.[53] However, at the same time, this type of project indicated that the collaboration with ACC continued to be so close that it was difficult to claim neutrality towards the *5–7 outsiders* who came forward in 1937–1938. This manifested itself in particular in their relationship with Rothas Sugar Ltd.

F.L. Smidth & Co.'s contact to Ramkrishna Dalmia had immediately turned their neutral status into a topic for discussion. *The Merger's* attempt to prevent Danish assistance to *outsiders* was aimed directly at eliminating their neutral status, and when an order was received by F.L. Smidth & Co. from Dalmia in October 1937 for a factory to be built in Dehri on Sone in northeast India, this caused increased concern among AAC's management. According to Holck-Larsen, leading ACC people were "... afraid that you [F.L. Smidth & Co. i København] will be able to help Mr. Dalmia much more than, for instance, Krupps or Polysius would be able to".[54] Their anxiety was not reduced by the fact that Dalmia's intention was to establish another five cement factories which, assisted by the Danes, might be serious competitors to ACC.[55]

Dalmia's Rothas group might also have good reason to be concerned when collaboration was now initiated with the very technology supplier that was in charge of the development of the factories of their competitor. It was possible to put pressure on the Danes, however. One option available to Dalmia was used immediately in 1936 when he bought yet another factory to be established in Karachi, but this time from Polysius, which could then be played off against the Danes in the competition for future orders.[56] Another easy and obvious option for a new actor like Dalmia was to blacken F.L. Smidth & Co.'s reputation with accusations of partiality due to their close collaboration with existing companies. This soon became a factor which the Danes needed to take into consideration. Already in 1936, when Dalmia first mentioned his plans to build more factories, he thus requested access to information from the Danes regarding raw material deposits in the South Indian geography.[57] On this occasion, the FLS people chose to make their knowledge available, although this had been acquired through their collaboration with their old Indian business partners. When this resulted in Rothas placing their orders with Polysius after all, the challenges to Danish loyalty peaked.[58] In this situation it was obvious to everyone that the Danes had good reasons to nurture their relationship with ACC. But there was also a limit to their resistance against Dalmia as they were committed to collaborate with him in Dehri on Sone, and he was still a potential major customer. It was obvious that Dalmia was willing to compromise on their confidence-based relationship, and the Danes had no tools to control his business.

A consequence of their long-standing close relationship with the older business partners was therefore that F.L. Smidth & Co. had to continuously seek to guard against the risk of accusations of partiality. The need to be particularly careful of Dalmia increased over time, and ACC began to put pressure on him to get information of his plans, which they could use as a countermeasure against Rothas Industries Ltd. The issue became blatantly obvious in July 1937, when a leading member of staff at *The Merger* supplied the FLS people with information he had overheard about Rothas Industries Ltd.'s expansion plans and in return expected access to the knowledge possessed by the Danes of their competitor's raw material strategy, to be used for preventive purchases of the relevant areas containing lime deposits.[59] In order to nurture their relationship with ACC, the FLS people could choose to deliver what was asked for, but they considered the risk this implied to be too great. As expressed by O.V. Mørch:

> Obviously, since Mr. Dalmia is our customer we cannot give his competitors any details about such a vital matter, and we would therefore ask you to treat this matter with the utmost delicacy so that we cannot afterwards be blamed for being indiscreet in any way. As you will be aware, conditions in India are quite favourable for the spreading of news, and Mr. Dalmia is very likely to have his informants in places where you least expect it.[60]

"... Competition of a Life and Death Nature ..."

In 1938, the tensions between the Danes and Dalmia developed into open conflict. The releasing factor was the time pressure Dalmia had imposed on himself by advertising in August 1937 that cement would be available for sale as of 1 January 1938. This meant that there was hardly time for the first factory in Dehri on Sone to become operational and ready to produce cement in large quantities by this deadline, and at ACC they were well aware of this. In order to put pressure on Dalmia, ACC therefore signed a contract, using a front man, for a large consignment of cement to be delivered on exactly 1 January 1938. This meant that Dalmia might be forced to buy expensive cement from other suppliers – most likely from ACC. So when Dalmia himself therefore visited the building site in September 1937 to speed up the production start, Aage Smith expected that he would be deeply sceptical of the FLS engineers. "Knowing our connection with A.C.C. it is easy to understand that very small incidents may make Mr. Dalmia and Mr. Jain inclined to think that our erectors may be sabotaging the erection work and also delay the start of the works". Aage Smith expected that Dalmia would do everything in his power to either get the Danes to throw more resources at the work in the shape of more engineers and fitters, or back down on the price. Dalmia did in fact react promptly by dismissing FLS-constructor Konstantin-Hansen and sending a fierce complaint to the FLS management containing an implicit threat to damage the reputation of the Danes:

> We know that your firm has got a very good reputation and even though you are no longer interested in selling your machinery to us,

we do not even dream that you would have asked your Erector to put obstacles in our work. But, due to his nature, he is not only putting hindrances in the way of speedy erection, but also dissuading our other workers and fitters from helping us. We must say that we find the position intolerable and difficult to keep them here, as they always accuse us of something or other. We have not experienced such difficulties in the erection of our other factories in the past and the erection of other units by the Erectors of other manufacturers in other places is going on very satisfactorily.

However, Dalmia's aggressive style backfired on himself. In light of the fact that his collaboration with the Danes was about to be ditched, the German technology suppliers started increasing the prices of their offers for Dalmia's factory projects. At the end of September, Dalmia therefore had to eat humble pie and inquire when F.L. Smidth & Co would become free of their contract with ACC and would again be able to deliver price-regulating offers for new factories. At the same time, he contacted ACC regarding the delivery of the large amount of cement (40,000 barrels) he had now ordered from ACC. A scenario of competition was looming, and one which in Aage Smith's words was of a "... 'life and death' nature ...".[61] In 1938, Dalmia once more resorted to accusations of sabotage, and this time they served, in the eyes of the FLS people, as an alibi for not paying for the machinery deliveries at the very time when Rothas Industries Ltd.'s capital reserves had been exhausted and production had not yet been commenced.[62] In April the FLS head office was informed that Konstantin-Hansen had once more been dismissed, primarily with reference to his behaviour. As Dalmia himself described the matter: "Mr. Hansen is of intemperate habits and indulges in strong drinks at night; his subordinate staff are often so annoyed with his behaviour that they threaten to resign".[63] Dalmia interpreted Hansen's behaviour directly as a conscious attempt to delay the factory building process and turned this into an argument for withholding payments to F.L. Smidth & Co. The construction management was now taken over by Rothas' own engineers, and in May, O.V. Mørch summarised the situation briefly, mentioning the measures they felt obliged to take in light of the increasingly poor relationship:

> You will see that Dalmia again asserts that we are too friendly to the ACC, and he uses that as an excuse for keeping back payment. You will see that we have answered very strongly and that we propose to take action against Rohtas Industris Ltd. if they do not pay at once.[64]

The countermeasures O.V. Mørch referred to was legal action. However, the FLS people were only willing to take this step because there were no other solutions. Thus, O.V. Mørch proceeded:

> We are very sorry that we are compelled to take this action, as sooner or later it may come out that we are suing Rothas for the third instalment of the contract and that they have only paid 50% so far. ... On the other hand, if we do not take action quickly then Rothas people will have used all their money, or the debenture holders may have seized their factories and we shall get nothing at all. ... The case must then go on and it is possible that the Rothas people will then pay as they will be afraid of publicity and we will then also avoid this publicity, which is certainly also disagreeable to us.

When the threat of legal action was about to become a reality at the end of May 1938, and F.L. Smidth & Co. had hired lawyers in Bombay to take action – and this immediately caused Dalmia to start paying – the victory came at a high cost. Not only did the Danes then realise that their relationship with a potential major customer had been seriously damaged. They could also expect that the knowledge of a customer's dissatisfaction with the Danish products and services and the suspicion that this was caused by unfair treatment might damage F.L. Smidth & Co.'s reputation with other customers.[65] This meant that Dalmia had hit F.L. Smidth & Co. hard regarding one of the most important Danish competitive advantages, i.e. their possibility to capture and fill out the position as the centre and connecting link in the constellations, networks and collaboration contexts that had been established around the world's cement industry during the previous half-century.

Notes

1 Unless otherwise stated, the following is based on Dwijendra Tripathi & Jyoti Jumani: *The Concise Oxford History of Indian Business* (Oxford, 2007).

2 John M. Hurd: "Railways," in *The Cambridge Economic History of India. Vol. 2. c. 1757 – c. 1970*, ed. Dharma Kumar and Tapan Raychudri (Cambridge, 1983), 737.

3 R.M. Lala: *The Creation of Wealth. The Tatas from the 19th to the 21st Century*, 3rd ed. (Penguin, 2004).

4 John Keay: *The Honorable Company: A History of the English East India Company* (London, 1991).

5 P.J. Cain and A.G. Hopkins: *British Imperialism, 1688–2000*. 1993, 2nd ed. (Harlow, 2002), 288–289.

6 Povl Drachmann: *F.L. Smidth & Co. 1922–1932* (Copenhagen, 1932), 83, 87.

7 A.J. Francis: *The Cement Industry 1796–1914: A History* (London, 1978), 257.

8 Tripathi and Jumani, *The Concise Oxford History of Indian Business*, 82–83. *50 Years. The Cement Industry in India 1914–1964* (Bombay: Cement Manufacturers Association, 1964), 7. Rangaswamy Srinivasan: *The Fall of Arbuthnot and Co.* (Madras, 2009). Aage Smith: *Nogle Træk af*

Indiens Cementfabrikkers Historie I Aarene 1930–1940; *Rotary Kilns Supplied by F.L. Smidth & Co.*, 1938 (FLSA).

9 Tripathi and Jumani, *The Concise Oxford History of Indian Business*, 85–86. *50 Years. The Cement Industry in India 1914–1964* (Bombay: Cement Manufacturers Association, 1964), 7. *F.L. Smidth & Co.: Rotary Kilns supplied by F.L. Smidth & Co.*, 1938 (FLSA).

10 Tripathi and Jumani, *The Concise Oxford History of Indian Business*, 64.

11 Knudaage Riisager: *F.L. Smidth & Co. 1882–1922* (Copenhagen, 1921), 256. Povl Drachmann, *F.L. Smidth & Co.*, 83, 87.

12 *The Cement Industry in India 1914–1964* (Bombay: Cement Manufacturers Association, 1964), 7.

13 Aage Smith: *Nogle Træk af Indiens Cementfabrikkers Historie I Aarene 1930–1940* (FLSA). *The Cement Industry in India 1914–1964* (Bombay: Cement Manufacturers Association, 1964), 7.

14 Gita Piramal: *Business Legends* (Penguin Books, 2010).

15 Piramal, *Business Legends*.

16 Riisager, *F.L. Smidth & Co.*

17 *Aage Smith to O.V. Mørch*, 10 February 1933, Indien 1931–35 (FLSA).

18 View the survey of Danish-led cement factories in Asia up until 1922 in Riisager, *F.L. Smidth & Co.*, 211–214. Burner master Christensen's presence in Shahabad 1932 appears from *Aage Smith to F.L. Smidth & Co., Copenhagen*, 21 February 1933, Indien 1931–35 (FLSA).

19 Unless otherwise stated, the following is based on information in Ejnar Lassens Landorph's private archives, kept in the Danish National Archives (Rigsarkivet), which consist primarily of letters home to his family in Denmark from the periods he was posted in Canada and India.

20 *Ejnar Lassen Landorph to Peter Frederik Lassen Landorph*, 20 January 1921 (ELL).

21 *Ejnar Lassen Landorph to Peter Frederik Lassen Landorph*, 6 March 1923 (ELL).

22 *Aage Smith to F.L. Smidth & Co., Copenhagen*, 22 May 1932, Indien 1931–1935 (FLSA).

23 *Aage Smith to F.L. Smidth & Co., Copenhagen*, 25 May 1932, India 1931–1935 (FLSA).

24 *Aage Smith to F.L. Smidth & Co., København*, 8 February 1933, India 1931–1935 (FLSA).

25 *O.V. Mørch to Aage Smith*, 10 February 1933, India 1931–1935 (FLSA).

26 *O.V. Mørch to Aage Smith*, 10 February 1933, India 1931–1935 (FLSA).

27 Aage Smith: *Nogle Træk af Indiens Cementfabrikkers Historie I Aarene 1930–1940* (FLSA).

28 Aage Smith: *Nogle Træk af Indiens Cementfabrikkers Historie I Aarene 1930–1940* (FLSA).

29 *Aage Smith to F.L. Smidth & Co., Copenhagen*, 25 May 1932, Indien 1931–1935 (FLSA).

30 *Aage Smith to F.L. Smidth & Co., Copenhagen*, 19 December 1932, Indien 1931–1935 (FLSA).

31 Statements referred from *O.V. Mørch to Aage Smith*, 10 February 1933. Indien 1931–1935 (FLSA).

32 *Aage Smith to F.L. Smidth & Co., Copenhagen*, 28 July 1933, Indien 1931–1935 (FLSA).

33 *O.V. Mørch to T. Stig-Nielsen*, 20 January 1933, T. Stig-Nielsen, Oriental 1933; *Aage Smith to F.L. Smidth & Co., Copenhagen*, 22 May 1932, Indien 1931–1935 (FLSA).

34 *Aage Smith to F.L. Smidth & Co., Copenhagen,* 28 August 1933; *O.V. Mørch to Aage Smith,* 9 September 1933, India 1931–1935 (FLSA).

35 *O.V. Mørch to Aage Smith,* 10 April 1934; *O.V. Mørch to Aage Smith,* 24 November 1934; *Aage Smith to F.L. Smidth & Co., Copenhagen,* 2 December 1934; *Aage Smith to F.L. Smidth & Co., Copenhagen,* 18 February 1935; *O.V. Mørch to Aage Smith, 1 March 1935,* Indien 1931–1935 (FLSA).

36 *O.V. Mørch to Aage Smith, 22 July 1933; Aage Smith to F.L. Smidth & Co., Copenhagen,* 28 August 1933, India 1931–1935 (FLSA).

37 *O.V. Mørch to Aage Smith,* 6 April 1935, India 1931–1935 (FLSA).

38 *Aage Smith to F.L. Smidth & Co., Copenhagen,* 7 April 1935; *O.V. Mørch to Aage Smith,* 12 April 1935, India 1931–1935 (FLSA).

39 *Aage Smith to F.L. Smidth & Co., Copenhagen,* 19 November 1934, India 1931–1935 (FLSA).

40 *O.V. Mørch to Aage Smith,* 28 March 1935, Indien 1931–1935 (FLSA).

41 Aage Smith: *Nogle Træk af Indiens Cementfabrikkers Historie I Aarene 1930–1940* (FLSA).

42 *Aage Smith to F.L. Smidth & Co., Copenhagen,* 28 October 1935; *Aage Smith & Co. to F.L. Smidth & Co., Copenhagen,* 1 November 1935; *Aage Smith to F.L. Smidth & Co., Copenhagen,* 13 December 1935, Indien 1931–1935; Aage Smith: *Nogle Træk af Indiens Cementfabrikkers Historie I Aarene 1930–1940* (FLSA).

43 *N. Holck-Larsen to F.L. Smidth & Co., Copenhagen,* 6 July 1936, Indien 1936 (FLSA).

44 *Niels Holck-Larsen to F.L. Smidth & Co., Copenhagen,* 23 July 1936, Indien 1936 (FLSA). Tripathi & Jumani, *The Concise Oxford History of Indian Business,* 105.

45 *Niels Holck-Larsen to F.L. Smidth & Co., Copenhagen,* 15 August 1936, Indien 1936 (FLSA).

46 *Aage Smith to Niels Holck-Larsen,* 27 August 1936, Indien 1936 (FLSA).

47 *O.V. Mørch to H. Holck-Larsen,* 26 August 1936; *O.V. Mørch to H. Holck-Larsen,* 15 September 1936, Indien 1936 (FLSA).

48 *H. Holck-Larsen to F.L. Smidth & Co., Copenhagen,* 1 October 1936, Indien 1936 (FLSA).

49 *F.L. Smidth & Co., Copenhagen to H. Holck-Larsen,* 20 October 1936, Indien 1936 (FLSA).

50 Aage Smith: *Nogle Træk af Indiens Cementfabrikkers Historie I Aarene 1930–1940; Aage Smith to F.L. Smidth & Co., Copenhagen,* 7 January 1937; *Aage Smith to F.L. Smidth & Co., Copenhagen,* 14 January 1937, Indien 1937 (FLSA).

51 *O.V. Mørch to Aage Smith,* 30 January 1937, Indien 1937 (FLSA).

52 Aage Smith: *Nogle Træk af Indiens Cementfabrikkers Historie I Aarene 1930–1940* (FLSA).

53 *E.C. Reid to F.L. Smidth & Co., Copenhagen,* 28 October 1937, Indien 1935–1939 (FLSA).

54 *H. Holck-Larsen to F.L. Smidth & Co., Copenhagen,* 22 October 1937, Indien 1936 (FLSA).

55 Aage Smith: *Nogle Træk af Indiens Cementfabrikkers Historie I Aarene 1930–1940* (FLSA).

56 Aage Smith: *Nogle Træk af Indiens Cementfabrikkers Historie I Aarene 1930–1940* (FLSA). *The Cement Industry in India 1914–1964* (Bombay: Cement Manufacturers Association, 1964), 8.

57 *H. Holck-Larsen to F.L. Smidth & Co., Copenhagen,* 14 November 1936, Indien 1936 (FLSA).

58 Aage Smith: *Nogle Træk af Indiens Cementfabrikkers Historie I Aarene 1930–1940* (FLSA).
59 S. Slyter to *F.L. Smidth & Co., Copenhagen,* 8 July 1937, Indien 1937 (FLSA).
60 *O.V. Mørch to Aage Smith,* 10 July 1937, Indien 1937 (FLSA).
61 *Aage Smith to F.L. Smidth & Co., Copenhagen,* 30 September 1937, Indien 1937 (FLSA).
62 *Aage Smith to F.L. Smidth & Co., Copenhagen,* 7 February 1938; *Aage Smith to F.L. Smidth & Co., Copenhagen,* 16 February 1938, Indien 1938 (FLSA).
63 *J. Dalmia to F.L. Smidth & Co., Copenhagen,* 26 April 1938, Indien 1935–1939 (FLSA).
64 *O.V. Mørch to Aage Smith,* 12 May 1938, Indien 1938 (FLSA).
65 *Rothas Industries Ltd. to F.L. Smidth & Co.,* 19 May 1938; *O. V. Mørch to Rothas Industries Ltd.,* 21 May 1935; *F.L. Smidth & Co., Copenhagen to Rothas Industries Ltd. 23 Maj 1938; Rothas Industries Ltd. to F.L. Smidth & Co.,* 24 May 1938; *O.V. Mørch to Brix-Andersen,* 28 May 1938, Indien 1938 (FLSA).

References

A.J. Francis: *The Cement Industry 1796-1914: A History* (London, 1978).

Dwijendra Tripathi & Jyoti Jumani: *The Concise Oxford History of Indian Business* (Oxford, 2007).

Gita Piramal: *Business Legends* (Penguin Books, 2010).

John M. Hurd: "Railways," in *The Cambridge Economic History of India. Vol. 2. c. 1757 – c. 1970,* ed. Dharma Kumar & Tapan Raychudri (Cambridge, 1983).

John Keay: *The Honorable Company: A History of the English East India Company* (London, 1991).

Knudaage Riisager: *F.L. Smidth & Co. 1882–1922* (Copenhagen, 1921).

Peter J. Cain & A.G. Hopkins: *British Imperialism, 1688–2000.* 1993, 2nd ed. (Harlow, 2002).

Rangaswamy Srinivasan: *The Fall of Arbuthnot and Co.* (Madras, 2009).

Povl Drachmann: *F.L. Smidth & Co. 1922-1932* (Copenhagen, 1932).

Russi M. Lala: *The Creation of Wealth. The Tatas from the 19th to the 21st Century,* 3rd ed. (New Delhi: Penguin, 2004).

The Cement Industry in India 1914–1964 (Bombay: Cement Manufacturers Association, 1964).

7 A Robust Non-FDI Strategy

Control Without Economic Investment

This book has provided an insight into the extent to which companies can achieve control of the investments of other companies without any appreciable use of FDI – and to what degree such types of control may constitute the foundation for internationalisation and the creation of income-generating activities in other countries. By looking into the strategic considerations, network formations and social relations and events closely linked to the everyday activities of the people involved, the text explores how strategies based on tools other than FDI formed the basis for F.L. Smidth & Co.'s control of the Asian market for technology and machinery for the cement industry during long periods across the first half of the 20th century. Based on extensive influence on and control of the investments made by the main actors of the cement industry, the Danish engineering company was able to establish itself as a de-facto monopolist in the field as regards deliveries, development and maintenance of production plants for the industry. This was the case in the individual markets where their level of control both varied and fluctuated over the years in question. But for periods, their control was pervasive and included more or less the entire continent.

This culminated during the years around 1930 when the Danish control stretched from Japan in the east to India in the west and its strength reached a climax.

At this time, FLS had been retaining a constant grip of activities in Siam and Southeast Asia since the market for cement technology had begun to develop in the 1910s. The foundation was the installation of a Danish company management at the Siam Cement Company, which emerged from and was based on a strongly asymmetrical knowledge base to the advantage of the Danes, and which was established within a (high) political framework promoting strong business ties between two politically equal nations. The control was extensive. The risk that the Danes in charge of the Siam Cement Company would buy machinery from other suppliers than their old parent company in Copenhagen was never present.

DOI: 10.4324/9780429446184-7

And as regards critical decisions involving both their Siamese employees and their Danish support base, they primarily consulted the FLS headquarters in Copenhagen. The entire construction became rooted and consolidated by the materiality from which it originated and which it formed and was interwoven in. This implied the fitting of the sophisticated machinery, which was constantly being further developed by the inclusion of new facilities, meaning that a need was maintained to supply external expertise with a large cultural capital in the shape of updated technological know-how in key operational positions, i.e. Danes trained and sent out by F.L. Smidth & Co., and also the establishment of the physical frameworks constituting the factory landscape, which consolidated the position of the Danes as people in social control and in charge of the day-to-day operations and development of the company. And finally the large distance between Siam and Denmark and the climatic, cultural and social differences between the two geographical areas, which deeply affected the private lives of the Danish expatriates and thus contributed to maintaining their loyalty towards their Danish parent company and ensured their function as the auxiliary arm of the company, financed by their customer's budget.

In China, F.L. Smidth & Co.'s grip of the market, which had been established and developed since the 1890s, was regained around 1930, following a period of serious challenges as a result of new competition from German machine suppliers and by the civil war in the 1920s. As in Siam, the Danish position might be advantaged by the wish of the Chinese to collaborate with partners they need not fear would be the spearheads of political or business-related agendas from the big western colonial powers. All activities were therefore interwoven with high political agendas and in official diplomatic initiatives to establish ties between Denmark and the new Chinese regime under Chiang Kai-shek. And as in Siam, the Danish control was based on the installation in the Chinese companies of Danish company managers accommodated at the factories and benefitting from the strongly asymmetrical knowledge base and social relations, which were being currently consolidated and maintained through the purchase of the most recent state-of-the-art machinery and production technology from Copenhagen.

In Japan around 1930, F.L. Smidth & Co. had just completed extensive renovation programmes of the main actor of the well-established Japanese cement industry, centred around the Asano Cement Company and the Onoda Cement Company, both of which had been accumulating extensive experience of cement production since the end of the 19th century. In only a few years, machines and production facilities manufactured by and delivered from Copenhagen had become the standard at the most recent and technologically most updated sections of the largest Japanese factories. The Danes had succeeded in establishing a strong network position with extensive and thorough influence on the decisions made by the Japanese companies regarding investments in and maintenance of production equipment. What was of decisive importance was the creation of Danish-Japanese relations at the highest levels of company ownership and management, including close personal acquaintances that could be used to influence the lower management hierarchies at the Japanese companies and the decision-making processes among their engineers. The relations between the top managers of the companies were interwoven with the efforts of the Danish-Japanese diplomatic services to create ties between the two nations at levels up to their royal and imperial families. And the Danish-Japanese relations within the cement industry were interwoven into a broader effort to establish business-related and cultural collaborations between the two countries.

In India in 1930, F.L. Smidth & Co. had been in charge of the establishment and development of the main part of the country's cement factories since the first of these were established almost 20 years earlier. Their status was that of a de facto monopolist at both the British-owned and Indian-owned companies and cement producers, of which the latter counted some of the heaviest actors in the Indian business community emanating from the Swadeshi movement's aim for liberation from British supremacy. At the British-owned factories, Danes had been installed in the factory managements from the beginning – in line with the situation in Siam and China. And during the years around 1930, the Indian-owned companies initiated a thorough reorganisation of their management layers, meaning that from then on, F.L. Smidth & Co. came to both control and supply candidates for key positions in the works managements of their respective factories. Thus, the Danes systematically ousted previously employed British engineers and work managers who had been involved in the management and operation of the Indian-owned cement companies. At the same time, Danes slipped into key position in the overall cartel-like bodies through which the Indian cement manufacturers coordinated prices, market conditions, the development of the production apparatus, etc. This became the beginning of a movement towards a vertical integration which would formally secure F.L. Smidth & Co. sole and exclusive rights and total control of the technological development of almost the entire Indian cement industry. And although this movement was halted before the Danish control came to be formalised, it was in fact a reality from the beginning of the 1930s.

However, the Danish opportunities for control were not confined to columns in the individual companies or countries. In Asia as a whole, during the years around 1930, the Danes were clearly approaching a position as coordinator for the main actors in the cement industry of the continent. This was the case in the western sphere, India, where the Danish role in the cartel collaboration between the cement manufacturers in *Associated Cement Companies* not only secured them a very strong position up through the 1930s for control of the investments in the large country's cement-producing facilities but also extensive influence on the organisation and the development of the industry in general. In the eastern-southeastern sphere, at the beginning of the 1930s, F.L. Smidth & Co. were about to become the central liaison and a channel for coordinating the interests between the main actors of the cement industry both internally in China and across the national boundaries between Japan, China and Siam/Southeast Asia. The expatriate Danes in the Chinese factory managements were not only efficient guardians of the interests of their Danish parent company at their respective factories; they were also important pawns in a game in which F.L. Smidth & Co. could take on the role as coordinator of major cartel-like collaborations regarding the regulation of market conditions and production structures between the Chinese cement manufacturers and their customers in the Chinese cement market – and between the cement industries in China, Siam/Southeast Asia and Japan. The Danes had some, albeit not full, influence on the willingness of the various partners to enter into such network constellations, and with their role as co-ordinator of the activities within these followed a large control potential. A potential, that is, without the backing of any noticeable cash inflows from Denmark and which rather presupposed that no such support was provided.

Consequently, the case study of F.L. Smidth & Co.'s establishment in Asia has delivered insight into internal and external factors which may promote companies' use of non-FDI-based strategies for the acquisition of control across national boundaries of the investments of other companies. The case is an example of how knowledge capital can be used as a tool to control systems in which technological advantages are of essential importance, and of how the lack of access to large capital reserves in companies is not necessarily an obstacle to influence – but at times rather the opposite. And it illustrates how a company's point of departure in a small home economy may provide decisive advantages and tools. Partly in high political contexts in which it may, paradoxically, be an advantage to be able to refer to a politically/financially insignificant and harmless point of departure. Partly because a small overseeable home context can create opportunities for coordination which may be decisive for the joint control and coordination of efforts. In the present case, in concrete terms for the creation of decisive knowledge advantages through collaborations and work distribution among companies, educational and research institutions and the government. And for a joint effort in the foreign markets among companies, official representations, individuals and so on for the establishment of network positions when entering new markets.

In combination, all these tools were the preconditions for FLS to become a born-global success in the world's most distant and foreign markets during a short number of years at the beginning of the 20th century without the need for massive capital investments and the risk these would imply and which might have threatened the existence of the relatively weak company in terms of capital. The case shows well-known advantages of seeking collaboration in markets – rather than the integration of activities in companies – which have been highlighted in a number of contexts from Alfred Marshall's first cluster formation theories in *Principles of Economics* (1890) and *Industry and Trade* (1923) to cluster research in the most recent years – and many other texts.

This book includes different factors in an analysis of the internationalisation of a company, leaving a clear picture of the need to apply a differentiated use of the concept of *control* as a precondition for analysing and understanding multinational enterprise.

Challenges to the Strategy

The culmination of the Danish level of control during the years around 1930 also meant that the following decade provided examples of some of the biggest challenges encountered by F.L. Smidth & Co. in Asia before World War II in terms of pursuing a strategy that was not based on FDI. Both internal and external factors and circumstances were the reasons for this.

In China, the strategy had already been seriously challenged several times by internal factors. The challenges emanated primarily from a constant risk caused by opportunism, incompetence, long periods of no contact between the customer and F.L. Smidth & Co. in Copenhagen and personal challenges among the expatriate Danes in the factory managements. The Chinese had been able to utilise these types of phenomena during the previous decades to counteract situations in which the Danes had overexploited their opportunities for control and had – to a large extent in concrete terms – written out cheques for themselves on behalf of the Chinese. During the 1930s, this still occurred, for instance, when close Chinese contacts passed away. When control was to a large extent supported by the cultural and social capital of individuals, such single events might have far-reaching consequences. At a more fundamental level, it was decisive for the Danish position, however, that the strategy was now also being challenged by the fact that the asymmetrical knowledge base was becoming levelled out by the Chinese. As the inflow of well-educated Chinese with the required engineering competences grew, the need for Danish presence in the day-to-day management of factories decreased accordingly. Due to the more balanced knowledge distribution between the Danes and the Chinese, the Danes lost an essential control tool in situations where decisions were to be made regarding future investments by the Chinese cement producers, causing the Danes to more often having to compete on equal terms with their German competitors in particular. And for this reason, it became a serious problem for F.L. Smidth & Co. that they could not engage in equal price-based competition with the Germans due to the lack of abundant capital reserves in the small Danish home economy. This meant that the Danes had suffered a decisive loss of control in China, as the Japanese invasion of mainland China led to further and strongly dramatic deterioration of their opportunities for influence.

In Japan, the Danish possibilities to draw on an asymmetrical knowledge base had already from the beginning been notably smaller than was the case in other parts of Asia. In many ways, the Japanese market resembled those in Western Europe. The Japanese had developed their own cement industry in line with countries such as England and the USA, and technology-developing constellations were even in the pipeline in Japan which matched those in Germany with Polysius and in Denmark with F.L. Smidth & Co. At the same time, Danish possibilities were not promoted to any major extent by the political context, whereas Japan's ambitions to take on the role as colonial power were not inferior to those in the west. Even though Danish influence was considerable around 1930, it was never mentioned that Danes should be installed in the managements of the Japanese factories, which would have enabled them to prolong their control of the investments of their customers. On the contrary, the Danish knowledge capital was under constant pressure in the shape of Japanese wishes to gain access to this, as well as to transfer production of machines and facilities from F.L. Smidth & Co.'s machinery works in Denmark to Japanese machinery works – and, quite simply, as a result of Japanese copying of the Danish technology. In the 1930s, this pressure continued to increase, and F.L. Smidth & Co. had to fight hard to maintain control of their own technology and to contain the adverse effects of the Japanese requests to surrender it. They succeeded in speeding down the process, but from an overall perspective, the Danish attempts at gaining control turned out to be futile. Towards the end of the 1930s, F.L. Smidth & Co. had to finally give in and accept complete delocalisation of all elements in the manufacture of machinery and facilities for the Japanese cement factories.

India was the only Asian country in which F.L. Smidth & Co.'s position remained unaffected by decisive challenges at the end of the 1930s. Quite paradoxically, their extraordinarily strong influence and powerful position in relation to Associated Cement Companies and the resulting risk of accusations of partiality from actors outside of the cartel now became one of their biggest challenges. This might well have been a clear disadvantage for F.L. Smidth & Co.'s reputation as a potential business partner among all actors in the cement market, but for the time being, their grip of the market was not being seriously threatened.

In other words, at the end of the 1930s, the strategy of F.L. Smidth & Co. had up to this point with very little use of FDI turned out to be extremely robust in Asia for decades. Considerable fluctuations had occurred since their first market entry in the 1890s, but they had succeeded in maintaining such extensive influence and control of the main actors of the cement industry that the Danish grip of the market had been retained. On the other hand, however, after almost half a century as a market leader, their general situation was beginning to look less positive during the course of the 1930s. For the FLS people, the robustness of their strategy was therefore a current theme for discussion, which implied that they needed to consider whether it was necessary to develop fundamentally new strategies. Might the challenges of the 1930s be a warning of what would follow after World War II?

The Robustness of the Strategy after World War II

For the present, a broader assessment of the robustness of the strategy on which L. Smidth & Co. had based their business in Asia during the first half of the 20th century must be based on our knowledge of their global activities in the period. However, if existing summary and anecdotal knowledge of their business areas after World War II is included, this offers an idea of whether new approaches to development were used, or whether the existing strategies were retained.[1] At the same time, this may indicate the extent to which the strategies explored in the previous chapters of this book reflect not only a distinct development in the Asian context but are in fact a more general expression of F.L. Smidth & Co.'s strategies for the establishment and control of their grip of the global market.

There may be every reason to assume that the challenges encountered by F.L. Smidth & Co. in Asia in the 1930s would continue and gain in strength. Decolonisation after World War II resulted in the gradual phasing out of Danish possibilities to appear as an alternative to the companies originating in imperial powers with pronounced power-political expansive agendas. This meant that a decisive element in the political small-state advantage was about to disappear. At the same time, the possibilities to draw on asymmetrical knowledge conditions must be expected to dwindle in step with the economic growth in the Asian countries and the enhancement of their educational and knowledge levels. To counteract this, it was essential to make sure that the efforts to maintain a Danish technological competitive advantage became extremely successful. Whether this was achievable or not depended to a large extent on their possibilities to continue to profit from their role as research centre for the cement industry. If these possibilities began to disappear in some markets, their strong position in the centre of a leading competing constellation in the global cement industry would generally become weaker. There was every reason to fear such a negative trend in light of the developments seen in China and Japan up through the 1930s. At worst, these might release a vicious spiral, causing F.L. Smidth & Co. to lose their centre position and consequently their competitive advantages.

In light of this, it was not surprising that, during the second half of the 20th century, the development of F.L. Smidth & Co.'s line of business became strongly characterised by diversification and vertical integration, in contrast to their previous highly specialised niche position. This growth in business areas occurred in waves, which to posterity may seem like sometimes desperate endeavours to provide the company with new strategic legs for support.

F.L. Smidth & Co. Becomes a Conglomerate

Diversification and vertical integration were part of F.L. Smidth & Co.'s business concept from an early stage. Already in 1889, the establishment of the cement factory Aalborg Portland extended their engineering business to also include the market for building materials, and in only a few years, the company was efficiently controlling the Danish cement market and its factories. From around 1900, machinery works were also established in Denmark, Germany, England and the USA, and in 1916 the construction group Danalith was founded. This meant that F.L. Smidth & Co. were able to manufacture their own machinery and sell this to their customers, and to build the factory facilities in which this was to be fitted. At the end of the 1930s, F.L. Smidth & Co.'s transportation section was separated out as an individual company, DanTransport, and like Danalith this became an example of a new business line which started as an FLS supplier but soon expanded and provided services to other customers as well. This also applied to the insurance company Forenede Assurandører, which was established in 1919 because no existing insurance company had sufficient capacity to insure site development projects of a calibre like that of a complete cement factory. In only a few years, this company came to be preferred by Danish business customers in general. Moreover, during the 1920s, F.L. Smidth & Co. established an asbestos cement works, Dansk Eternit Fabrik, and a concrete plant in Denmark. This meant that their development towards a group was well underway as World War II began, and their hunt for new business lines was intensified in order to keep the company running, including windmill development projects and peat extraction.

In other words, their movement towards diversification had begun much earlier, but after 1945, this was intensified to an extent and at a speed that caused the image of F.L. Smidth & Co.'s core business to sometimes fall apart. Usually, the process was started by looking for possibilities to make use of the engineering skills which were already available in the group and covered different fields of expertise. This resulted in a powerful business expansion with companies which in various ways were owned or controlled by F.L. Smidth & Co. and/or descendants of the company's three founders. Many of the affiliated companies and businesses were located quite far from their core business and point of departure. Thus, their shareholdings in the cable and wire production at *Nordiske Kabel og Trådfabrikker* were expanded significantly from the 1950s, which provided the FLS owners with control of one of Denmark's largest industrial enterprises at the time. At the beginning of the 1970s, their field of activity included a considerable haulage contractor business, which at this time had expanded its activities to comprise both transportation of contractor's machinery, tourist coaches and tourist ferry services. To this were added companies that produced electronic equipment, machines for concrete tube production, construction cranes and fork-lift trucks. At the same time, F.L. Smidth & Co. participated in the search for oil and gas via the company Greenland Petroleum Consortium A/S, and involvements in the electronics industry also came to be included in their portfolio.

While they were focusing strongly on growth, and also because of this, F.L. Smidth & Co. began to fall behind from the 1950–60s in terms of keeping up their technological advantage within their traditional core business: technology for the cement industry. Their many engineering expertise and business areas began to compete internally in the group, while at the same time, competition on cement technology prices in the world market remained strong. In other words, to maintain their position, it was decisive that they sharpened their focus on their old niche areas, and the conditions for this to happen were gradually being eroded as the company's focus was being spread across a large number of activities. It was, therefore, necessary to concentrate their efforts on recapturing their technological lead position, and from the 1970s, a new focus was aimed at the delivery of what were now called *turnkey projects*, i.e. the sale of cement factories where F.L. Smidth & Co. were in charge of planning and establishing the project, and all the customer needed to do was, metaphorically speaking, to insert the key in the ignition lock and start the production. This type of project has been part of F.L. Smidth & Co.'s raison d'être since the early years – as this book has illustrated. However, from the 1970s, these became framed as innovation. The degree of discontinuity during the 1960–70s was expressed, for instance, when Erik B. Rasmussen stepped in as the new group manager in 1986, and on this occasion stated that

> What really surprised me when entering this position was that FLS did not really possess any particular expertise regarding the delivery of complete turnkey plants. I thought this was the company's main line of business. In actual fact, however, FLS had only just entered into this type of business in any serious manner. Previously, they had confined themselves to machine deliveries etc., which typically cover 35% of a project's total costs. Now, they had embarked on the last 65%. Taking on the full responsibility.[2]

In other words, the company's historical identity had sunk into oblivion.

In line with efforts in the 1980s to reclaim their position as a supplier of cement factories, the company launched some of its largest ventures – which were, at the same time, some of those furthest removed from their cement business. What sparked this was the recession of the 1980s, which was a hard time for the cyclical cement industry globally – and consequently for F.L. Smidth & Co.'s core customers. They were hoping that the different lines of business might support each other and compensate mutually, so that good times in one area would offset difficult times in the other. In 1987, *FLS Aerospace* was established, which soon became one of Europe's leading companies within aircraft maintenance. At the same time, *FLS Miljø* was established, taking as its point of departure decades of experience from the cement industry with smoke cleaning and waste incineration (in rotary kilns) combined with the previous wind energy projects, among others. The hope was that FLS Miljø would become as important for the environmental area as their original activities had been for the cement industry. Their strategy to develop the company as a conglomerate was now so predominant and explicit that in 1989 this led to a change of name from F.L. Smidth & Co. to *FLS Industries,* using the plural form to indicate a broad range of activities.

Returning to the Roots 2000–2020

Following decades of attempting to fortify their foundation by spreading their activities over a range of business areas, it became clear to FLS in 2000 that this very strategy was about to cause the bottom to drop out of the company. At this time, neither *FLS Aerospace* nor *FLS Miljø* had delivered satisfactory results for at least ten years, and in 2001, the price of FLS shares reached the lowest level of the past 13 years. This was a serious crisis, and the future for the old highly esteemed Danish company appeared to be uncertain. This sparked off a fundamental change of strategy, which can be characterised as a U-turn away from the attempts they had been making for decades to fortify their foundation by diversifying into a range of business areas. To a large extent, this was a return to what had formed the basis of F.L. Smidth & Co.'s market acquisitions before World War II.

The historical line became extremely evident when the newly appointed chairman of the board, Jørgen Worning, in 2002 explained their radical decisions to sell off many business areas in order to focus on technology for cement production and mineral extraction. Now their original technological niche position within cement production was highlighted as the core of their strategic focus:

The new board has been holding a number of strategy meetings. We have reached the conclusion that FLS will return to its roots. In

> *other words, we will construct and design cement factories and manufacture building materials. We will only do business in these two areas … . **We will return to our roots – cement.** With the right management, we have a future. F.L. Smidth's roots will carry the future. We will resign from our other activities so as to concentrate on our engineering business and on building materials.*[3]

The new strategy meant that FLS intended to sell off all their other activities in only 16 months, and even if they did not manage to meet this tight deadline, their plan was implemented at speed. The heaviest elements in their portfolio were removed with the phasing-out of *FLS Miljø* in 2004/2005 and the sale of *FLS Aerospace* in 2004, and their focus on the technology niche was now so explicit that their direct ownership of the cement factory *Aalborg Portland,* which had been a core element in F.L. Smidth & Co.'s activities since 1889, was abandoned. The factory was sold to Italian *Cementir* in 2004.

In 2005, the change of strategy led to yet another change of name, from the conglomerate name *FLS Industries* to *FLSmidth & Co. A/S* – marking a symbolic return to their historical point of departure. The reason for the change of name was explained by the then managing director Jørgen Huno Rasmussen as yet another sign of their focus on their historical point of departure: "No one abroad knows FLS Industries, but everyone knows and respects F.L. Smidth & Co. We have one of the best brands in the world, and we do not want to waste this".[4] This was a manifestation of the company's strategic return to its roots, which had been established more than 100 years earlier. But it also demonstrated how companies, over very long time spans, sometimes even centuries, can use completely different tools than direct investments to build their international positions.

Notes

1 The following is based on Søren Ellemose: *FLSmidth – et eventyr i cement* (København: Jyllands-Postens Forlag, 2005). Cecillie Wallengren, Signe Foersom, Torben Seeman Hansen and Jesper B. Larsen: *FLSmidth – grænseoverskridende i 125 år* (København, 2006).
2 Ellemose, *FLSmidth*, 139.
3 Ellemose, *FLSmidth*, 240.
4 Ellemose, *FLSmidth*, 283.

References

Cecillie Wallengren, Signe Foersom, Torben Seeman Hansen & Jesper B. Larsen: *FLSmidth – grænseoverskridende i 125 år* (København: FLSmidth A/S, 2006).
Søren Ellemose: *FLSmidth – et eventyr i cement* (København: Jyllands-Postens Forlag, 2005).

Index

Printed in the United States
by Baker & Taylor Publisher Services